CW00525016

John Triseliotis
Selected writings on
adoption, fostering and
child care

John Triseliotis
Selected writings on adoption, fostering and child care

Edited by Malcolm Hill

Published by British Association
for Adoption & Fostering
(BAAF)
Saffron House
3rd Floor, 6–10 Kirby Street
London EC1N 8TS
www.baaf.org.uk

Charity registration 275689 (England and Wales)
and SC039337 (Scotland)

British Library Cataloguing in Publication Data
A catalogue record for this book is available
from the British Library

ISBN 978 1 907585 91 3

Project management by Miranda Davies, BAAF
Designed by Helen Joubert Associates
Typeset by Avon DataSet Ltd, Bidford on Avon
Printed in Great Britain by TJ International
Trade distribution by Turnaround Publisher Services,
Unit 3, Olympia Trading Estate, Coburg Road,
London N22 6TZ

BAAF is the leading UK-wide membership
organisation for all those concerned with
adoption, fostering and child care issues.

MIX
Paper from
responsible sources
FSC
www.fsc.org   FSC® C013056

Contents

John Triseliotis
14 September 1929 – 29 September 2012

John Triseliotis was brought up in rural Cyprus. He worked initially as a teacher before becoming engaged in social work in London and Cyprus. He gained a PhD and for many years combined teaching, research and administrative roles at the University of Edinburgh. His particular interests included adoption, fostering and ethnicity. He progressed quickly to become Professor of Social Work at the University of Edinburgh, where he was also Director of Social Work Education. He was awarded an OBE in 1989. After his formal retirement, he was appointed Visiting Professor at the University of Strathclyde, continued to research and write and undertook expert witness work for courts.

In addition to his wider influence as a researcher, adviser, teacher and campaigner, John was an active member of BAAF's Publications Advisory Group and regularly reviewed books for *Adoption & Fostering* for which he also wrote articles and was a dedicated peer reviewer.

Acknowledgements

This publication was made possible and worthwhile by the quality, quantity and high reputation worldwide of the writings of John Triseliotis. I would like to thank John's widow and children, Vivienne, Paul and Anna, for their support for this project.

We are grateful to BAAF, Routledge, Wiley and the National Children's Bureau for giving their permission to reproduce John's work for free. Thanks are also due to Professor Peter Stathopoulos, colleague and friend of John, for providing details of John's publications in Greek.

Miranda Davies has displayed her characteristic skill, reliability and helpfulness in her role as production editor.

About the editor

Malcolm Hill is Emeritus Professor of Social Work at the University of Strathclyde, formerly Director of the Glasgow Centre for the Child & Society at the University of Glasgow. He worked as a social worker in London before moving to Edinburgh to undertake a PhD under the supervision of John Triseliotis. The two later collaborated on several studies about adoption and children looked after in public care.

Introduction

Malcolm Hill

This volume of selected writings by John Triseliotis illustrates the major contribution he made over many decades to the fields of social work in general and of adoption and fostering in particular. Through his research, writing and teaching he influenced many professionals, students and others. John was ahead of his time in many ways. After his appointment to an academic position at Edinburgh University in the 1960s, he embarked on a string of research studies alongside his teaching and tutoring commitments – unusual then but now a common expectation. Although much of his fieldwork was carried out in Scotland, his studies concerned issues of universal applicability, resulting in a worldwide reputation. From his early days, he was interested to hear and convey the viewpoints of children and service users, which only later became standard practice. His work is suffused with evidence and informed commentary about issues related to children separated from their birth families that remain relevant today, including the nature of attachments, identity and multiple heritage.

John's earliest major published work, the summary and discussion of which open this anthology, was concerned with adopted people's interest in and understanding of their birth families. This study, *In Search of Origins*, was hugely influential in affecting the law and practice about adoption in England and Wales and elsewhere. It helped change public as well as professional and academic under-standing and attitudes towards adoption. Subsequently he wrote and researched on a wide range of topics, mainly on services for separated children, of which only a sample could be included here. The breadth of John's overall work is demonstrated by, for instance, his early writings on social work in Cyprus, and for a UK audience, about what

1

came to be called "ethnicity", a topic on which he continued to offer informal help to policy-makers later in his career (Triseliotis, 1972; 1977; Brown *et al*, 1994). As in his work on adoption, John emphasised that people often have dual or multiple identities that validly reflect their origins. It is not necessary for them to choose or for others to expect everyone to adhere to a single "mainstream" identity.

In the 1990s, with Professor Peter Marsh of Sheffield University, John carried out ground-breaking research about the impact of social work education across Britain (Marsh and Triseliotis, 1993). This remains of enduring relevance given current debates about the best ways of reforming social work education in England and the introduction of the Assessed and Supported Year in Employment (ASYE) for newly qualified social workers in England from 2012. John additionally published about social work in his first language, Greek (e.g. Triseliotis and Kousidou, 1989).

People who reviewed John's books highlighted key points about his writings that were also apparent in his verbal presentations. Several stated that he displayed great expertise yet covered complex issues in a clear accessible manner (Mann, 1980; Stein, 1996; Neil, 1997). One reviewer, a practitioner, began by stating: 'If it is always a pleasure to read a new book by John Triseliotis, how much greater pleasure to receive a copy and be given the opportunity to review it' (Cottingham, 1988, p. 395). His co-written general texts about fostering and adoption were commended for their blend of theory, values, evidence and suggestions for practice (Berridge, 1996; Feast, 1997; Neil, 1997). A reviewer of a collection containing one of the last articles John wrote commented that 'Triseliotis's paper stands out', because it 'offers deeper, more critical and hard-hitting thinking' (Clapton, 2012, p. 165). Critical comments are hard to find in the reviews and normally involved gaps in coverage. Occasionally, interpretations were contested. Kelly (2000) argued that some of the conclusions reached in a book about fostering services were unfair, though his overall appraisal was positive, stating that the book should be 'required reading for all people responsible for children in care' (p. 85).

This volume can only contain a small proportion of John's writings, which extended across six decades. The selection has been made to illustrate the range and continuing relevance of his work, especially in relation to child and family services. These are arranged chronologically. Although each has a particular focus, nearly all are multi-layered. The rest of this introductory chapter provides short overviews of the main themes that John covered in these and his other writings, with brief references, where appropriate, to identify links with later and current literature.

Adoption, origins and contact

Undoubtedly, adoption was the field in which John first established his international reputation and he wrote on many different aspects throughout his career, often drawing on his own substantial portfolio of research. He anticipated issues that only later became very prom-inent and remain highly relevant, such as openness, counselling and intercountry adoption. His work continues to be regularly cited as a benchmark by present-day researchers in the adoption field (e.g. Smith and Logan, 2004; Neil et al, 2011; Feast et al, 2013).

In the 1960s adoption in Britain was dealt with separately from other children's services and was largely a matter of childless couples assuming full parental responsibility for babies born outside marriage, then a much stigmatised status. It was taken for granted that an adopted child had no contact with his or her original birth family. However, unusually, Scotland had since 1930 allowed adult adoptees access to their birth records,[1] but only in 1966 did the law allow bona fide researchers access. John realised the significance of this and 'seizing the opportunity, he embarked on one of the first systematic evaluations of adoption' (Parker et al, 2013, p. 5). In this study John interviewed 70 adoptees who had sought out their records. Many had not found out they were adopted until they were in their teens or older, testifying to the secrecy surrounding adoption at that time.

His analysis revealed that, as adults, some were content with information about their birth parents while others wished to make contact. He found that those who had a warm and close upbringing

---

[1]   Finland has similar legislation.

with their adoptive family were more likely to be satisfied with information only, while more of those seeking contact had unhappier childhoods. It would have been easy to conclude from this that searching was a sign of something wrong, which was then a common viewpoint. However, John recognised that the searchers were all expressing an understandable curiosity about their origins in order to better understand themselves and their situations. Almost everyone displayed sensitivity about the feelings of their adoptive parents.

The subsequent book describing the research, *In Search of Origins* (see Chapter 1), continues to be referred to widely in the field of adoption for its illumination of the nature of adoption as having distinctive and life-long emotional and psychological processes. Forty years after its publication, Sen (2013) reviewed *In Search of Origins* in a series about classic texts. He identified the continuing legacy of the book's recognition of people's need to know about their birth roots. Sen also saw in the book a feature that characterised John as a person and informed his subsequent work – namely, the empathy for different viewpoints. At the same time as highlighting adopted people's needs, 'he is also sympathetic to adoptive parents' own situation' (p. 76) and the importance to them of feeling the child is rightfully theirs.

As John was carrying out his research, the Houghton Committee was deliberating about possible changes to adoption law in England and Wales. It was initially sceptical about permitting more openness in adoption. The Committee was especially loath to give adoptees a right of access to identifiable information about their birth parents, which was seen as confidential. Also, giving adoptees knowledge of the details might destabilise relationships with their adoptive parents. 'However, having heard further representations and evidence from Triseliotis's research on the Scottish system' (Smith and Logan, 2004, p. 37), the Committee eventually decided to recommend a change in the law to give adopted adults access to their original birth entry from the age of 18.

The Children Act 1975 gave adopted people aged 18+ in England and Wales the right to obtain a copy of their original birth certificate and this entitlement was extended to Northern Ireland in 1987. The Children Act 1989 provided for the establishment of a contact register where adopted adults and birth relatives could record their whereabouts to facilitate communication should the other party be interested. The Adoption and Children Act 2002 extended the availability of information in certain circumstances (Smith and Logan, 2004). Not surprisingly, it has been found that adoptees in England and Wales show similar curiosity about the reasons for their adoption and about what their birth family look and behave like, as had been revealed in Scotland (Howe and Feast, 2000). It seems, though, that a higher proportion of people adopted from institutions overseas may not be interested in finding out more about their origins, sometimes because it seems highly unlikely there would be any information to trace (Feast *et al*, 2013).

Changes in rights of access to records were accompanied by wider moves towards what was known as openness in adoption, encompassing not only adults but also children, who were increasingly seen as entitled to a good understanding of their origins and in some cases to ongoing contact with birth relatives. Since the 1970s, frankness from an early age with regard to communication about adoptive status has become broadly accepted and it seems that nearly all people adopted in recent decades knew about their adoptive status from a young age (Howe and Feast, 2000). Based on his own and other research, John was an early advocate for enabling children to have contact with their birth families in the minority of cases where they had a meaningful attachment (see Chapter 2). Not only could this help children after adoption, but it could also make adoption possible in cases where courts were reluctant to sever contact (Triseliotis, 1985). During the 1980s, many agencies thought it necessary to stop birth family contact in order to facilitate the child's attachment to new adoptive parents.

The issue of contact in adoption remains contentious. Quinton *et al* (1997) stated that openness and contact had become so well established that it might be assumed there was unequivocal research evidence about the benefits. They accepted that many adoptees report gains and that mostly contact does not threaten the stability of placements, partly because adopters tend to reduce or stop it when they think it is having negative effects. However, they argued that most research on the effects had been small scale, short term and lacking in standard measures. Furthermore, Quinton and Selwyn (2006) suggested that the case for openness was mainly based on ideas about the rights of people to know about their origins, citing the adoption handbook of Triseliotis *et al* (1997) rather than "sound" evidence about psychosocial benefits, which they indicated was a preferable basis for policy-making. This viewpoint is sustained in part by the belief that only comparative longitudinal research can provide good evidence, while as we see below, John based his views on more plural evidence and ethical considerations. Moreover, he was understandably affected by hearing first hand from a few individuals who had been obliged to cease contact with a parent as part of their plan for adoption. He described three teenagers, one in tears, who said they missed their parents very much but were not allowed to see them. He also reported on some children who were very pleased to be in touch with family members (Triseliotis, 1991c). Conscious of the limited systematic evidence available, he felt that such cases at the very least posed questions about blanket policies on contact. On the other hand, from his research he was aware that many, if not most, adopters *at that time* did not wish to consider contact.

In any case, growing acceptance of openness in adoption has meant that nowadays it is more commonplace for some kind of contact with the birth family to continue after adoption, though in most cases this is indirect (so-called letterbox contact) and infrequent (once or twice a year). It seems that agency policies encouraging adopters to be open about contact where appropriate have widened the proportion willing for this to happen (Thomas, 2013).

Recent studies have continued to show the complexity of adoption with contact and its effects. As John found with adult adoptees, face-to-face contact between adopted children and birth families often entails a mix of benefits and challenges. It helps children deal with issues of dual identity and loss (Smith and Logan, 2004; Neil *et al*, 2011). But even indirect contact through correspondence is not straightforward, as adults and children can find it hard to know what to say, while words can be misinterpreted and replies may not be received. Exchange of photos usually works well, however (Young and Neil, 2009).

After *In Search of Origins*, John carried out several studies, large and small, about adoption. He contributed to the substantial body of research showing that adoption is usually very successful as regards emotional well-being, social competence and coping with life (see Chapters 2 and 11). He conceptualised the processes leading to good outcomes in terms of identity, security and attachment, drawing on ideas from Erikson and Goffman about the development of the self and social stigma. Adoption typically provided children not only with love and confidence, but also a sense of stability and being normal, which was often lacking even in the most loving foster homes (see Chapters 2 and 3).

A keen observer of trends in adoption, he recognised that changes in policy and practice in the 1970s had led to adoption being increasingly seen as a desirable outcome for children in care. As they were older than the infants traditionally adopted and often had a history of changeable and/or poor care, they posed greater challenges. He identified that in such cases adopters needed to offer not simply love, but a 'treatment type of role with many of the children' (Chapter 4, p. 104). In the 1980s, this led to new methods of assessment, matching and support. John recognised the importance of the rapid growth of group work for children and adults, both before and after adoption. Consequently, he edited a book incorporating many contributions from practitioners who were expert in this emerging field (Triseliotis, 1988a). John's introductions to sections of the book discussed theoretical and experiential aspects of group work in a way that was 'comprehensive and illuminating' (Cottingham, 1988, p. 395). Adoption counselling services developed, as Triseliotis (1973; 1980b) had recommended, not only in relation to adopted adults searching, but also for adopters with children who had "special needs" (in the terminology of the time). The Adoption and Children Act 2002 helped expand the availability of adoption support services and recent research has confirmed their value to adopters, except those with the highest level of need (Thomas, 2013).

Ever alert to new developments, John was successful in obtaining funds to study the new legal provision for adoption allowances. This was a further measure intended to assist adoptions from care (e.g. by foster carers, by those on low income, where children's substantial impairments entailed high costs). As with birth family information and contact, the proposed introduction of payments in some circumstances aroused concerns and opposition. Many people thought payments to adopters would distort the motives for and experiences of adoption, but the evaluation found that financial security tended to enhance rather than detract from loving relationships. In the event, allowances have become widely accepted. The allowances study included many adoptions from long-term foster care, so the research also gained insights into the similarities and differences that adoption brought to adults and children (see Chapter 3; Hill *et al*, 1989). More recent work has shown that the majority of foster carers who adopt do so with an allowance, though some foster carers are still deterred from adoption at least partly on financial grounds (Kirton *et al*, 2006). In the USA open adoption is most common when adopters were formerly foster carers and in many cases the adopters continue to receive an allowance (subsidy) (McRoy *et al*, 2009).

Similarly, John led a study of freeing for adoption, another legal innovation, introducing the option of an intermediate stage en route to adoption where parental consent was legally affirmed or dispensed with. This meant that adopters could take on a child without the anxiety that parental agreement would later be withheld and birth parents could withdraw from involvement prior to the adoption hearing. Freeing worked reasonably well at first, alongside tighter timescales for legal proceedings (Lambert *et al*, 1990), but increasingly it was thought not to be suited to all the circumstances in which it was being used. During the first decade of the new millennium the provision to make new freeing orders was discontinued in favour of placement orders (England and Wales[2]) and permanence orders with authority to adopt (Scotland[3]), though they remained for longer in Northern Ireland.

John continued to show an interest in contact between adoptees

---

[2]   By the Adoption and Children Act 2002.
[3]   By the Adoption and Children (Scotland) Act 2007.

and birth family members. When well past the usual retirement age, he joined Julia Feast and Fiona Kyle in a retrospective study of the three main perspectives in adoption on this issue: adopted people, birth parents and adoptive parents. Interviews were undertaken with at least two and sometimes all three in the same family (Chapter 12; Feast *et al*, 2011). Feast noted that the research had been inspired by *In Search of Origins*. The findings highlighted the complex feelings of all involved. Even though the adoptions took place many years previously, before participants were prepared for openness, the great majority regarded the search and contact as mainly positive, though a quarter of adoptive parents demurred. Initially reunions were intense, but in most cases they led on to more "friend"-like than parent–child relationships, which were often sustained for several years. Birth fathers tend to be less prominent in the search processes and associated research than birth mothers, but this study included both. It found less stress among the men, perhaps because they feel less threatened (Feast *et al*, 2011). Further insights into the viewpoints of birth fathers have been provided over a number of years by Clapton (2003) and Clifton (2012).

Permanence – over five decades

For many years now, adoption has become closely associated with ideas about permanence, defined by John as having a family base for life (see Chapter 4). A wish to provide permanence was a major factor in the trend in North America and the UK for adoption to be increasingly used for children in care[4] whose return home was unlikely or would be unsafe. Permanence entails a sense of belonging and security, which can be assisted by legal certainty about the future, though not necessarily so (Triseliotis and Hill, 1990; Thoburn, 1994).

John's career began well before the start of the "permanence"

---

[4] For much of John's career children in foster and residential care were referred to as "in care", but following the Children Act 1989 the phrase "looked after" was substituted, though it remains usual to refer to adoptions from care and leaving care. Both "in care" and "looked after" are used here.

movement but his early work, emphasising lifelong security and identity, pre-figured some of its key principles. Over the years there has been a range of ways of interpreting how best to achieve permanence. At one end of the spectrum were those who identified the word exclusively or primarily with adoption. Given that he was an adopter himself and had already carried out research showing the benefits of adoption, it could easily have been thought that John would espouse this viewpoint. In fact, his views were closer to the other end of the spectrum, which saw permanence as achievable in a range of ways and which stressed the importance of support and services to birth families, who were struggling, so that they could offer permanence rather than lose their children to care or adoption. He set out a framework for considering permanence that embraced several stages and aspects of work with vulnerable children, from prevention via care and (supported) restoration to permanent fostering and adoption (see Chapter 5). His view was that permanence outside the family through adoption could only be justified provided that efforts and services were made to achieve it within the child's own family (Triseliotis, 1985; see Chapter 4). Once more, engagement with these issues was prescient, and some of his concerns about the lack of support given to birth families pre-figure current critiques of the direction of the present 'early intervention' agenda (Featherstone *et al*, 2013).

During the 1970s a number of local authorities developed coherent policies to promote permanence,[5] including Lothian Region on John's doorstep at the University of Edinburgh (McKay, 1980; Hussell and Monaghan, 1982). A key ingredient of permanence planning was to set time limits (e.g. two years) for children in care, after which adoption would be sought if there was no immediate prospect of return home. The rationale was that too many children were "adrift" in care with no definite long-term plans, uncertainty about their futures and in a placement that could not be a lifelong base. Whereas formerly adoption was usually considered only at a parent's request,

---

[5]   Sometimes called permanency.

now authorities sought to persuade parents to agree in appropriate cases and, if necessary, asked courts to dispense with the consent of those who were unwilling or could not be found. New ways of recruitment were developed to increase the pool of adopters beyond childless couples. John was involved in some of the evaluations of the permanence policy in Lothian, which showed good results, especially for children with disabilities (Borland *et al*, 1991).

In 1991, John reviewed the progress of permanence planning (see Chapter 4). He praised the growth in numbers of children adopted from care and improvements in information sharing and post-adoption support. He asserted that adoption was the preferred option for 'some vulnerable children with no one else to turn to'. It was also good that in the UK adoption policy had become directed to children with special needs within the country, whereas other countries in Western Europe tended to be dominated by overseas adoption (Triseliotis, 1989b). However, he also criticised instances where, in his view, the clean-break philosophy had severed meaningful ties between children and members of their birth families so that they could be more readily adopted. Other critics of the permanence movement pointed to its inadequate attempts to return children home before going for adoption, neglect of permanent fostering and irrelevance to teenagers who made up an increasing proportion of the in-care population (Thoburn, 1994; Gilligan, 1997).

Permanence remained an important ideal during the 1990s, but receded in significance. Triseliotis (1998/9) discussed eight different reasons for the reduced influence. He suggested that the decline in the proportion of children leaving care by adoption was in part due to criticisms of what he called the "excesses" of the permanence move-ment. Jones (2003) similarly provided a critique of the concept and policy emphasis of permanence, based on its oversimplification of children's complex connections, playing down of disruption risks and neglect of intensive work with birth families. Partly in consequence, the Children Act 1989 placed emphasis on "partnership" with birth families. Another important factor causing doubts about permanence through adoption for older children, especially those over 10, was evidence that adoptive family stress was sometimes persistent and that placement breakdowns were high. Even for 6–11-year-olds where adoption is the plan, more than a quarter will not be found placements or their adoptive placement will break down (Simmonds, 2009).

Nevertheless, permanence associated with adoption gained a new impetus after 2000. There were many reasons for this, among them evidence about the negative consequences of delaying the adoptive placements of children who entered care at an early age as a result of serious abuse (Quinton and Selwyn, 2006). The government prioritised adoption and introduced tighter time-scales and targets for decision-making. This led to a doubling in the number of adoptions in England, though the figures tailed off after 2005 (Kirton, 2013; Thomas, 2013). While the increase in adoptions has been broadly welcomed, Thoburn (2003) warned that tight targets could lead to higher breakdown rates. The Coalition Government from 2010 onwards has again promoted adoption as a means of enabling children to leave care, while otherwise paying little attention to children's services.

Foster care

Most children separated from their parents are placed in foster families. John devoted much attention to fostering, sometimes in comparison with other arrangements, including adoption, and sometimes in its own right. As with adoption (Triseliotis *et al*, 1997), he co-wrote an important comprehensive text covering the history of foster care, relevant policy, theory and research, and practice issues (Triseliotis *et al*, 1995b).

His first substantial study of foster care set out to fill a gap in knowledge about what happens 'as foster children cope in adult life' (Triseliotis, 1980a, p. 131). Contrary to some later research on leaving care and after, many of the respondents in this study were coping well. This may reflect the fact that in those days a lower proportion of children who were fostered had experienced serious abuse. John noted the almost universally low level of educational achievement, which was later highlighted in the research of Jackson (1989; 2013) and others, leading eventually to policy measures such as virtual school heads and dedicated teachers to help improve attainments among looked after children. John's study of formerly fostered adults affirmed the positive potential of long-term foster care to help children overcome major social disadvantages, by showing warmth and commitment despite ups and downs. These findings have been replicated in more recent research involving adults who have been fostered (e.g. Schofield, 2003; Randle, 2013), which have confirmed the interplay between warmth, security and resilience. Compared with adoption, though, fostered young people had tended to experience more negative experiences and stigma outside the family (Chapter 2).

John also found that children in long-term foster homes had often been unsettled by a turnover of children staying short term. Since then, it has become more common to separate out foster homes that specialise in different planned lengths of stay, though, in practice, it is not always easy to reconcile carers' designation with a child's needs when plans change.

In his subsequent reviews of foster care research, John showed that when children of similar ages and challenges were compared the success of foster care was almost as good as adoption (Chapter 11). The main problem, as Sinclair (2005) has noted, is that it is hard to achieve foster placements that do survive to become long term.

At a time when young people with significant behavioural and other problems, including persistent offending, were being fostered when previously they would have been placed in residential care (Sellick, 2006), John and colleagues examined foster care for teenagers as part of a spectrum of care (Triseliotis *et al*, 1995a). The findings about the progress of those in the sample who were fostered showed a tendency towards extremes in outcome compared with other arrangements, as foster care included some of both the most and least successful. Other research and consultations have suggested that most young people in care in their teens prefer residential care, either because they feel close to their own family and do not want another or – the opposite – they are so disillusioned with their previous birth family or fostering experience that they do not want to repeat it.

However, in this research, when young people living away from home were asked which of the two forms of care they liked better, they were evenly divided. In practice, few said they had been given a choice.

Usually the *Messages from Research* series, initiated under the Department of Health and Social Security (DHSS) and continued under the Department of Health (DH), Department for Education and Skills (DfES) and Department for Education (DfE), confined itself to studies based in and covering England and Wales, but the 2005 review of foster care (Sinclair, 2005) included two Scottish studies, one led by and the other involving John (Chapter 9; Walker *et al*, 2002). In the first of these, John undertook with colleagues the first national survey (and still the only one) of local authority foster care services and foster carers in Scotland in the late 1990s (see Chapter 9). This took place shortly before the big expansion of fostering by the independent sector (Sellick, 2006; 2011), which was therefore not included. Issues of recruitment and retention were and remain a vital consideration given the big rise in the proportion of children in public care fostered since the 1980s. Overall recruitment and loss were in balance, though less so in large urban centres. Some authorities had an average retention period of 10 years plus that others could aspire to. Even though there was not a large shortage, the high usage rate compared with availability meant that at the point of placing a child there was usually little or no choice. Hence matching was rarely possible. The study demonstrated the valuable role performed by foster carers' link or support workers, who were nearly all well regarded. More carers were critical of children's social workers and of levels and reliability of fostering allowances. A little later, a comprehensive English study produced very similar findings about foster carers' views of their roles and of social work agencies (Sinclair *et al*, 2004).

Part of the Scottish survey addressed a hitherto neglected aspect of foster care research – why foster carers cease to foster (see Chapter 8). The main reasons given for stopping were very diverse. Some no longer fostered for the very positive reason that they had adopted their foster child(ren). Otherwise, in about half the cases the explanation was specific to fostering, i.e. dissatisfaction with poor support or with the fostering experience including the child's behaviour and the stresses of caring. For a similar proportion, ceasing to foster related to a change in circumstances, mainly retirement, illness, moving or starting work. The characteristics of continuing and ceasing carers were similar, except that the latter included more with poor health or problems with the agency. They were also more likely to have fostered children of a type or age they had not wanted.

Triseliotis *et al* (2000) concluded that in order to improve retention as well as for the inherent benefits, local authorities should develop a more collegiate approach to foster carers as professionals, with adequate support and payment – implications echoed by Sinclair *et al* (2004). In general, specialist or professional fostering schemes have a good record of recruiting foster carers from non-traditional backgrounds, and retaining carers who value the autonomy, support and higher level of pay and recognition (Walker *et al*, 2002; Sinclair, 2005). Mostly the outcomes of such projects have been positive, though serious offending has proved hard to impinge on (Biehal, 2009). Against expectations, a national quasi-experimental evaluation of Multidimensional Treatment Foster Care (MTFC), based on a well-regarded US programme, showed better short-term results for offending behaviour compared with ordinary services, but the difference had disappeared at stage two of the study (Biehal *et al*, 2012).

Unusually and regretfully, it was not possible for the Scottish fostering survey to include children's perspectives. Other studies have filled the gap, in particular highlighting the importance to foster children of being treated "normally", like any other child. Moreover, their everyday experiences are typically very similar to those of most other children, with their status as foster children playing only a part of their overall identity (Sinclair *et al*, 2001; Heptinstall *et al*, 2001).

The care continuum

Although much of John's work concerned adoption and fostering, he was always very conscious of other forms of care, including work aimed to prevent children being separated from their families. He provided an integrated account of the care spectrum when he presented a framework recognising different stages or extents of intervention in family life, drawing on empirical evidence and theoretical considerations (see Chapter 5). One reviewer commented that, although this framework contained little that was original, it was valuable in having universal applicability and highlighting the need for policy and practice not to become too compartmentalised (Jones, 1993).

As a key principle, John re-stated the conceptualisations by the US writers Maluccio and colleagues (1986) that permanence embraced achievement of stability within the child's own family as well as in alternative families. He recognised that general services to tackle, for instance, poverty or drug misuse were vital alongside a wide range of more targeted interventions in order to help prevent reception into care or help with restoration. John observed that the courts had an important part to play in sharpening up assessments and plans. The need to convince a court of the requirement for adoption meant that social workers were compelled to demonstrate that concerted rehabilitation efforts had been made, while US evidence showed that some children could return home successfully when court appearances motivated parents. Much later, a model combining intensive parenting support with court-based time limits was successfully applied in New Orleans and is now being trialled in Glasgow (Walker *et al*, 2013).

John's own empirical work was largely concerned with children placed away from home, but certain insights into preventive services were provided by the teenagers study referred to above (Triseliotis *et al*, 1995a). This research included a sample of young people who were offered formal or informal supervision with a view to managing individual or family problems without recourse to placement away from home (see Chapter 6). Relationships with social workers were generally good, but young people were often unclear about the purposes of contact and explicit contracts were rarely used. Alongside direct counselling, social workers linked young people to a range of other services, but it was rare for this to be part of a co-ordinated multi-agency strategy. One option used was a then new development of outreach by residential workers, which has become more common since. With a few exceptions, the young people, parents and social workers regarded changes and benefits resulting from supervision as small scale.

For some time, notions about prevention have become reframed in terms of family support (e.g. Dolan *et al*, 2006). Many commentators have lamented the fact that in the UK it is rare to have concerted high-frequency multi-agency intervention targeted at "high-risk" families, as in the USA (Farmer, 2009), though some have argued that universal family centres and neighbourhood work can and should be preferable (Holman, 1988). Other services have operated at a more intermediate level, such as Sure Start. However, there has been a growth in the number of specialist intensive family support teams in both the statutory and voluntary sector, often adhering to a multi-systemic approach (Walker, 2010).

Residential care

When John began his career, residential care was used more com-monly than now. Quite large institutions were still commonplace, with many of the features of "batch living" described by Goffman (1991). By the time John first came to carry out research in this area, concerted efforts had made children's homes more individualised and positive. Notably, many family group homes existed, headed by house parents who were often a married couple, so that the setting resembled in some ways a large family, with perhaps six to 10 children. Another form of care then fashionable was the therapeutic community. While the emphasis of the family group home was on love, care and approximating normality, therapeutic communities aimed to resolve or reduce residents' psychological problems, particularly by analysing, using and modifying group processes among residents.

It was in this context that John obtained a grant from the ESRC to compare residential and adoptive upbringing, as part of the group of Studies in Deprivation and Disadvantage. Triseliotis and Russell (1984) recruited two samples of adults in their 20s who had either been adopted or spent a large part of their childhood in residential care. It was not possible to match the samples, so there were significant differences other than the form of care, which as John acknowledged, would also affect outcomes. However, in order to make the two groups more comparable as regards having experienced at least a few years in care, nobody adopted before the age of two was included. Similarly, the residential group had experienced continuity of care in their final home for at least six years.

When the research took place, residential care was still regularly used for younger children on a long-term basis: the residential group in the study had spent on average 11 years in that setting. They had experienced residential care at a time when family group homes and therapeutic communities were among the ideal kinds of setting, but despite this, most gave negative accounts testifying to the persistence of features of traditional institutional care: absence of affection, turnover of staff, rigid rules and lack of privacy. While the outcomes for the residential group were generally poor, some had done better through success at work or in marriage.

A decade later, the study about social work services for teenagers included residential care (Triseliotis *et al*, 1995a). By this time, concerns about the negative impact of residential care on younger children, combined with a growth in the numbers of foster homes, meant that residential care had largely become a service for teenagers, still sometimes referred to as adolescents but increasingly as young people. The term "children's home" had largely gone out of fashion and places where children lived in non-family groups and did not have schooling on the premises were now known as residential units. Typically 10 to 20 young people lived together. Residential boarding schools, many of which had formerly been approved schools (known as List D schools in Scotland), continued to provide an important resource.

This study highlighted the importance to young people of having at least one person who is committed to them over an extended period, be that a parent, foster carer, residential worker, social worker or teacher. This chimes with evidence and ideas related to resilience (Daniel and Wassell, 2002; Gilligan, 2008). Each form of provision had examples of success and failure. Residential schools had helped young people make good progress more often than other forms of care that appeared to be linked to their stability, flexibility and supportive educational arrangements. Grimshaw with Berridge (1994) reached similar conclusions.

Since 1995, further major changes have occurred in residential care, which mean that the findings of this study and many earlier ones may no longer be readily applicable to current provision. There has been a substantial fall in the numbers of children placed in residential care, reflecting a widespread preference for family-based care, though the high cost of residential provision has been an important factor too (Clough, 2005). The term "residential unit", which itself largely replaced children's home during the 1990s, has itself come to be displaced in some areas where, for instance, children's houses may be preferred. The size of establishments, apart from residential schools, has fallen further so they now often cater for five or fewer children. Nevertheless, significant numbers of children are still placed in residential schools, especially in Scotland. There have been notable improvements in qualification levels among staff and of post-appointment training, which has recently been boosted by the espousal by a number of authorities of a social pedagogy approach akin to that on the continent (Bayes, 2009; Coussée et al, 2010).

Although most of his research concerned family-based care, John recognised that residential care has an important part to play within the care spectrum and sometimes as part of a package or sequence combined with other forms of intervention, especially for older children (Chapter 5; Triseliotis et al, 1995a; cf. Clough et al, 2006). His views that residential care is desirable when young people are opposed to family care and in cases where severe behavioural difficulties relate to earlier distorted family relationships accords with the opinion of experts in this field (Bullock, 2009). John assisted with a comparison of a project aimed to demonstrate that foster care could cater for young people who would otherwise be in secure residential accommodation (Walker et al, 2002). This study showed that the (short-term) outcomes from the fostering scheme could sometimes be impressive, as other studies about challenging teenagers in foster care have demonstrated (Biehal, 2009). However, similar numbers of young people in the project did not do well. Interestingly, young people from the comparison group in secure residential accommodation often provided favourable reports and showed signs of positive change, at least in the short run.

Birth family contact in foster and residential care

Just as one of John's abiding interests concerned adopted people's mental and in some cases physical interactions with their families of origin, so he also gave much attention to issues of contact between children in care and their birth families. John was influenced by early child care research evidence about the benefits of contact both for the child's well-being and for the potential to return home. The link between high contact frequency in care and subsequent reunification has been one of the most consistent findings over several decades (Sinclair *et al*, 2004), but this is likely to reflect better relationships and prospects, so does not necessarily mean that increasing contact will be beneficial in more adverse circumstances. Some writers have in any case questioned the validity of such findings in relation to children who have been abused, who make up a greater percentage of looked after children nowadays (Quinton *et al*, 1997). Nevertheless, John's own research included examples of previously neglectful parents who made major changes, for example through tackling alcohol misuse (Triseliotis, 1989b; Hill *et al*, 1992). A recent thorough literature review concluded that 'contact is a necessary but not a sufficient condition for reunification' (Sen and Broadhurst, 2011, p. 300).

While John took account of research evidence about the effects of contact, he also pointed out legal and ethical considerations associated with children's rights. He noted that the Children Act 1989 (and equivalent legislation in Scotland and Northern Ireland) required local authorities to promote parental contact provided it is in the child's interest, which remains the case. He stressed that this is not about contact for its own sake, or for the parents' benefit, but about 'maintaining meaningful links' that are important to the child (Chapter 5).

This viewpoint was supported by Sinclair *et al* (2005) in relation to their large survey of foster placements. They stated:

Contacts should often be maintained, not because they are likely to have a good effect, but because parents or children want them. It is wrong to prevent them unless it can be shown that they are damaging. (p. 117)

Contact is crucially affected by the attitudes of foster carers, whose emotional investment often makes it harder for them to accept shared care or difficult birth parent behaviour than residential carers. Triseliotis *et al* (2000) found that difficulties in managing birth family contacts were prominent among foster carer complaints about their role, though it should be emphasised that this applied only to a minority (see Chapter 9). A recent survey of English foster carers reported that more than a quarter described difficulties relating to contact (Austerberry *et al*, 2013). As Triseliotis *et al* (2000) found, often the same foster carers were also dissatisfied with support from the child's social workers and were more likely to think these prioritised the birth family's viewpoint. It is not easy to tease out the chain of cause and effect here, but it does indicate that where foster carers are finding it hard to be inclusive, social workers have to try particularly hard to take account of their misgivings. A common response to the tensions between foster carers and birth parents has been for contact to occur much less often within the foster home than formerly. It seems there has been a cultural shift among social workers and their managers. The reasons for this include legal prohibitions on parents knowing the whereabouts of the child, practical difficulties for foster carers who are looking after several children and carers' fears of birth family violence or substance misuse (Sen, 2010; Sen and Cormack, 2011). A consequence is that contact now often happens in "neutral" territory such as a social work office or family centre, where it is hard for the child or family members to feel at ease. This in turn impacts on assessment of parent-child relationships.

Based in part on his work as an expert witness exposed to social work assessments and reports, John felt that in too many cases judgements by social workers and others were made about the relationship between a child and parent on the basis of brief contacts in highly artificial and/or stressful situations, where a child's overt reactions did not necessarily reflect their overall feelings (see Chapter 13). He concluded that sometimes contact was terminated without valid evidence of deleterious effects. He also repeated findings from attachment experts that children can feel close to more than one parental figure, so that an existing close tie need not preclude achieving a "permanent" bond with a foster carer or adopter.

It must be acknowledged that not everyone agrees with this viewpoint. Some writers have concluded that agencies and courts sometimes take too long to assess birth family relationships and prospects for going home. In some cases this has resulted in return to an unhappy or even abusive situation. Also, it is argued that delays leave children in unsettled placements when they could have been adopted earlier at a time when it was easier to form new relationships (Ward *et al*, 2011; Turney *et al*, 2012; Thomas, 2013). It remains 'difficult to identify the particular circumstances where reunification should (not) be attempted' (Kirton, 2013, p. 100), though Farmer (2009) shows that returning a child a second time when a previous attempt has failed has little chance of success. Farmer also concluded that in all tricky decisions about when or if to return a child home, careful social work judgement is required, alongside assistance from other professionals and well-planned and supported arrangements, whatever the decision. John likewise highlighted the need for thorough assessment and stated that the reason some attempted rehabilitations did not work was because of 'failure to address the original problems' and ineffective family work (Triseliotis, 2012, p. 265). Others have identified that in most cases the wider help given to families to assist reunification is often minimal (Biehal, 2007).

Evidence and ethics

When he began his academic career, John was unusual in his emphasis on research as a basis for understanding and his commitment to amassing empirical data through his own efforts. He was, therefore, a pioneer of evidence-based policy and practice long before it became fashionable. His research always had an applied aim that would help practice, whether this involved greater understanding of issues facing service-users or evaluations of particular innovations. He also conducted literature reviews to distil the key messages needed to inform professional activities, such as adoption counselling (Triseliotis, 1988b).

Since 2000, it has become commonplace for policy-makers to stress the importance of striving for positive outcomes for children and for using evidence about what produces good long-term outcomes. From his first research, John was interested to explore the long-term effects of different kinds of experience and several of his studies compared outcomes for young people exposed to contrasting placement types (see Chapter 2; Triseliotis and Russell, 1984; Triseliotis and Hill, 1990; Triseliotis et al, 1995a). For practical reasons, these comparative studies were retrospective and did not have matched samples, so John recognised that there were limitations in interpretation. In his reviews of the literature about placement outcomes, he examined several different dimensions, such as breakdown rates, changes in the young person and reported satisfaction. He avoided all-or-nothing conclusions. For instance, he recognised that more adoptions are successful on multiple criteria than long-term fostering, but the latter has its successes too, as when a lasting bond forms yet, for whatever reason, the young person, the foster carers or both do not want adoption (see Chapter 11).

Whenever possible, John liked to include multiple perspectives in his research. This was partly a matter of practice principle – that it was important to incorporate the viewpoints of service-users. Also he espoused the epistemological axiom that there can be multiple truths and different paths to truth (see Chapter 7). Ahead of developments in approaches to participatory research with children (Tisdall et al, 2009), John ensured that children's viewpoints were obtained and respected (see Chapter 3; Triseliotis et al, 1995a). John himself was skilled at encouraging children to talk about sensitive matters. Furthermore, including professionals, carers and/or different family members made it possible to identify both congruence and contrasts in attitudes and interpretations, as well as providing checks on measures of progress and outcome (Triseliotis et al, 1995a; Hill et al, 1996; see Chapter 12).

John was also keen to use several methods in the same study, as these could provide checks on each other as well as provide unique data. Typically he would combine semi-structured interviews with one or two standard measures, e.g. to assess self-esteem or behaviour issues. Case records were an important source of data, though inevitably affected by their variable quality and completeness.

Within the literature on research related to children and social work is a strand that privileges quantitative studies and sources of evidence claimed to be more objective, particularly randomised-control trials and large prospective surveys (e.g. Newman *et al*, 2005; Sheldon and Mcdonald, 2009). John accepted the value of such studies, but also knew they were often difficult to fund or implement. He advocated careful sampling and a systematic approach to questioning and analysis, but also valued flexibility to pursue matters that emerged in interview. Hence he supported the use of both quantitative and qualitative data-gathering (see Chapter 7). He believed that in-depth discussion was needed to make sense of the findings of standard measures. His preference for research that combined the merits of quantitative and qualitative data is in the mainstream of social work research, where most studies have adopted mixed designs and data sources to provide multiple complementary perspectives on "reality". Sen (2013) noted that the analysis of individual experiences in *In Search of Origins,* informed by the writer's practice, research and theoretical knowledge, was an example of the power of qualitative research, with an enduring influence on policy and practice.

While John was a flag bearer for research, he also emphasised that findings should be placed in the context of relevant theory (see Chapters 3 and 12) and the legal policy context (Triseliotis, 1995b; Triseliotis *et al*, 1997). He also recognised that 'no research is free of value biases' (Triseliotis, 1991b on intercountry adoption, p. 46), which could, for example, affect the way a research problem was formulated and each stage from sampling to analysis. He noted how research on ethnic identity had been fraught with divergent interpretations. He made clear that ethics should be central to policy-making together with empirical data and not necessarily disregarded because of evidence about outcomes. He was an early critic of policies that discouraged foster carers from adopting and, as we have seen, of the clean-break philosophy within permanency planning. In these and other respects, he wanted to see more nuanced and flexible approaches with regard to how and when it is appropriate to help a child maintain multiple attachments or, equally, to move a deprived child to circumstances that can aid recovery (Triseliotis, 1989b).

John expressed strong ethical concerns with respect to intercountry adoption, even though research showed that for many individual children this could be a good solution. He reviewed evidence in the early 1990s and showed that the outcomes of most international adoptions, which were usually also transracial, were generally good (Triseliotis, 1991b). On the other hand, children adopted transracially – whether within or between countries – have been found to face discrimination and feel cut off from their cultures of origin (Triseliotis, 1989b). Many studies in the following two decades have confirmed that even children adopted from very deprived institutions tend to do well in later childhood and adulthood, though a minority have higher rates of mental health difficulties (Feast *et al*, 2013). Nevertheless, John opined that the "effectiveness" of adoption should not override immoral processes that characterised the processes preceding many international adoptions, including bribery, coercion and trafficking (see Chapters 4 and 10). As we have seen in relation to permanence, and especially the deliberate breaking of birth family ties to assist adoption, John felt strongly that it was vital to have a legitimate justification for such profound actions. Similarly in relation to intercountry adoption, he argued that this should only occur when full safeguards for children's rights were in place (see Chapter 10). That necessitated, in his view, either birth parent consent or court-sanctioned grounds for dispensing with consent in the child's best interest. He deplored the lack of regulation that was common until the 1990s and was concerned that as national and international agreements were introduced they were often ineffective. Simmonds (2009) largely concurred with this viewpoint and stated that moving children cannot be justified simply because they are going to more advantageous circumstances. He commented: 'the point at which adoption becomes necessary for the child and ethically defensible is something that continues to exercise policy-makers, legislators and practitioners' (p. 224). A number of former source countries have now banned intercountry adoption, but what John referred to as "the trade" has grown elsewhere, particularly from Africa (Selman, 2009).

John was very conscious that the impulse for children to be transplanted from one country to another and the associated corruption reflected deep poverty in many countries and the relative wealth of would-be adopters. Hence he was in favour of strategies to reduce poverty and to ban private and independent adoptions. He drew an interesting parallel with the work of Richard Titmuss on blood donation to argue for altruistic gift mechanisms to prevail over market forces in adoption (see Chapter 10). He recognised poverty as a major factor in prompting not only intercountry adoption but all adoptions, so that tackling this should be a vital accompaniment to any policy for separated children (Triseliotis, 1995).

The social work role

As a social work educator for many years, John was naturally interested in how social workers performed in relation to children and families, and how well. Many of his studies relied in part on social workers as informants and obtained feedback from other key parties about social work.

He was a strong believer in the capacity of social workers to provide well-rounded assessments, notably for courts, and to offer intense and constructive support and counselling, as well as link young people and parents to other services. His research pointed to examples where this indeed occurred (e.g. Triseliotis *et al*, 1995a), but also to shortcomings as perceived by birth families and foster carers. He regretted the fact that working with families as a whole seemed to have become rare outside specialist agencies (see Chapter 6; Marsh and Triseliotis, 1993; Triseliotis *et al*, 1995a). He was sceptical about the value of psychoanalytical group work, but believed in the helpfulness of activity-based, task-centred and support groups. He described the influence of ideas about learning, role and dynamics in the varied types of group, which emerged in the 1980s and continue to this day as part of foster care and adoption assessment, preparation and support. Integral to most of these approaches has been the emphasis on positive contributions by group members as learners and problem-solvers (Triseliotis, 1988a). He cited early research evidence about the benefits of group training on placement stability. Curiously, subsequent systematic evaluations of group training have not been able to demonstrate any benefits for fostered children, although they have shown that foster carers tend to like the training and it does alter their parental attitudes and practices (Minnis and Divine, 2001; Pithouse *et al*, 2002).

Through his children's research, John had become aware of gaps in social work expertise, so he was keen when the opportunity arose to assess the impact of social work training (Marsh and Triseliotis, 1996; Triseliotis and Marsh, 1996). While social work programmes received much positive feedback, many students and supervisors identified inadequacies in skills training and in applied teaching more generally. Insufficient detail had been learned about child protection and accommodated children. It remains the case that social work courses, even with the advent of full degree programmes, are spread thinly across a wide range of knowledge and skill areas, so that many students start to practice with limited child care expertise (CWDC, 2009; McIntyre and Orme, 2011).

In his later years, John expressed disappointment in what appeared to be a diminution in direct work by social workers. In what was his final published article, he noted that 'there had been much soul searching in social work journals regarding the loss of skills and the importance of building relationships and trust with services-users' (Triseliotis, 2012, p. 265). For a range of reasons, other experts have voiced similar concerns about the need for statutory social work organisations to allow more time for professional relationship-based work (e.g. Munro, 2011), perhaps within smaller family-focused departments (Holman, 2001). John recognised that the demands of dealing with child protection as well as the increased requirements of multi-agency meetings and "managerialism" left most (local authority) social workers with little time for frequent contact and in-depth work with children or carers (cf. Kirton, 2009; Dickens, 2010). These factors help explain findings from John's research that the frequency of contact and quality of help offered were highly variable and, though sometimes very good, could be poorly regarded by young people, birth parents and foster carers (Triseliotis, 1995a; see Chapter 9). He recognised that social workers nowadays make more concerted efforts to promote contact between separated children and their birth families than in previous decades, but also believed that crucial assessments were too often superficial (Chapter 13). Nevertheless, he commended the skilled and sensitive approach of some practitioners supervising contact. It remains a challenge, especially within local government, to reconcile the multiple duties and accountability structures for children's social work, with its ideals of being relationship based and reflective and having a capacity to tolerate yet minimise risk (Wilson *et al*, 2008). Turney *et al* (2012) have argued in favour of thorough contextual and historical assessment of families. They also warn of the importance of being aware of the opposite dangers of either being deflected from effective engagement with parents by focusing solely on the child, or allowing enmeshment in family dynamics to distract from a clear view of what is best for him or her. John knew that to manage such complexities well for the benefit of children required skilled, well-trained social workers working within a supportive organisational environment and with the time to build good relationships with children, family members and carers.

And now read on

The above synopsis has illustrated how John anticipated, charted and contributed to many developments related to children separated from their birth families. His research and writings covered issues and dilemmas likely to remain pertinent for many years to come. For example: When birth families have major difficulties providing adequate care for a child, how much effort should be put into enabling the child to return home? In what circumstances is it legitimate to make a permanent alternative arrangement? When and how should fostered and adopted children remain in touch with birth relatives? A major preoccupation for John was in comparing the short-term and long-term consequences of different kinds of care. Doubtless in years to come new research will shed fresh light on such issues, but John's commentaries about evidence will still need heeding. It is vital to take account of the complexity of care situations. Judging progress involves many criteria that often produce mixed results and statistical evidence should combine with deep understanding and careful listening to the key parties involved. Key to John's approach to work and to life was sympathy for disadvantaged people and a willingness to engage with multiple viewpoints.

Many academics, practitioners and students have stated that John's writings are interesting, relevant and incisive, as his verbal present-ations were. Hopefully the reader will now proceed to obtain pleasure and insights from the work reprinted in the rest of this book.

References

Austerberry H., Stanley N., Larkins C., Ridley J., Farrelly N., Manthorpe J. and Hussein, S. (2013) 'Foster carers and family contact: foster carers' views of social work support', *Adoption & Fostering* 37:2, pp. 116–129

Bayes K. (2009) *Higher Aspirations, Brighter Futures*, Glasgow: Scottish Institute for Residential Child Care

Biehal N. (2007) 'Reuniting children with their families', *British Journal of Social Work* 37:5, pp. 807–823

Biehal N. (2009) 'Foster care for adolescents', in Schofield G. and Simmonds J. (eds) *The Child Placement Handbook*, London: BAAF

Biehal N., Ellison S. and Sinclair I. (2012) 'Intensive fostering: an independent evaluation of MTFC in an English setting', *Adoption & Fostering* 36:1, pp. 13–26

Borland M., O'Hara G. and Triseliotis J. (1991) 'Placement outcomes for children with special needs', *Adoption & Fostering* 15:2: pp. 18–27

Brown J., Chakrabarti M. and Triseliotis J. (1994) *Fostering an Anti-racist Perspective in Social Work Education and Training through Networking*, Glasgow: University of Strathclyde

Bullock R. (2009) 'Residential care', in Schofield G. and Simmonds J. (eds) *The Child Placement Handbook*, London: BAAF

Clapton G. (2003) *Birth Fathers and their Adoption Experiences*, London: Jessica Kingsley

Clifton J. (2012) 'Birth fathers and their adopted children: fighting, withdrawing or connecting', *Adoption & Fostering* 36:2, pp. 43–56

Clough R. (2005) 'Children in residence', in Axford N., Berry V., Little M. and Morpeth L. (eds) *Forty Years of Research, Policy and Practice in Children's Services*, Chichester: Wiley

Clough R., Bullock A. and Ward A. (2006) *What Works in Residential Care*, London: National Children's Bureau

Coussée F., Bradt L., Roose R. and Bouverne-de-Bie M. (2010) 'The emerging social pedagogical paradigm in UK child and youth care', *British Journal of Social Work* 40:3, pp. 789–805

CWDC (Children's Workforce Development Council) (2009) *Submission to the Social Work Task Force*, London: DfES

Daniel B. and Wassell S. (2002) *Assessing and Promoting Resilience in Vulnerable Children*, London: BAAF

Dickens J. (2010) *Social Work and Social Policy*, London: Routledge

Dolan P., Canavan J. and Pinkerton J. (2006) *Family Support as Reflective Practice*, London: Jessica Kingsley

Farmer E. (2009) 'Reunification with birth families', in Schofield G. and Simmonds J. (eds.) *The Child Placement Handbook*, London: BAAF.

Farmer E., Moyers S. and Lipscombe J. (2004) *Fostering Adolescents*, London: Jessica Kingsley

Feast J., Kyle J. and Triseliotis J. (2011) 'Adoptive fathers' experiences of search and reunion', *Adoption & Fostering* 35:1, pp. 57–64

Feast J., Grant M., Rushton A., Simmonds J. and Sampeys C. (2013) *Adversity, Adoption and Afterwards*, London: BAAF

Featherstone B., Morris K. and White S. (2013) 'A marriage made in hell: early intervention meets child protection', *British Journal of Social Work*, doi: 10.1093/bjsw/bct052

Gilligan R. (1997) 'Beyond permanence? The importance of resilience in child placement practice and planning', *Adoption & Fostering* 21:1, pp. 12–20

Gilligan R. (2008) *Promoting Resilience*, London: BAAF

Grimshaw R. with Berridge D. (1994) *Educating Disruptive Children*, London: National Children's Bureau

Heptinstall J., Bhopal K. and Brannen J. (2001) 'Adjusting to a foster family: children's perspectives', *Adoption & Fostering* 25:6, pp. 6–16

Hill M., Lambert L. and Triseliotis J. (1989) *Achieving Adoption with Love and Money*, London: National Children's Bureau

Hill M., Lambert L., Triseliotis J. and Buist M. (1992) 'Making judgements about parenting: the example of freeing for adoption', *British Journal of Social Work* 22:4, pp. 373–91

Hill M., Triseliotis J., Borland M. and Lambert L. (1996) 'Outcomes for teenagers on supervision and in care', in Hill M. and Aldgate J. (eds) *Child Welfare in the United Kingdom and Ireland*, London: Jessica Kingsley

Holman B. (1988) *Putting Families First*, London: Macmillan

Holman B. (2001) *Champions for Children*, Bristol: Policy Press

Howe D. and Feast J. (2000) *Adoption, Search and Reunion*, London: The Children's Society

Hussell C. and Monaghan B. (1982) 'Child care planning in Lambeth', *Adoption & Fostering* 6:2, pp. 21–25

Jackson S. (1989) 'The education of children in care', in Kahan B. (ed.) *Child Care: Research, policy and practice*, London: Hodder & Stoughton

Jackson S. (ed.) (2013) *Pathways through Education for Young People in Care: Ideas from research and practice*, London: BAAF

Jones A. (2003) 'The fiction of permanence', in Douglas A. and Philpot T. (eds) *Adoption: Changing families, changing times*, London: Routledge

Kirton D. (2009) *Child Social Work, Policy and Practice*, London: Sage

Kirton D. (2013) 'Kinship by design in England', *Child & Family Social Work* 18:1, pp. 97–106

Kirton D., Beecham J. and Ogilvie K. (2006) 'Adoption by foster carers: a profile of interest and outcomes', *Child & Family Social Work* 11:2, pp. 139–146

Lambert L., Buist M., Triseliotis J. and Hill M. (1990) *Freeing Children for Adoption*, London: BAAF

McKay M. (1980) 'Planning for permanent placement', *Adoption & Fostering* 4:1, pp. 19–21

McIntyre G. and Orme J. (2011) 'What a difference a degree makes', in Taylor R., Hill M. and McNeill F. (eds) *Early Professional Development for Social Workers*, London: Venture Press

McRoy R.G., Lynch J., Chanmugam A., Madden E. and Ayers-Lopez S. (2009) 'Children from care can be adopted', in Wrobel G.M. and Neil E. (eds) *International Advances in Adoption Research for Practice*, Chichester: Wiley

Maluccio A., Fein E. and Olmstead K.A. (1986) *Permanency Planning for Children*, London: Tavistock

Marsh P. and Triseliotis J. (eds) (1993) *Prevention and Reunification in Child Care*, London: Batsford

Marsh P. and Triseliotis J. (1996) *Ready to Practice?*, Aldershot: Ashgate

Minnis H. and Devine C. (2001) 'The effect of foster carer training on the emotional and behavioural functioning of looked after children', *Adoption & Fostering* 25:1, pp. 44–54

Munro E. (2011) *The Munro Review of Child Protection*, London: Department for Education

Neil E., Cossar J., Jones C., Lorgelly P. and Young J. (2011) *Supporting Direct Contact After Adoption*, London: BAAF

Newman T., Moseley A., Tierney S. and Ellis A. (2005) *Evidence-based Social Work*, Lyme Regis: Russell House Publishing

Parker R., Hill M. and Feast J. (2013) 'The life and work of John Triseliotis', *Adoption & Fostering* 37:1, pp. 5–8

Pithouse A., Hill-Tout J. and Lowe K. (2002) 'Training foster carers in challenging behaviour: a case study in disappointment, *Child & Family Social Work* 7:3, pp. 203–14

Quinton D. and Selwyn J. (2006) 'Adoption: research, policy and practice', *Child & Family Law Quarterly* 18:4, pp. 459–77

Quinton D., Rushton A., Dance C. and Mayes D. (1997) 'Contact between children placed away from home and their birth parents: research issues and evidence', *Clinical Child Psychology and Psychiatry* 2:3, pp. 393–411

Randle M. (2013) 'Through the eyes of ex-foster children: placement success and the characteristics of good foster carers', *Practice* 25:1, pp. 3–19

Schofield G. (2003) *Part of the Family: Pathways through foster care*, London: BAAF

Sellick C. (2006) 'From famine to feast: a review of the foster care research literature', *Children & Society* 20:1, pp. 67–74

Sellick C. (2011) 'The rise of independent foster care', in Taylor R., Hill M. and McNeill F. (eds) *Early Professional Development for Social Workers*, London: Venture Press

Selman P. (2009) 'From Bucharest to Beijing', in Wrobel G.M. and Neil E. (eds) *International Advances in Adoption Research for Practice*, Chichester: Wiley

Sen R. (2010) 'Managing contact in Scotland for children in non-permanent placement', *Child Abuse Review* 19:6, pp. 423–37

Sen R. and Broadhurst K. (2011) 'Contact between children in out-of-home placements and their families and friends networks: a research review', *Child & Family Social Work* 16:3, pp. 289–309

Sen R. and McCormack J. (2011) 'Foster carers' involvement in contact: other professionals' views', *Practice* 23:5, pp. 279–92

Sheldon B. and Macdonald G. (2009) *A Textbook of Social Work*, London: Routledge

Simmonds J. (2009) 'Adoption: developmental perspectives within an ethical, legal and policy framework', in Schofield G. and Simmonds J. (eds) *The Child Placement Handbook*, London: BAAF

Sinclair I. (2005) *Fostering Now*, London: Jessica Kingsley

Sinclair I., Gibbs I. and Wilson K. (2001) 'A life more ordinary', *Adoption & Fostering* 25:4, pp. 17–26

Sinclair I., Gibbs I. and Wilson K. (2004) *Foster Carers: Why they stay and why they leave*, London: Jessica Kingsley

Sinclair I., Wilson K. and Gibbs I. (2005) *Foster Placements: Why they succeed and why they fail*, London: Jessica Kingsley

Smith C. and Logan J. (2004) *After Adoption*, London: Routledge

Thoburn J. (1994) *Child Placement: Principles and practice*, Aldershot: Avebury

Thoburn, J. (2003) 'Home news and abroad', in Douglas A. and Philpot T. (eds) *Adoption: Changing families, changing times*, London: Routledge

Thomas C. (2013) *Adoption for Looked After Children: Messages from research*, London: BAAF

Tisdall E.K.M., Davis J.M. and Gallagher M. (2009) *Research with Children and Young People: Research design, methods and analysis*, London: Sage

Triseliotis J. (ed.) (1972) *Social Work with Coloured Immigrants and their Families*, Oxford: Oxford University Press

Triseliotis J. (1973) *In Search of Origins*, London: Routledge & Kegan Paul

Triseliotis J. (1977) *Social Welfare in Cyprus*, London: Zeno Booksellers and Publishers

Triseliotis J. (1980a) 'Growing up in foster care and after', in Triseliotis J. (ed.) *New Developments in Foster Care and Adoption*, London: Routledge & Kegan Paul

Triseliotis J. (1980b) 'Counselling adoptees', in Triseliotis J. (ed.) *New Developments in Foster Care and Adoption*, London: Routledge & Kegan Paul

Triseliotis J. (1983) 'Identity and security in adoption', *Adoption & Fostering* 7:1, pp. 22–31

Triseliotis J. (1985) 'Adoption with contact', *Adoption & Fostering* 9:4, pp. 19–24

Triseliotis J. (ed.) (1988a) *Group Work in Adoption and Foster Care*, London: Batsford

Triseliotis J. (1988b) 'Adoption services and counselling', *Adoption & Fostering* 12:2, pp. 31–37

Triseliotis J. (1989a) 'Foster care outcomes', *Adoption & Fostering* 13:3, pp. 5–17

Triseliotis J. (1989b) 'Some moral and practical issues in adoption work', *Adoption & Fostering* 13:2, pp. 21–27

Triseliotis, J. (1991a) 'Perceptions of permanence', *Adoption & Fostering* 15:4, pp. 6–15

Triseliotis J. (1991b) 'Intercountry adoption: a brief overview of the research evidence', *Adoption & Fostering* 15:4, pp. 46–52

Triseliotis J. (1991c) 'Maintaining the links in adoption', *British Journal of Social Work* 21, pp. 401–414

Triseliotis, J. (1993) 'The Theory Continuum', in Marsh P. and Triseliotis J. (eds) (1993) *Prevention and Reunification in Child Care*, London: Batsford

Triseliotis J. (1995) 'Adoption: evolution or revolution?', *Adoption & Fostering* 19:2, pp. 37–44

Triseliotis J. (1998) 'When is evaluation a scientific activity, when is it not?', *Scandinavian Journal of Social Welfare* 7:2, pp. 87–93

Triseliotis J. (1998/99) 'Is permanency through adoption in decline?', *Adoption & Fostering* 22:4, pp. 41–49

Triseliotis J. (2002) 'Long-term foster care or adoption? The evidence examined', *Child & Family Social Work* 7:1, pp. 23–33

Triseliotis J. (2012) 'Classic Text Review of Social Work with Families by E. Sainsbury', *Practice* 24:4, pp. 265–67

Triseliotis J. and Hill M. (1990) 'Contrasting adoption, foster care and residential rearing', in Brodzinsky D.M. and Schechter M.D. (eds) *The Psychology of Adoption*, Oxford: Oxford University Press

Triseliotis J. and Kousidou T. (1989) *Social Work in Adoption and Foster Care*, Athens: Centre for Child Care Mitera

Triseliotis J. and Marsh P. (1996) *Readiness to Practice*, Edinburgh: The Scottish Office

Triseliotis J. and Russell J. (1984) *Hard to Place*, London: Heinemann

Triseliotis J., Borland M. and Hill M. (1998) 'Foster carers who cease to foster', *Adoption & Fostering* 22:2, pp. 54–62

Triseliotis J., Borland M. and Hill M. (2000) *Delivering Foster Care*, London: BAAF

Triseliotis J., Feast J. and Kyle J. (2005) *The Adoption Triangle Revisited: A study of adoption, search and reunion*, London: BAAF

Triseliotis J., Sellick C. and Short R. (1995b) *Foster Care: Theory and practice*, London: Batsford

Triseliotis J., Shireman J. and Hundleby M. (1997) *Adoption: Theory, policy and practice*, London: Cassell

Triseliotis J., Borland M., Hill M. and Lambert L. (1995a) *Teenagers and the Social Work Services*, London: HMSO

Triseliotis J., Borland M., Hill M. and Lambert L. (1998) 'Social work supervision of young people', *Child & Family Social Work* 3:1, pp. 27–36

Turney D., Platt D., Selwyn J. and Farmer E. (2012) *Improving Child and Family Assessments*, London: Jessica Kingsley

Walker H., Wilson P. and Minnis H. (2013) 'The impact of a new service for maltreated children on Children's Hearings in Scotland', *Adoption & Fostering* 37:1, pp. 14–27

Walker M., Hill M. and Triseliotis J. (2002) *Testing the Limits of Foster Care*, London: BAAF

Walker R. (2010) 'Family intervention model to keep children out of care', *Community Care*, 6 March

Ward H., Brown R. and Westlake D. (2012) *Safeguarding Babies and Very Young Children*, London: Jessica Kingsley

Wilson K., Ruch G., Lymbery M. and Cooper A. (2008) *Social Work: An introduction to contemporary practice*, Harlow: Pearson

Young J. and Neil E. (2009) 'Contact after adoption', in Schofield G. and Simmonds J. (eds) *The Child Placement Handbook*, London: BAAF

Book reviews

Berridge D. (1996) Review of *Foster Care: Theory and Practice* (Triseliotis *et al*, 1995b) *Child & Family Social Work* 1:1, pp. 71–72

Clapton G. (2012) Review of *Adoption & Fostering*, special edition on '30 Years of Child Care Practice and Research' (2010), *Children & Society* 26:2, pp. 164–66

Cottingham U. (1988) Review of *Group Work in Adoption and Foster Care* (Triseliotis, 1988a) *Children & Society* 2:4, pp. 395–97

Feast J. (1997) Review of *Adoption: Theory, policy and practice* (Triseliotis *et al*, 1997) *Children & Society* 11:4, pp. 271–73

Jones D. (1993) Review of *Prevention and Reunification in Child Care* (Marsh and Triseliotis, 1993) *British Journal of Social Work* 23:6, pp. 690–92

Kelly G. (2000) Review of *Delivering Foster Care* (Triseliotis *et al*, 2000) *Adoption & Fostering* 24:3, pp. 85–6

Mann P. (1980) Review of *New Developments in Foster Care and Adoption* (Triseliotis, 1980) *British Journal of Social Work* 10:4, pp. 531–32

Neil B. (1997) Review of *Adoption: Theory, policy and practice* (Triseliotis *et al*, 1997) *Adoption & Fostering* 21:2, pp. 68–69

Sen R. (2013) Classic text review of *In Search of Origins* (Triseliotis, 1973) *Practice* 25:1, pp. 75–77

Stein M. (1996) Review of *Teenagers and the Social Work Services* (Triseliotis *et al*, 1995a) *Adoption & Fostering* 20:1, pp. 60–61

1   *In Search of Origins*: summary and discussion

This collection begins with the concluding chapter of In Search of Origins: The experiences of adopted people *(Routledge & Kegan Paul, 1973). This was John's first major book about adoption. It made a significant contribution to the greater openness that occurred from the 1970s onwards as regards communication with adopted children, adults seeking information on their background and contact with birth family members. The book is based on a detailed examination of the experiences and views of 70 adult adoptees, who either wanted more information about their birth families or wished to find one or both parents.*

The main aim of the study was to establish the past and current circumstances of adopted people who sought information about their origins and to examine their motivation for the search, their needs and general outlook. Adoptees in Scotland can usually expect to obtain from official records information about where and when they were born, who their original parents were and where they lived and what the occupation of the father or mother was at the time of birth. Because most adopted children are "illegitimate", it is seldom that information about the father is available.

Each year only, a very small number of adopted people feel the impulse to seek out this type of genealogical information. Because most of those featuring in the study embarked on their search without prior knowledge of their special right, it can be assumed that if other adoptees felt the same need they would have done likewise. For the vast number of adoptees the impulse to search was in response to some deeply felt psychological need and rarely to a matter-of-fact attitude.

Two groups of adoptees were identified whose stated search goals differed from the start. The goal of the first group was to find one or both of their natural parents while that of the second was to obtain background genealogical information. The two groups differed from each other in a number of ways, thus affording an opportunity not only for comparison but especially for gaining certain insights into the feelings, thinking and general needs of adopted people and in particular of those preoccupied with their origins. The adoptees who wanted to meet their natural parents were far more strongly motivated and more determined than those interested only in background information.

The adoptees in the sample came from different parts of the country and some were living outside Scotland at the time of the enquiry. A small number referred to their adoptive parents as foster parents, the word "adoptive" not being much in use in their areas for this form of substitute parent–child relationship. This lack of differentiation between adoption and foster care could easily lead to misunderstandings where social workers were selecting families to act as foster parents rather than as adoptive ones.

A very high percentage of adoptees in the sample came to know about their adoptive status well after the age usually recommended by the literature on adoption. Three out of every five were told or found out after the age of 10. The later parents postponed the revelation the greater the possibility that the adoptee would find out from outside sources. In the absence of a control sample it is difficult to say whether adoptees who do not search into their original background are told at an earlier or at a similar stage. The fact that a great number of adoptees came to know about their adoptive status during adolescence and after made it possible for the study to reflect on certain developments in their lives that could not have been complicated by the knowledge of adoption.

Though the stage of "telling" did not seem to be of paramount importance, adoptees who were told when under the age of 10 were the more satisfied and the reverse was true of those who were told later. The majority of the adoptees thought that the age of four to eight was the most appropriate for "telling". Finding out from outside sources was strongly resented and the parents' reluctance to tell was bitterly criticised. Those who found out late or came to know about their adoption from outside sources were the most hurt and upset. It shook the faith of many of them in their parents and where it was accompanied by other adverse experiences within the family, irreparable damage was caused to the relationship between the adoptee and his parents.

The general reaction to being told by or finding out from outside sources, especially in adolescence and adult life, was mostly painful and distressing. On the basis of the adoptees' comments the view was formed that adoption is felt as a form of abandonment or rejection irrespective of the quality of other experiences. When knowledge of adoption is delayed till adolescence or adult age, the feeling of "rejection" seems to be infinitely greater than when revelation takes place in earlier years. It appears that when knowledge of adoption comes early – possibly before the age of eight or 10 – there is time for the trauma to heal where accepting and cherishing relationships prevail. The scar, however, appears to remain for ever and is liable to open up under extreme forms of stress. When knowledge of adoption is delayed till adolescence and beyond, the possibility of a healing process is considerably diminished.

Among adoptees the initial reaction to late discovery of the adoption situation was one of shock and stunned numbness. Later it was followed by grief accompanied by intense criticism and anger towards the parents for holding back. The adoptees' grief took the form of directing most of their thoughts and feelings to objects or information associated with their birth parents but especially the mother. The process of grief seemed difficult for many because they had no, or very little, information about the "lost" set of parents to whom to attach the feeling.

Adoptees who were told at some time below the age of 11 could not remember reacting so strongly or painfully at the time except where the revelation took a destructive and vindictive form. Otherwise some parents were able to transmit through "telling" a feeling of pride and well-being, which the adoptees valued immensely. When the meaning of adoption, i.e. "surrender" and "loss", started to seep in, a kind of retrospective thinking and grieving began; it was far more manageable compared with those who only came to know about their adoption in their teens or later.

There was a general reluctance among adoptive parents to reveal or share information about the child's original genealogy and also how he came to be adopted. Though this attitude, as well as the reluctance to reveal the adoptive situation at all, had some cultural sanction in certain parts of the country, in most other cases inform-ation was deliberately withheld because of the parents' fears and anxieties. The adoptees interpreted their parents' failure to share with them as reflecting a lack of trust and precariously built relationships. Many regretted the fact that "telling" about adoption and gradually sharing information was not used as an opportunity to develop and cement family relationships. Though some adoptees were prepared to recognise that their parents withheld or distorted certain particulars because they wanted to protect them, they still maintained that truth and honesty would have helped to enhance their respect for them. It would have been easier, they argued, to come to terms with painful facts about themselves than to live with lies and have their trust in their parents shaken. Secrecy and evasiveness gave many the feeling that adoption was something shameful or not the done thing. This feeling, which was often reinforced by community attitudes, contrib-uted to the development of a poor self-image and to a reluctance among adoptees to reveal their adoption even to people very close to them.

Adoptees who were given no information about their background, or to whom some information was disclosed but in a hostile way which was often depreciative of the natural parents, were generally keen to find their birth parents. Their total attention and impulses were in this direction. In contrast, those who were told something positive about their natural parents were now mostly inclined to search for additional information about their genealogical back-ground. Similarly, where the adoptees had some knowledge about their origins the strength of their motivation for the search was weak. The opposite was true in cases where there was a lack of such information.

There was a stage in the adoptees' life, mostly before the age of about 11, when they did not seem particularly interested to talk about their adoption and in fact would not have welcomed frequent discussion. It was at the start of their early teens that they mostly found themselves desperately wanting to hear from their parents about their adoption, about their origins and about their first set of parents. This need reached its climax in adolescence and it appeared to be closely associated with the adoptees' efforts to establish their identity as individuals, wanting at the same time to integrate their first parents into their system in order to feel more complete. Satisfaction of this need at the adolescent stage, the adoptees maintained, would have helped them to understand themselves and other people better and possibly to forestall their subsequent preoccupation with their first set of parents. The adoptees were quite clear, however, that some preoccupation with one's origins never stops except with death.

It was a characteristic of most of the families in which there was little or no communication about the adoption situation, that there was a lack of communication about other things as well. For some families this reflected a traditional pattern of functioning, while for others it was the result of "family malfunctioning". While the former was mostly a characteristic of working-class families the latter transcended social class barriers. In both instances the adoptees felt deprived of what they saw as their birthright to know. Though almost all the adoptees were emphatic that both the telling and sharing of detailed information were of great importance, they also conveyed the view that these aspects were meaningless unless seen in the context of the totality of life situations and experiences.

Besides many adoptees' frustrations and criticisms about the stage at which their adoptive status was revealed to them and about the kind of information they were given, there was a fundamental disappointment in the quality of their family relationships. Many of them perceived their adoptive home life as unsatisfactory, lacking in feeling and warmth, and as having failed to develop in them a sense of attachment, belonging and pride in being adopted. They did not meet with any form of discrimination in favour of other siblings within the adoptive home but claimed that their experiences of an unhappy home life were also shared by the parents' own children, where these existed. For the group of adoptees who experienced their adoptive home life as unsatisfactory, preoccupation with this took precedence over all other types of relationships, such as wife and husband or mother and child.

In a small number of cases, however, earlier "good" relationships seemed to be distorted by recent events such as death of a parent, property disputes, illness, etc. Many adoptees attributed their own unhappiness, sense of emptiness, isolation and sometimes distress to either the poor quality of their home life or to the fact of being adopted.

Where the adoptees' perception was generally of an unsatisfactory home life it was usually accompanied by a poor self-perception, too. Many had a negative image of themselves and talked of their inner "void", their desolation and general incapacity to form meaningful relationships with other people. They felt ashamed and embarrassed at being adopted and illegitimate. A fair number had already received psychiatric treatment while others were in obvious need of such help. The search itself was helping many to keep themselves together and the process was assuming greater importance than the goal. Their main criticism of their home life was about the lack of emotional satisfactions, absence of warmth and failure to develop in them a sense of belonging. The greater the dissatisfaction with their family relationships and with themselves, the greater the possibility that they would now be searching for their original parents. The better their image of themselves and of their parents, the greater the possibility that they would be looking for background information.

Though adolescence was the most common period when the adoptees first thought of enquiring into their origins, it was some subsequent life crisis that eventually decided them to act. The most usual events that generated an impulse to search were death of one or both parents, illness, expectation of a child, pending marriage or separation or when inner pressures could no longer be contained. The most severe crises were precipitated by events which carried a sense of loss or abandonment, such as death of a parent, especially when followed by the remarriage of the surviving one and separation from or desertion by a parent, husband, boyfriend or girlfriend. Crises of this nature seemed to affect worse those who were less well settled and more vulnerable. The current experience of loss appeared to reawaken the "rejection" or "abandonment" felt through the loss of the first parents. The death of one or both adoptive parents was usually followed by a strong desire for the first set of parents, especially the mother, but its intensity varied depending on the quality of the adoptees' earlier home life.

The adoptees' expectations from the search were closely associated with the type and amount of information revealed, with the quality of their home life, the perception of themselves and with the nature of their current stress. Though all of them wanted to find answers to such questions as to who their natural parents were, why they were given up for adoption and whether their first set of parents wanted them and loved them, many were also hoping to develop a relationship of friendship with them. There was a hope that their original parents would make up to them what they had missed from their earlier relationships. The ones who were mainly satisfied with their adoptive home life were looking for information that would help them to complete themselves, while the more disillusioned ones were hoping for nourishment from mainly the mother.

The outcome of the search left many adoptees with mixed feelings. Those who were looking for additional information were generally satisfied with the results but ideally they would have liked more detailed particulars. They were surprised to find the paucity of the official records which often did not go beyond what they already knew. Those who set out hoping to meet their parents were less satisfied. Though they welcomed what information they obtained they were mostly unsuccessful in their attempts to attain their main goal. After the initial search a very small number were thinking of giving up, but the rest – and these were mostly the ones who were feeling under the greatest pressure – were determined to go on. For them the search and its continuation seemed to protect them from their loneliness and unhappiness.

A very small number were eventually successful in finding a parent or a blood relation. With one exception, there was no indication that earlier expectations were fulfilled or relationships developed. Where a meeting occurred it was usually followed by some disillusionment in the adoptee, with a tendency for the latter to transfer on to the original parents many feelings that were formerly held about the adoptive ones. The adoptees claimed, however, that following these contacts they found it easier to come to terms with their condition and circumstances.

Almost all the adoptees, irrespective of the objectives and outcome of their search, were in favour not only of retaining the system by which they were able to obtain information, but also of improving it.

In conclusion, the majority of adoptees searching into their genealogical background and especially most, but not all, of those trying to find their birth parents were unhappy and lonely people and a considerable number had had psychiatric help. They generally hoped that the search would lead to new nurturing relationships or at least to the development of a more secure personality. A number of important factors jointly or separately seemed to combine to bring about the search for the natural parents. These were: the non-disclosure of background genealogical information or the revelation of only hostile particulars; unsatisfactory adoptive home relationships; a negative self-image; and having had psychiatric help. Late knowledge of adoption had no significant influence on the search goals. A core of 22 adoptees in the Meet the Natural Parents group shared three important characteristics: the non-disclosure of background information or the revelation of only hostile particulars; unsatisfactory adoptive family relationships; and negative self-image. Only one adoptee in the Background Information group shared all these three characteristics.

The study identified three main areas which have important implications for adoption practice: the developing child's need for a warm, caring and secure family life; the adoptees' vulnerability to experiences of loss, rejection or abandonment; and the adopted person's need to know as much as possible about the circumstances of their adoption and about their genealogical background in order to integrate these facts into their developing personality.

The unhappiness and disillusionment of many adoptees who featured in the study were often associated with an emotionally sterile early family life, which was later reinforced by other adverse life experiences. Being adopted, as such, did not appear to be the real cause for the breakdown of the personal relationships described. The adoptees wished for parents who were happily married, who could display their love and affection, making them feel secure and wanted. Provided that the home was a loving one and the child accepted for what it was, bringing up an adopted child did not seem to differ from rearing an own or any other child. This conclusion was mainly reached because the adoptive parents' attitude towards their own children (where these existed) did not differ from that towards the adopted ones. In other words, the parents' attitude towards their adopted children was a reflection of their general child rearing practices. A further observation pointing to this conclusion was the adoptees' varied coping with late revelation, which was related more to their perception of the quality of their adoptive home life rather than to the stage of "telling".

The adoption situation itself presents three main tasks which, if badly managed, could complicate the child–parent relationship. Where this happens the likelihood is that the difficulties will be projected on to the adoption situation. The first task is the degree of the parents' acceptance of their own condition and of the reality of their adoptive parenthood, emotionally coming to accept and recognise the child as their own. The undue stress often laid on the differences between adoption and biological parenthood tends to create considerable guilt feelings among parents who want to see the child as their own and relate to it unconditionally. While it is necessary for the parents to acknowledge the existence of the first set of parents, it is also imperative that at the same time they should come to feel that the child is rightfully theirs and to respond to it as if it were theirs by birth. After all, most of the adoptees interviewed said very clearly and definitely that though they knew they had a biological set of parents, it was to their adoptive mother and father that they responded as true parents and for whom they had real feelings. The words "mother" and "father" had emotional meaning only in relation to their adoptive parents and such feelings were evoked only in relation to them. They saw their adoptive parents as their true and rightful parents and even where the relationship failed, most of them still maintained very warm feelings for them. If adopted children want, and try, to see their adoptive parents as their real parents, it also follows that successful parenting must involve the emotional acceptance of the children as one's own, without inhibition or guilt.

Whether adoption agencies can select homes which can offer such qualities as "love", "warmth" and "acceptance" as outlined by the adoptees is debatable. These are all intangible qualities that are difficult to identify at the selection stage. Social workers and other similar professionals can reach only a limited level of agreement in their assessments of people and this makes any selection a precarious procedure. Interpretations of what is a "warm", "loving" and "secure" couple can differ and are open to a fair amount of speculation and guesswork. It is even more difficult to identify with certainty the kind of attitudes at the selection stage which point to likely relationship difficulties later on. Even if it were possible to make accurate assessments at the selection stage, there would still be no guarantee that people's attitudes, needs and reactions would not change under the impact of new experiences which might affect the parent–child relationship. General statements at the selection stage regarding a couple's feelings about their childlessness and infertility are usually not indicative of future reactions to a real child. When applicants are under scrutiny and over-dependent on the agency, they are unlikely anyway to share their true feelings. More careful selection could have perhaps eliminated the most gross aspects of emotional and physical neglect the study came across but perhaps not the rest. Similarly, the current practice of theoretical preparation for adoptive parenthood seems to be of limited value as it deals with the parents in isolation. Practice suggests that it is with the real experience of caring for a child that some couples may need help, and ideally they should then feel able to consult with the placing agency. It could be argued, however, that the current methods of selection with the stress on the authority of the agency and the dependence of the client, do not encourage adoptive couples to go back to the agency for consultation without feeling a failure.

The adopted person's vulnerability to experiences of loss, abandonment or rejection is mostly related to his feelings about being given up by his original parents. The degree of acceptance of this condition varies among adoptees. Later losses or serious crises or disappointments in life seem to reactivate such feelings. Yet again, where the adopted person had developed a feeling of well-being and belonging later experiences of "rejection" or "loss" seemed to affect him less compared to those who did not come to feel in this way. Where the distress or unhappiness arising from such new experiences is focused on the adoption situation, the adoptee may be better helped by someone with knowledge and understanding of adoption.

Telling about adoption and sharing background information involves some very deep emotions on the part of the adopters and of the growing child. Irrespective of the adopters' readiness at selection stage to be honest and open with the child, when they are faced with the actual task some will find it difficult and will tend to postpone it until the child comes to find out from another source. This usually sets in motion a cycle of inhibitions, mistrust and speculation. For a number of reasons there will always be parents who find themselves unable to cope with some of the tasks that are peculiar to the adoption situation, such as "telling", the disclosure of information and the handling of adolescent behaviour which focuses difficulties on the adoption situation.

The various issues outlined above point to the obvious need for adoption agencies to see their work as part of an ongoing process rather than as a once and for all activity; in other words, to see adoption as part of a continuum and give equal emphasis to its different stages. The process of "selection" will have to be seen as an opportunity for preparation and for mutual trust to be developed between the agency and the parents. The agency's general approach and the organisation of its adoption work will determine, to a large extent, how far parents and children alike will feel able to call at the agency for consultation and advice, if necessary. It is hoped that the adoption agency of the future will always be available to natural and adoptive parents, as well as to adopted children and adults. Consultative services to these groups should be built into the structure of each agency and be made available and accessible, without unnecessary barriers, secrecy and evasiveness.

In Chapter 10 [*In Search of Origins*] there is a detailed discussion about the type of information that adoptees would ideally like to have about their origins and general background, including their original parents' medical history. The study has also shown that adolescence is the most crucial period during which adoptees become intensely preoccupied and curious about themselves and experience a strong urge to find out about their first pair of parents. They make a desperate attempt at this stage to complete themselves by integrating within their system their two pairs of parents. If knowledge about the first pair of parents is not forthcoming, such integration may not take place or it may turn out to be very precarious and likely to collapse under stress. Most adoptive parents seem to respond appropriately to their children's questions about their first parents, without feeling threatened or anxious. As a long period elapses, however, between the stage at which agencies pass on information to the parents and the stage at which the latter have to share it with their children, it would be advisable for agencies to make it a practice to give all relevant background particulars in writing. In this way not only are memory failures avoided but also, and equally important, is the avoidance of misinterpretation or misperception of verbal information.

Irrespective of the approach suggested above, a minority of parents may still not find it easy to share what they know or they may be dead at the time when the adoptee is most curious to find out more. It is also not unusual for some adolescents to find it easier to accept information and advice from an outside source rather than from their own parents. For these reasons it is again important that the adopted person, and especially the adolescent, comes to know that he can go at any time to the agency that arranged his adoption and ask for details about his origins and why and how his adoption was arranged. There is no obvious reason why the agency should not respond to this need and discuss and share with the adoptee alone, or in his family's presence, information from its records. Such a service would require that every agency keeps a very detailed account about the circumstances and genealogy of each child it places. The law could also help by directing that the birth certificate should bear the address of the agency that made the original arrangements so that adoptees would know where to go. Adoption agencies, by making themselves available, can be of great help not only to adoptees who happen to go through some crisis which they connect with their adoption, but also to some parents who find it difficult to cope with the child's repeated questions about his origins. The following extracts, from a letter addressed by a mother to her adoption worker, illustrate the latter point:

> Dear . . .
>
> I happened to have the radio on this morning when you were being interviewed . . . I was especially interested in the enquiry which is being made as to the advisability of adopted persons being allowed to find out from the register their parents' names . . . we feel quite strongly about this.
>
> Bruce, on two or three occasions, asked who his 'other mummy' was and he found it very hard to believe that I did not know. On the last occasion, in desperation, I said that when he was grown up he could go to a big office in Edinburgh and find out for himself. Since then he has never mentioned the subject again.
>
> We feel from our experience with our own adopted child that adopted children should be given the option of being able to trace their true mother . . .

Because of personality or other special factors it is very possible that for a very small number of adoptees no amount of information or counselling will be of much help to them. They may see a meeting with their original parents as the only solution to their problems and in this respect the agency may have to exercise its judgment whether to act as a go-between for the child and his first parents. When a situation like this arises, perhaps only experienced reality can help people to come to some terms with their losses. This could eventually help them to emerge strengthened out of their isolation and distress. In an unpublished study by Triseliotis and Hall, the majority of mothers surrendering their children in Edinburgh in 1970 said they would not object to a future meeting between themselves and their child if this were suggested as necessary for their child's welfare and mental health.

The placing agency should ideally offer similar facilities and opportunities for counselling to the natural father or mother who, years later, may be focusing his or her possible unhappiness and guilt on the relinquishment of the child. In extreme cases the agency would again have to exercise its judgment whether a meeting between the original parent and the adoptee were advisable. For such an arrangement to take place it would be necessary for the adoptee to be adult enough to cope with this and for the agency to have prepared the ground well. So far, adoption agencies have only rarely known of natural parents calling years later to ask for news about a relinquished child.

The experience from Finland confirms most of our findings and recommendations. The main adoption agency there, which places about 225 children each year (45% of the total adoptions in the country), provides for adoptees of any age calling in there to obtain background information about their biological parents. About 50 to 70 young people, mostly adolescents, go to the agency each year for information about their origins. Sometimes the initiative is taken by the adoptive parents who may call with the child. The service seems to have been of infinite benefit to the users without damage to the interests of other parties.[6]

The adoptees' quest for their origins was not a vindictive venture, but an attempt to understand themselves and their situation better. The contribution of the law and of adoption agencies towards such an

---

[6] Paper prepared by Elina Rautanen and read at the conference of the Association of British Adoption Agencies in Blackpool, December 1971.

objective can be of immense value to those who happen to feel in a limbo state. The self-perception of all of us is partly based on what our parents and ancestors have been, going back many generations. Adoptees, too, wish to base themselves not only on their adoptive parents, but also on what their original parents and forebears have been, going back many generations. It is the writer's view, based on his findings, that no person should be cut off from his origins.

Final note
The final report of the Departmental Committee on the Adoption of Children (Cmnd 5107), published in October 1972, made certain recommendations that give expression to the findings of this study. The report recommends that the adoption agency or, where there is no agency, the local authority, should be named on the adoption order, so that an adopted person may himself later be in a position to approach the agency for information that the adopters are unable or unwilling to provide. Furthermore, adoption agencies should be required to retain their records for 75 years. The committee also recommended that an adopted person aged 18 years or over should be entitled to a copy of his original birth certificate. This recommendation would cover all adopted adults in England, Wales and Scotland.

2 Identity and security in adoption and long-term fostering

This chapter, reprinted from Adoption & Fostering *(7:3, pp. 22–31, 1983), was an early example of comparing the experiences and current circumstances of young adults with contrasting care histories. One group had been placed for adoption between the ages of three and seven and the second group comprised people who had been fostered on a long-term basis. Three key ingredients were identified as promoting a sense of security in the adoptive or foster families: feeling wanted, knowledge of one's background and being perceived by others as worthwhile.*

The possible similarities and differences between people who grow up adopted and those in long-term fostering is a topic about which questions are frequently asked. Particular emphasis is usually placed on the possible qualitative similarities and differences between these two forms of "substitute" care. Since the implementation of legislation concerning approved adoption allowances in February 1982, a number of agencies have put up schemes providing for allowances to be paid to some foster parents who decide to adopt the children in their care. The underlying assumption appears to be that adoption is preferable for children in long-term foster care who have possibly lost contact with their parents. While some wonder whether it really makes any difference since the child will continue to live in the same household, Andrews (1971) suggests that the binding nature of adoption is of deep psychological significance to the long-term foster child. There are also those who suggest that long-term foster care (and residential care, for that matter) is an indication of failure in the agency's work, and that the eventual aim should be to do away with it altogether (Watson, 1968). Madison and Schapiro ask whether long-term foster care is third best after own family and adoption (1969).

Background

In this article I will be drawing from a larger study which contrasted people who grew up adopted with people who grew up in long-term fostering – average 11 years with the same foster parents – to examine mainly issues in identity formation. (The larger study covered also those who grew up in residential care, but no reference will be made to this group as the material contrasting late adoptions and residential care will appear in a book to be published by Heinemann.)[7] The adopted group referred to here were placed with their adoptive parents when aged between three and seven, and those in long-term fostering when aged between a few months and nine years old. (Only an insignificant percentage of fostering arrangements broke down before the child reached the age of 16.)

At the time of interview the 44 adoptees were mostly in their mid-20s and the 40 in the foster care group were in their early 20s. Both groups, but particularly those fostered, came from very disadvantaged natural families. The adoption of the adopted group was delayed mostly because they were seen at the time as an "at risk" group. This was either because of their own poor physical health or their parents' personal, mental or social circumstances. Only an insignificant proportion of the fostering placements were initially arranged with long-term aims in mind. Most of them drifted into long-term *de facto* adoptions through lapse rather than good planning.

A sense of personal identity

Concepts such as identity, security and a sense of belonging are elusive and difficult to define or measure. Fanshel *et al* (1978) had to abandon their attempts to measure feelings of being "wanted" or of "belonging", which are said to be very basic qualities for identity building, because it proved to be 'an extraordinarily difficult task'. It may, therefore, be seen as foolish to pursue this matter within the limited methodology available. Nevertheless, a start has to be made somewhere, recognising

---

[7]   The book referred to is *Hard to Place* (Triseliotis and Russell, 1984).

that biases may unintentionally enter into the discussion. For an evaluation of the respondents' respective sense of identity, attention was paid to the quality of their descriptions of experiences and to a range of self-rating questionnaires.

Personal identity is the result of multiple psychological, social and cultural influences that combine towards the building of an integrated and unified self. By personal identity I mean the kind of consciousness we all carry about "who" we are and the kind of self-image we have of ourselves. Depending on its quality and strength, the sense of self gives us a feeling of separateness from others, distinguishing us from our environment, while at the same time enabling us to enter into daily social interactions and relationships with a degree of confidence.

For the purposes of this article three areas were selected for study which are said to make a big contribution to identity building:

1. a childhood experience of feeling wanted and loved within a secure environment;
2. knowledge about one's background and personal history;
3. the experience of being perceived by others as a worthwhile person.

A childhood experience of feeling wanted and loved within a secure environment

Studies in child development may disagree about the exact stage in childhood when identity begins to be formed and when it stops, and which are the most crucial stages, but most of them agree that warm, caring and satisfying emotional experiences are important ingredients to the development of a secure self. Depending on the quality of the experience, it is claimed, a sense of self-image, bodily and mental, is cultivated from the moment the young infant begins to recognise another face, and continues throughout childhood and possibly beyond. Leaving aside possible genetic processes, the child's person-ality and sense of self is to a large extent dependent on repeated confirmatory emotional and other learning and socialising experi-ences throughout childhood. The implications of all these is that it is not possible for a person to develop a secure identity if he does not experience a sense of belonging within a secure family and social environment. Negative childhood emotional, social and learning experiences, such as discontinuity of care, emotional neglect and anxious parenting, and a lack of security can contribute to undermine the development of a secure sense of identity.

It was with these concepts in mind that all respondents in the study were asked to describe and rate the quality of their childhood experiences while growing up adopted or fostered. (The pros and cons of this approach are discussed in the book to be published by Heinemann referred to earlier.) Positive accounts given by both groups of respondents included: 'being brought up as their (parents') own'; 'being made to feel secure through their love'; 'enjoying my parents' love, care and kindness'; 'they were a real mum and dad to me'; 'loved for myself'; 'wanted and loved'. These accounts did not imply the absence of conflict but the subjects were referring to the totality of the experience and not to isolated parts.

About half of the respondents in each of the two groups spoke with real enthusiasm and satisfaction about their growing up experiences and the quality of care they received from their adoptive or foster families. Both groups indicated that strong feelings of attachment and psychological bonds developed between themselves and their "substitute" parents. These close relationships carried on into adult life and were a source of continued mutual satisfaction and support. These respondents felt secure, wanted and loved by their "parents" and experienced a strong sense of "belonging". A further third of those adopted, but only about a fifth of those formerly fostered, were equally satisfied with their substitute care experiences, but added some minor qualifications which did not overall detract from what appeared to have been a basically good and enjoyable upbringing.

Only a very small proportion of adoptees rated or described their experiences as of "mixed" quality or unsatisfactory. This contrasted with about three out of every 10 of those fostered. Asked how close they felt to their "substitute" mothers, about eight out of 10 of those adopted, and seven out of 10 of those fostered, said they felt close or "very" close. This closeness continued into adult life but dropped to about six out of 10 for those fostered while remaining about the same for adoptees.

Some of the feelings of dissatisfaction expressed by those fostered were mostly related to the quality of the relationships between themselves and their foster families or to the disruptions that occurred in their lives. A fair amount of resentment, as I have said elsewhere, was felt by some of those who were fostered in conditions of "group" care or of "professional" type fostering, where short and long stays were taken on simultaneously (Triseliotis, 1980). The goings and comings of the short stays had created a sense of insecurity and impermanence to the long stays. While almost all adoptees, with few exceptions, felt that they had a family for life, there were various shades of uncertainty among some of those fostered, particularly among those whose relationships with their foster parents broke down, and by those brought up in conditions of "group" foster care.

In general, former foster children were more conscious of their fostering status than adoptees of their adoptive status. The older the fostered person at placement the greater this awareness along with significant memories about the "failures" of their natural families or broken promises. Adoptees, overall, perceived themselves as growing up "normal" or "like any other kid", but a fair proportion of those fostered were aware of differences in their situation in spite of most foster parents' efforts to make them feel one with the rest of the family. Occasional "welfare" visits, very sporadic appearances by a parent, comments at school about who their real parents were, and the goings and comings of other foster children in some families, all contributed to a sense of "unusualness" in their situation which was not apparent among most adoptees. Having also surnames which were different from those of the foster family was just one more example which to them stressed a "difference" in their situation from that of other children. In spite of this sense of "difference" no one expressed a preference for growing up in a children's home.

Whatever the principles of fostering may be, when it comes to long-term fostering some of the psychological implications are different from those of short- and medium-term fostering. In the latter cases the children are expected to rejoin their families. On the other hand, the child in long-term foster care usually lacks continuity of contacts and psychological bonds with natural parents, and is left in limbo searching for ways to cement his relationship with those caring for him. (In fact only an insignificant proportion of those fostered had seen a natural parent at some stage in the five years before they reached the age of 17.) While both adoptees and those formerly fostered carried within them a sense of "rejection" by the original family, these feelings appeared stronger among those fostered, part-icularly those who failed to develop strong attachments to their foster parents. Adoptees who happened to fall out with their parents did not sever contact altogether, but about one in every six of those fostered had cut off from their foster parents. Fostered people who experienced such a break felt even more bitter than some of those brought up in residential care, who were disillusioned by their residential life.

It looked as if fostered people, having experienced family life, felt its loss more than those who had not lived with a family for any length of time. Some regretted this disruption as it deprived them, in their view, of having "a family for life" with its network of support systems not only for them but also their future children. A situation like this highlighted the contrasting difference between a successful fostering outcome, which fortunately was the case for most, and the sadness generated by breakdowns and disruptions. Most of the sadness was related to the fact that they were left with no family to fall back on. The tendency then was to seek refuge in early marriage, join the armed forces or seek out siblings in the hope of making some viable arrangement.

How secure was it?

Because a sense of security seems to be vital in identity formation, the study tried to identify and assess how secure respondents in each group felt during their childhood years. While adoptees, with only three exceptions, did not perceive their situation as insecure or impermanent, this was not true for many of those fostered. Except for those who were unaware of their fostering status until their teens, most of the rest had some or more awareness of the precariousness of their position. In their comments they demonstrated some awareness of the possibility of discontinuity in their lives resulting either from the action of a local authority or of a foster parent or as a result of their own behaviour. Fears of being reclaimed by a parent added to this insecurity. Similar fears were also found among foster parents who sometimes openly or unintentionally conveyed these to the children.

Typical comments from formerly fostered people:

I remember getting closer to my foster parents as time went on and my own mum stopped coming to see me. My foster parents became my real parents. If they had taken me away then my whole world would have collapsed.

My foster parents were rather scared of social workers because they were attached to me and they were afraid I might be taken away . . .

I was happy with the Ts [foster parents] but when they were moving to England, the welfare came round and said that I couldn't go with them because my father wouldn't agree. I remember thinking at the time 'but he never comes to visit me'. [To the child's consternation the Children's Department acceded to the father's wishes.]

Typical comments from foster parents:

. . . we would have been terribly shaken if they had taken him away. After all these years he got into our ways and it would not have been good for the child or for us to take him away . . . losing a foster child is like losing one of your own . . .

. . . that is one of the curses of fostering. The taking away . . .

. . . having had them so long and being taken away . . . that was the only thing we dreaded . . .

Formerly fostered children, who were very close and attached to their foster parents, were quite apprehensive about the possibility of disruption in their lives. Those brought up in conditions of "group" foster care would equally be upset but not to the same extent. Even in homes where a certain amount of friction existed between the foster child and the foster parent, the threat of disruption again posed anxieties and it was rarely a hope of relief. It was perhaps to be expected that this type of insecurity was not present in the adoptive home, except in the three cases mentioned earlier. In two of these the parents' threat to have the children removed materialised in two children being taken into care. The main anxiety sensed by some adoptees was the discomfort of their parents in talking to them about their adoption and their original family. But many foster parents were also feeling likewise.

Many of those fostered were remarkably aware about the differences between fostering and adoption, particularly the amount of security that goes with the latter: 'Adoption is for ever' or 'in adoption no one can take you away'. About a third regretted the fact that their natural parents or the then Children's Department did not consent to their adoption by their foster parents. They felt they had missed everything that goes with adoption (no danger of being removed and having the same surname as the adoptive family).

Foster mother:

> 'Mr S [Children's Officer] was adamant against us adopting L. . . . He said, 'Please don't consider it . . . there has been trouble in her background . . .' They said they didn't want to give us a child we might be sorry about later . . .

Another case:

> Miss B [child care worker] told us that 'there is no use trying to do anything with these types of children, you will make nothing of it'.

In some other cases adoption could not go through because one or both parents refused their consent, something the children resented because there was no contact between themselves and their parents.

However wanted those fostered were made to feel by their foster parents, adoption would still have been desirable because it represented to them an official sanctioning of the arrangement with its accompanied stability. An official sanctioning of the arrangement through some legal process could have generated feelings of "entitlement" towards each other. Perhaps it is this sense of "entitlement" conveyed by adoption that enabled the vast majority of adoptees in the study to speak with greater assurance and with no ambiguity about their place within the adoptive family compared to those fostered. The threats posed to the child in long-term foster care were absent in the adoption situation. It may justifiably be argued that the child in long-term foster care cannot fully feel secure because of the uncertainty surrounding his position and that of his carers. This constructed insecurity seems to generate various degrees of anxiety to both cared and carers. Caught between foster parents, the majority of whom wish to offer him security and continuity of care, and the possibility of disruption, the child is left in an ambiguous position which inevitably has some bearing on his identity.

Knowledge about one's background and personal history

I wrote elsewhere about the importance of the past in contributing to the formation of a whole self (Triseliotis, 1973, 1974, 1980). Since then other studies have appeared to confirm these earlier findings and to dispel any doubts about the importance of the past and of one's origins. Erikson (1968), too, viewed the development of a person's identity in a psycho-historical context, which related to his/her sense of genealogy in the life cycle through which everyone has to pass. Erikson was referring to the development of any person and not necessarily to those growing up outside their families. It can be claimed that the adoption studies of the last 10 or so years in this area have contributed significantly to the understanding of the development of identity, not only in adopted children but also in children living with both their natural parents, and of those in other forms of "substitute" care, ranging from foster care, residential care, step-parenting and children conceived by Artificial Insemination Donor (AID).

For example, one of the clear findings of my earlier study (1973) was the importance of being honest and truthful with children, and how misguided were those parents using evasiveness and secrecy to hide the truth from children, be it in matters of origins, illness, death, etc. Section 26 of the Children Act 1975 was a milestone in child care legislation because, possibly for the first time, it statutorily acknowledged the psychological importance of background information being made available to adopted people in England and Wales. In effect the law came to recognise that there is a need in all of us to know about our personal history, that of our parents and of our ancestors. It is a human curiosity which has to be satisfied for a full completion of self.

Something like a quarter of those adopted in our study neither were told nor found out their true status until after the age of 12. There was also a strong tendency among many foster parents who had young infants placed with them not to reveal the fostering status to them until the children's early or mid-teens. Sometimes fostered people found out the truth about themselves accidentally, which they did not like at all. Overall about three-quarters of those adopted and half of those fostered said that there was little or no discussion about their families of origin and the circumstances surrounding their adoption or fostering. It ranged from total evasiveness to generalised discomfort on the part of the "caretaker" to refer to the family of origin.

Comments by some adoptees:

I cannot remember when my adoption was ever discussed with me and I never brought it up.

I couldn't talk to my parents about my adoption. It was one of those things you didn't talk about.

Comments by some of those fostered:

I was 12 or 13 before I realised I was fostered . . .

I was never given much information about my family. Just that my mother was unable to keep me . . .

I grew up thinking I was adopted . . . it was only recently I found out I was only fostered.

I said elsewhere, and it was also true here, that though self-knowledge and information about the past are very important, evasiveness on the part of the "caretakers" is not enough to destroy an otherwise strong and positive relationship. Yet it can cause distress and generate increased curiosity, threatening the strength of the relationship. Evasive foster parents usually manipulated the situation and managed to see child care workers at times when the children were at school. At other times they would find ways of sending the children away or be out of their homes. Later they would produce a range of unrelated explanations of why the "welfare lady" came.

While adoptees overall were fairly clear and explicit when they were searching for more information, those fostered appeared rather hesitant and in some ways inhibited. Their continued dependence on their foster parents, mingled with feelings of gratefulness towards them, appeared to make them cautious. When asked, for instance, whether aspects of their past still affected them, almost half of those adopted referred to such things as not knowing enough about their background or the circumstances of their adoption, but only 10 per cent of those fostered said so directly, and something like three-fifths said they were "uncertain".

Though in many cases the adoptive family had no information to pass on, this was not always true of the foster family or of the social workers responsible for the children. It was often sad to discover the total ignorance or confusion of some of those fostered concerning their backgrounds and first families. Sometimes important inform-ation was incorrect or distorted. If one reason given why some adoptive parents avoid talking to the child about his first family is fear of losing him, this fear must be stronger among long-term foster parents whose position is infinitely more precarious. The "ambiguity" present in long-term fostering, which is increased by the fact that the foster family is not an absolute certainty with which the child can identify without anxiety, is now compounded by the fact that many know nothing or next to nothing about their family of origin and about their personal circumstances.

Yet in spite of all these drawbacks, many of those fostered identified considerably with their foster families and tried to integrate them in their self-concept. As our other studies in residential care have also shown, children are eager, not to say desperate, to identify with the people who care for them. In the absence of such people they are left with a vacuum. While the majority of those fostered saw themselves as "fortunate" for having found a family with whom to identify as their own, those adopted gave little thought to that matter as they did not view their position as in any way "unusual". The latter group took their adoptive families much more for granted compared to those fostered.

The experience of being perceived by others as a worthwhile person

The pioneering work of Goffman (1963) and other sociologists has contributed to our understanding of how the images we develop about ourselves are considerably influenced by the way others see us. In effect, they say that our self-concept is partly based on the perceptions of others about us. Goffman developed the concept of spoiled identity to signify the impact of stigma and labelling on individuals and minority groups who are seen to depart from or defy the norm. Minority groups, such as blacks or the handicapped or those fostered or adopted, may be collectively perceived as "inferior", or "not whole", or as "worthless" or "bad", simply because they are different or do not conform to traditional expectations. Children brought up outside their own families may be seen as "different" either because of the way they are being brought up or the behaviour of their parents of origin.

An interesting example of this is evidence that before the last world war adoption was broadly seen as an "inferior" institution suitable mostly for the working classes (Triseliotis, 1970). The adoption situation contains all the ingredients that can attract stigma. Not only may the adoptee have feelings about being "illegitimate", but his adoptive parents may equally feel stigmatised for being unable to bear children in a society in which the bearing of children is the "norm". Thus both the adoptee and his adoptive family (not to mention the natural family) do not sustain the normative expectations of society. Goffman (1963) again points out how 'failure or success at maintaining such norms has a very direct effect on the psychological integrity of the individual'.

Fortunately adoptees in this study experienced fewer negative community attitudes arising from their adoptive status than those found in my earlier study (Triseliotis, 1973). Similarly they appeared less bothered about the unmarried status of many of their parents of origin. Perhaps this is an indication of changing community perceptions and of more enlightened attitudes.

Adoptee:

People round about had known I was adopted but it didn't make any difference to how I was treated.

Another:

Everybody who spoke to me about my adoption accepted me as one of the gang . . . I was always made to feel much the same as others.

There were a few exceptions, mainly at school, but the predominant climate was an accepting one. Yet perhaps because of fear about possible negative perceptions, about a quarter of adoptees were not keen on telling their friends that they were adopted. Some would tell if the topic came up. It was perhaps for similar reasons that some did not like their parents introducing them as their "adopted son or daughter". As one put it: 'Every time my mother did this, it used to screw me up.' The view was that this is something that should be reserved for real acquaintances, otherwise it left the adoptee with a feeling of having no personal boundary and of his integrity being violated. Their reactions are not unrealistic in view of studies suggesting, for example, that children already "labelled" as "backward" or "below average" do less well in class than when the teachers are unaware of such labels or are told that the children are bright.

Those fostered experienced somewhat more negative encounters compared to adoptees, particularly at school. The different surname to that of the foster parents usually attracted undesirable attention. Unkind comments usually made reference to the behaviour of the original family: 'What's wrong with your own family?'; 'Have you a father?'; 'Why couldn't your own parents keep you?'; 'What is it like to be a foster child?' or 'What have you done?' The feeling behind many of the questions asked of them were rarely benevolent and they were usually meant to draw attention to the difference involved. On a few occasions teachers had to intervene to put a stop to this type of "persecution". This led to a further awareness among foster children, that of being associated with the "welfare". This connection stressed to them the "failure" of their families and the fact that they were subject to surveillance. It was not surprising perhaps that some took the step, in their late teens, of changing their surnames to those of their foster parents to avoid "drawing attention" to themselves, and to demonstrate their desire to identify with the foster parents.

Fostered people, in general, tend not to think the payment of allowances to the foster parents stressed their "welfare" status. On the contrary, they were very critical of the "authorities" for being so mean. Poor allowances, a theme often referred to at home by foster parents, appeared to signify to those fostered the low image in which fostering is held. Fanshel et al (1978) wondered whether a child who is not living with his own family, or who is not adopted, 'may come to think of himself as being less than first rate, or an unwanted human being'. The evidence from the study suggests that the perception of fostering as a "low-status" institution, adds to possible feelings of low self-esteem and low status among those in long-term fostering.

Social functioning and competence

Not surprisingly, adoptees were reared mostly by middle and lower middle-class parents and those fostered by predominantly working-class families, half of the latter holding semi-skilled and unskilled jobs. (Because the adopted group were considered to be an "at risk" group at placement, the percentage of non-manual families adopting them was well below the percentage of those adopting "young, healthy" infants at the time.) The ethos and socialisation processes to which the two groups of children were exposed were considerably different. It may not be unrelated to this that a much higher proportion of adopted than of fostered people were encouraged to continue their education beyond the compulsory school leaving age, and obtain higher educational qualifications. As a result, significantly more of those adopted than fostered were now in non-manual occupations. In effect, formerly fostered people were less well equipped educationally compared to adoptees to compete in the job market. Generally, both adoptees and those fostered were resembling in their achievements their respective "substitute" families. Because of this, those fostered were more likely than adoptees to hold less secure jobs, have a rather higher incidence of unemployment and less satisfactory housing conditions.

There was also no doubt that the material conditions of the adoption group as a whole were significantly better than those of the fostered group. This in turn appeared to increase the confidence of many adoptees in coping with both concrete problems and other life situations. While better educational qualifications, which led to greater job security, accounted for part of the adoptees' relative economic comfort compared to that of those fostered, another factor was the support and backing they had from their families who were themselves of relative economic comfort. In other words, coming from an "advantaged" background adds to later life economic security. Though many foster parents were also most supportive to their foster children, the financial resources of many of them were insignificant.

Maybe those fostered could have done with more encouragement and greater stimulation of their ambitions, but on the other hand the foster parents were not treating their own children differently. Social workers, however, could help to heighten the educational ambitions of foster children because of the serious implications for their future employment and job security. Though many adoptees and all of those fostered came from some of the most disadvantaged families in the country, their economic circumstances at the time of interview were overall infinitely better than those of their families of origin. The respondents' financial and other concrete circumstances were much more related to what happened to them after coming into care than to anything before then.

Significantly more of those fostered than adopted expressed some doubts or misgivings about their capacity to cope with daily living. In effect they were somewhat less confident than adoptees about managing their social situation. Job insecurity, uncertainty about the future, especially among those who broke with their foster parents, all contributed to this. Because of their lower age at interview, many of those fostered had not yet faced the full impact of independent living. Irrespective of job security and income, almost a quarter of those adopted and over a third of those fostered expressed mixed feelings or dissatisfaction about their current standard of living. Asked about their satisfactions in life, over nine out of 10 of those adopted, and over seven out of 10 of those fostered, said they were "fairly" or "very satisfied" with the way things turned out for them.

Social behaviour

Juvenile delinquency among members of both groups was insignificant, but somewhat more adoptees appeared before the adult court compared to those fostered. The percentages for both groups were about average for the population as a whole. Offences following drink occurred almost exclusively among adoptees. Similarly, adoptees consumed significantly more drink compared to those fostered. These differences are difficult to explain, especially as they were not related to similar behaviour in the families of origin. Perhaps part of the explanation could be the older age group of adoptees at the time of interview, and the fact that a higher proportion of those fostered were still living under the protection of their foster parents.

There was very little difference in the proportion of respondents from either group who needed psychiatric help during their childhood or in the 12 months before the interview. The rate was also at about the same level as that found among the rest of the population. As far as friendships were concerned, almost a fifth of adoptees and double that percentage of those fostered rated themselves as having some problems in relating to friends. Overall, in terms of social behaviour, there was little difference between the two groups, except that adoptees were more likely to be heavier alcohol drinkers and have somewhat more court appearances compared to those fostered.

Summary and conclusions

Compared to those who grew up in long-term fostering, adoptees in general appeared more confident and secure with fewer doubts about themselves and about their capacity to cope with life. With very few exceptions, the adoptees' identification with their adoptive families was complete with none of the ambiguities found in the fostering situation. While adoptees had no doubts about "belonging" to their adoptive families and the family belonging to them, many of those fostered were aware that their legal position was unclear and that their lives could have been disturbed at any stage during the placement. They were equally aware of anxieties and fears among their foster parents and of the "welfare" component in their lives. In spite of strong psychological bonds between the majority of those fostered and their foster parents, the ambiguous nature of the arrangement seemed to have a qualitative impact on the former's sense of identity.

Confusion about the families of origin and why respondents were in care, along with some negative community perceptions, contributed to a picture of a certain amount of insecurity, of some "genealogical" confusion and of an element of difference or stigma involved in their situation. Adoptees overall displayed a strong sense of belonging to their adoptive families, lacked some basic information about their families of origin, and met with only an insignificant amount of prejudice for being adopted. Unlike many of those fostered, adoptees did not generally view themselves as "welfare" children. Yet it would be wrong to conclude, from what has been said, that long-term fostering is a failure because this is not so. What has been identified are certain conditions, some of them avoidable, which generate some anxieties and insecurities among those fostered and which were not present in the adoptive group.

On the basis of these findings and of other recent developments, the question could be posed, as some have already done, whether long-term fostering still has a future. McKay (1980), though questioning the impermanency involved in long-term foster care, still sees a role for what she calls "permanent substitute" family care involving adoption or long-term fostering. Families in this category are expected to assume a full parental role while being able to tolerate "legal uncertainties". Adcock (1980) argues that a child needs a permanent home which is intended to last, and is given the legal security to make this possible. Children growing up in long-term foster care, she goes on, 'cannot be said to have permanent homes because they have no legal security against interference from either their own families or . . . from social workers'. Zimmerman (1982) has found from a recent study that youngsters who grew up in stable foster care (ranging in length from one to 21 years) were currently functioning more successfully than those who were returned to their natural families. Hussell and Monaghan (1982) go further and argue for a complete severance of the links between a child and his parent(s) where the latter cannot fulfil all the tasks of parenthood. Visiting a child in care, the authors continue, is not sufficient to maintain it as part of its original family. The implication of their views is that all such children should be placed for adoption rather than go into long-term fostering. Adoption would then provide the "permanency" and kind of security that are missing from long-term fostering.

My own view is that long-term fostering will continue to have its place as the method of choice. One example of its role is when removal of a child from a "medium"-type fostering arrangement to adoption could prove too risky and disruptive because of the child's strong attachment to his caretakers. Provided the latter are willing to switch to a long-term commitment, and are prepared to limit the number of other foster children they take in, there is no reason why the arrangement should not be made permanent. In cases of this sort something stronger may be needed than the unimplemented provision of section 33 of the Children Act 1975 (custodianship), something approaching adoption. Full parental rights, for instance, should perhaps be transferred to the foster family and a guardian ad litem appointed to report to the court annually. All other "welfare" supervision should gradually cease.

What about the child who still has some meaningful bond with one or both parents, but the parent is unable or incapable of resuming full care? It is in fact becoming increasingly apparent that the more social workers are aware of the need to plan and make decisions early to safeguard a child's welfare, the more likely it is that a natural parent will still be around. In situations where the natural parent has no bond with the child, it may be easier to plan for adoption. Where one or both parents, though, have some psychological bond with the child which is sustained through visiting, then the choice may have to be either adoption with a condition for access to the parent(s), or long-term fostering sanctioned by law to guarantee both permanency and access. Arrangements of this kind will obviously demand responsible and mature behaviour by all the adults involved. Though practice experience in this area is still very limited, some such arrangements are known to have taken place and worked.

As already stated, as child care practice improves in this area, social workers will face more sharply than ever before the issue of parental rights. For example, a Scottish Sheriff Principal and a Lothian Sheriff recently cautioned councils and their social workers not to present courts with a *fait accompli*, by assuming parental rights as a step to a child's adoption. In the Sheriff Principal's view such a step may not be in the best interests of the child (reported in *Community Care* on 19 August 1982). In view of these developments it may be premature to declare long-term fostering as "dead" provided that such a choice is not used as a compromise to satisfy the parental rights lobby but a decision safeguarding the child's long-term welfare.

This and my other studies suggest that children can develop their personality and identity on the concept of two sets of parents, provided that there is clarity in their minds about what is happening and that the stability and continuity of care are maintained and not threatened. Access arrangements in adoption or in long-term fostering need not undermine these requirements. Access, after all, is provided for in many divorce cases, though I am aware that a high percentage of these peter out after the first year. Adoptive parents may be more flexible than we think in accepting access by a natural parent or close relative. Any petering out of access provision in some adoption or long-term fostering arrangements should be the result of the natural parents' choice rather than due to the attitudes of the "substitute" family. Finally, and as far as long-term foster care is concerned, it will continue to be the best available solution for some children. In spite of some drawbacks, properly planned and legally safeguarded it can provide for the needs of all concerned.

References

Adcock M. (1980) 'Permanent placement: a right', *Adoption & Fostering* 99:1, pp. 21–24

Andrews R.G. (1971) 'When is subsidized adoption preferable to long-term foster care?', *Child Welfare* 50:4, pp. 194–200

Erikson E. (1965) *Identity: Youth and crisis*, New York: W.W. Norton & Co.

Fanshel D. and Shinn E.B. (1978) *Children in foster care: a longitudinal study*, New York: Columbia University Press

Goffman E. (1963) *Stigma: notes on the management of spoiled identity*, Englewood Cliffs, NJ: Prentice-Hall

Hussell C. and Monaghan B. (1982) 'Going for good', *Social Work Today* 13:47, pp. 7–9

Madison B. and Schapiro M. (1969) 'Long-term foster care, family care: what is its potential for minority group children?', *Public Welfare* XXVII No 2

McKay M. (1980) 'Planning for permanent placement', *Adoption & Fostering* 99:1, pp. 19–21

Triseliotis J. (1970) *Evaluation of Adoption Policy and Practice*, University of Edinburgh

Triseliotis J. (1973) *In Search of Origins: The experiences of adopted people*, London: Routledge & Kegan Paul

Triseliotis J. (1974) 'Identity and adoption', *Child Adoption* 78:4, pp. 27–34

Triseliotis J. (1980) 'Counselling adoptees', in Triseliotis J. (ed.) *New Developments in Foster Care and Adoption*, London: Routledge & Kegan Paul

Watson K.W. (1968) 'Long-term foster care: default or design? The voluntary agency responsibility', *Child Welfare* 47:6, pp. 331–364

Zimmerman R.B. (1982) 'Foster care in retrospect', *Tulane Studies in Social Welfare* 14, pp. 1–119

3   Children's views

Here we see an illustration of John's commitment to obtaining children's viewpoints and his empathy with their perspectives. He analysed over 50 interviews undertaken with children who had been adopted with an allowance (i.e. a maintenance payment to the adopters). Over a third of the children did not know about the allowance so this was not discussed, but the interviews explored their reactions to adoption and views about the differences between it and foster care. Nearly all those aware of the allowance indicated that it did not diminish their sense of belonging within the family, though many did not want people outside the family to know about it. The chapter is reprinted from Hill, Lambert and Triseliotis, Achieving Adoption with Love and Money *(National Children's Bureau, 1989, Chapter 5). This book was based on two studies carried out separately in England and Scotland. All children's names are pseudonyms to preserve anonymity.*

In this chapter we consider the views and interpretations of a sample of the children for whom allowances were paid. Our main objective was to obtain insights into the children's understanding of what had been happening to them, their perception of fostering and the meaning they attached to their recent transition to adoption. We also wanted to find out whether they saw qualitative differences between foster care and adoption. After all, the distinction between long-term fostering and adoption is central to the notion of allowances. In addition, we wanted to establish what the children thought about their parents being "paid" to look after them. When the relevant legislation on allowances was being considered, many fears were expressed that the children might feel stigmatised or treated like a commodity. The only previous study of "subsidised" adoption (in the United States) did not include interviews with children (Waldinger, 1979; 1982) and we feel it is important to redress this balance.

Sample and interviewing methods

All the children and young persons described in this chapter were part of the Scottish study. In the first instance, we decided to exclude from our sample children who either presented substantial mental handicaps or were aged younger than about eight years. Our pilot study persuaded us that children with mental handicaps or who were too young were unlikely to have the understanding and expressive ability required to communicate effectively about adoption and money. Furthermore, for similar reasons, few parents had told such young children about the allowance. Previous studies have used similar thresholds for their interviews with children in care (Fanshel and Shinn, 1978; Rowe *et al*, 1984; Thoburn *et al*, 1986), although Thorpe (1974; 1980) talked with children as young as five.

We asked all parents of children who had been told about the allowance if we could interview the children. Permission was given in 26 cases and we spoke with 31 children in those families. We interviewed a further 21 children (in 12 families) who did not know about the allowance, after we had assured the parents that no reference would be made to it. Thus the eventual sample was 52 children. Since there were 10 sibling groups, this involved children from 38 different families. By the time of our interviews with the children, the adoptions had already been completed in all but a few cases. The age of the sample group ranged from eight to 19 years (see Table 3.1).

Table 3.1
The children's age at interview

Age	Total number of children	
	N	*%*
8–11	12	23
12–13	24	46
16–19	16	31
	52	**100**

Although one-fifth of the children interviewed had joined the family within the last three years, most of the rest were being adopted by foster parents who had looked after them since they were very young. Just over half of the 52 children had been with their families for eight or more years before being adopted by them. Thus the children in this part of our research had been fostered over a long period of time. They ought to have been among the more successful placements, since they had been with their families for so long and their foster parents wanted to adopt them.

Interviewing children on such very personal and sensitive matters presents researchers with many problems, which are discussed in greater detail in a separate paper (Hill and Triseliotis, 1988). Firstly, it may be difficult to obtain permission from parents to interview the children separately on issues that are not usually openly discussed in many families: Raynor (1980) and Jaffee and Fanshel (1970) had access to only about one-third of adoptees, mainly because of parental reluctance to facilitate access. We were fortunate in that the parents seemed to trust us sufficiently to allow us access for separate interviews with most of the children who fell within the sample population. As a result we had very few refusals. We may also have benefited from the considerable goodwill that the parents felt towards their respective social worker and from the fact that, by the time we visited to interview many of the children, we had met the parents at least once and sometimes twice. This also meant that the children had either met us beforehand or knew about us, and some trust was beginning to develop between us. All the children in our study were seen in their own homes and, with only a few exceptions, without their parents' presence.

Understandably, in a very small number of cases, parents did not want us to talk with the children because of concern that the child might be distressed, or simply because they felt that too much questioning had already been carried out by social work or legal representatives. A more significant influence on the sample size was secrecy about the allowance. Slightly more than 50 per cent of those with children able to understand had not told them of the allowance. As a result, in some instances it was agreed with the parents to interview some children to ascertain their views on adoption, while avoiding any reference to allowances because they had not been told about them. As appropriate, we reassured parents that we would be careful in our questioning, since we were aware of the "weight of responsibility" we carried, as Rowe *et al* (1984) point out in relation to these children to whom we were given access. However, many were very pleased for us to meet the children.

The second problem is methodological – how to communicate with children effectively about issues that can be difficult to put into words for either emotional or cognitive reasons. We sought to reduce some of the barriers to communication by using a range of techniques. There was little guidance about how to do this in the conventional research literature, so we drew on approaches developed by practitioners which use diagrams and exercises to engage children's interests and to help them express things that they might find difficult to talk about.

Usually we began with some informal conversation and asked about the child's favourite activities and interests. We then carried out a loosely structured interview covering the main themes of fostering, adoption, perception of original and new family, as well as the allowance. This was interspersed with engaging the child in filling out personal ecograms, listing important people, word choice, sentence completion and happiness scales. If they knew about the adoption allowances, they were also asked to respond to statements about them which we had compiled. There was a core of topics and elements used for all the children, plus others which were adapted selectively according to the age and nature of the child to encourage motivation and rapport. We modified the order and wording of schedules and questions to suit the child. This was done in the knowledge that the data analysis would be primarily qualitative. It was also more important to follow the children's train of thought than to aim for standardisation. All the interviews were tape-recorded to avoid taking notes which could hinder the establishment of rapport.

The use of several different sources of data from the children should have increased the reliability of the information yielded by the interviews. We also asked independently adopters and social workers what they had learnt of the children's knowledge and opinions. They had greater familiarity with the children and usually had themselves needed to ascertain the children's views in order to help decide if adoption was the best plan. Generally, the results from our direct contacts with children matched well with what we learnt from the families and social workers, though they also highlighted that communication with the children about allowances had in some instances been unclear. Most of the children lived great distances from each other and were under the supervision of different local authorities. Thus, it was unlikely that their responses were "contaminated" through contact.

Becoming a foster child

Eighty per cent of the 52 children featuring in this sub-sample had been with their new families for four or more years. In a few cases, this was the first and only family they had joined after leaving their family of origin. However, others had experienced varying periods in residential establishments or other foster homes.

Of the children who could remember the period with their natural families, the majority conveyed unhappy and distressing experiences and some were haunted by the possibility of further moves. Some children recounted distressing memories of ill-treatment at the hands of natural parents, witnessing fights and quarrels, or recalled unhappiness in children's homes or in foster care. Three had painful experiences from adoptions that broke down. On the other hand, a minority had cherished recollections with one or both natural parents or with a grandparent, but they realised that a return to live with them was not possible or desirable.

The children who had memories of unpleasant experiences with their original parents were much less inclined than others to want to resume any association with them, even if the events had happened a long time ago. Two teenagers from this group were both angry and amused that their respective fathers were contesting their adoptions:

When I heard about it, I couldn't stop laughing.

> *He doesn't really care about us, he hasn't written or contacted*
> *us, so why does he resist our adoption?*

Another teenager with unhappy memories remarked:

> *I don't know why he wouldn't agree [to the adoption]. I thought*
> *he wanted us to be happy because he knew we didn't want to*
> *stay with him . . .*

Children who had experienced many changes and instability in their own families or after admission into care, wanted to forget the experience and concentrate on their new lives, and valued their new-found stability:

> *In the Home, there is staff and the likes but you have got a lot of*
> *changes; it was seeing one of them for a while and then it would*
> *change to another. Here, there is no change of staff.*

Several children who had experienced a previous breakdown of adoption arrangements or frequent placement changes in care expressed much relief that things were now working well for them.

The meaning of fostering

Children placed when very young did not begin to understand what fostering meant until they were about seven or eight years old, although most of them had been told about it before then. Awareness about fostering and of its different status was gradual. Typical comments included:

> *Mum told us we were fostered but you really didn't under-*
> *stand . . . As we grew older she told us more and, of course,*
> *there were the letters from our real parents . . . so we knew*
> *there were other parents . . .*

> *They must have told me when I was five or so that I was fostered*
> *and I didn't really know what it meant . . .*

The few children whose foster parents delayed explaining to them their fostering status found it somewhat confusing when they found out or were told. Generally, the children did not mention that social workers had explained or discussed with them their fostering position or why they were in care.

At the time of the interviews, the children and young people in the sample were, on the whole, remarkably consistent and accurate in their explanations of fostering. Three main themes emerged:

1. something happens to "your" family;
2. someone else looks after you;
3. it is temporary and you have to move on.

(These were the responses of a group of children who were being adopted by their foster parents. It is possible that other foster children might respond differently.)

Family problems, rather than their own behaviour, were the main explanation offered by the children for their original family being unable to look after them. Practical difficulties, illness or relationship problems were seen as responsible for their separation from their first parents:

You are taken from your real family to another family because your family couldn't either cope, or didn't have the money or through, like, problems with mother and father.

Foster children may come from a broken home or because they don't have parents or whatever.

Not surprisingly, the children in this study tended to locate what happened to themselves in the micro-world of their natural families, e.g. alcohol, relationship problems or being in trouble with the police, rather than in any wider structural or organisational contexts.

Generally, the children's comments suggested factors not related to themselves, but a minority included an element of personal rejection when referring to the reasons for separation:

It is when your real parents don't look after you and they don't want you and you get taken away and put in somebody else's home . . .

The children's awareness that their own families were incapable, unwilling or unable to care for them was bound to have some impact on their self-image and feelings of self-worth or leave them with a sense of rejection. Similar feelings have been identified among adopted adults, although Triseliotis (1973) and Triseliotis and Russell (1984) concluded that the long-term impact of such an experience depends largely on the quality of subsequent relationships.

The second and third themes in the children's definitions of fostering were based on the idea of being looked after by people other than your parents on a temporary basis. Although many of the children had themselves been in the same foster home for a long time, they still regarded fostering as impermanent – sooner or later you went back or moved on. The comments made by the children conveyed both aspects:

> *Fostering is about people who like children and who take them into their own home until further parents are found for them, they are adopted or go back to their families.*

Eighteen-year-old Maureen captured the temporary nature of fostering, by saying that it is:

> *Just a part-time home until the situation in your family gets better...*

Another child referred to fostering as living 'somewhere else for a while', while a third added that it is when you are 'put into somebody else's home until you go somewhere else'. Although most of our sample children had stable fostering histories, they nevertheless perceived instability and lack of continuity as features of foster care. This was exemplified in the following remark, which emphasised the expectation of breakdowns and repeated changes of families:

> *It is just a set of two parents that look after children for a short time, then move on ... just keep moving on.*

It is not clear from our data whether social workers or foster parents reinforce this expectation of repeated changes, but many of these children had evidently concluded that discontinuity and "moving on" were characteristic of fostering. Some had experienced this themselves, while those with a more stable history had often seen other foster children come and go in their own household. There was also a feeling in some of the comments that in foster care, unlike adoption, the situation was in the control of others, which meant that the child and maybe the foster parents too could not predict how long they would be together. As a result, full commitment on either side was not possible. Although they looked upon fostering in this way, the children were not necessarily unhappy, as we shall see later. This illustrates the "ambiguous" and unusual position of the child in long-term foster care described earlier by Rowe *et al* (1984). Besides adoption, there are ways in which this ambiguity can be reduced (Triseliotis, 1983).

The meaning of adoption

As with fostering, the great majority of the children expressed clear views about what adoption meant to them. Asked how they would explain adoption to someone else, such as a teacher, they spoke almost unanimously about continuity and permanence. In other words, adoption, in their view, was the exact opposite of fostering: 'You cannot be taken away'; 'not get moved on'; or 'if parents are fed up they don't put you out'. Related themes were security and belonging, such as: 'a secure family life'; 'feel secure'; 'I belong'; or 'being a proper part of the family'.

A teenager who had been fostered for eight years and had now been adopted by his foster parents expressed the feelings of many others, saying:

> I've got parents, while before I didn't. I've got fond, loving parents . . . I am more secure, before I wasn't.

Another 16-year-old remarked that adoption is about 'having a real mum and dad' and not having to worry any more.

For some of the children, adoption also removed any differences existing between them and other children in the family, which had persisted even in long-term fostering: 'It would make us more part of the family, not just outside as it were.' In the sample, there was a very small group of children who were adopted just before the age of 18, which is the maximum age a person can be adopted in Britain. When one of them was asked what it meant to him to be adopted a week before he was 18, he replied: 'Secure, a secure home for life . . . even after you marry you can always come back here.'

A final aspect was the significance to the children of the change in their legal status. The symbolic significance to children of the new *legality* of their position should not be underestimated. Typical comments included: 'It is something permanent and by law', and simply 'It is legal.' One adolescent observed: '. . . if I had not been adopted, I would have been quite disappointed because by law I wouldn't be here actually.' Another added: 'Just now they are legally my mum and dad . . . nobody can take you away.' The law not only sanctioned a de facto situation, but it also conferred certain rights, including calling their carers "Mum" and "Dad" and using their surname without inhibition or guilt. There would also be no more social work visits, nor other people making decisions on their behalf and having the power to remove them. The law, through adoption, seemed to have provided a satisfactory resolution to a hitherto ambiguous situation, which, for many children, had been dragging on for a long time.

It would be wrong to surmise from the above that adoption invariably led to a sudden transformation in the children's feelings; this was not so. Some children conveyed two types of feelings simultaneously – of continuity and yet also of something new. As one put it: 'nothing suddenly changed'. One young girl remarked that: 'it [adoption] wasn't a big deal as I always thought of myself as adopted'. However, at the same time it would have been disappointing if adoption had not taken place. The act of adoption helped to tie up many loose ends. Many observed that, in everyday life, nothing changed, but they then elaborated on what they saw as the benefits to them of adoption, for example, 'greater security', 'not needing to go away', 'not different from others', 'have a home now', 'a home in adulthood', 'definitely part of the family', 'happier'. Some expressed great excitement, that they felt 'over the moon' after the adoption went through, or that they were so pleased they wanted to tell everybody.

One or two children voiced some reservations about being adopted. A teenager echoed his parents' disappointment that adoption had not solved his personal and social problems including continued confrontations with the law. Another added that it would take a long time before he became a 'full' member of his family: 'I wonder what a real mum and dad would be like, the same or different...?' And another felt 'anger' and 'frightened' but could not say what about or towards whom.

Differences between fostering and adoption

Once the children and young people had explained separately their understanding of fostering and adoption, they were asked to say what they perceived as being the main differences between the two.

Southon (1986) raises the question of whether adoption is 'better than fostering' and adds: 'If the plan for a foster child is changed to adoption, there's an implication that adoption is better than fostering.' But she goes on to point out:

> There are many instances in which children are left with their foster parents on a long-term fostering basis, even sometimes when they are legally available for adoption. Are those children in the end worse off than if they had been adopted? Need security, stability and certainty always depend on an adoption order?

Triseliotis (1983)[8] had studied this exact issue. He found that long-term foster care did carry "ambiguities" and "uncertainties" for the child, in terms of status, security and a sense of belonging, which were not found to be present in adoption. This does not imply that long-term foster care has no place in child care planning. There will still be children in foster care who do not wish to be adopted and foster parents who may not wish to adopt. Triseliotis (1980) also demon-

---

[8] Chapter 2, this volume.

strated how many adults who grew up in long-term foster care had found stability and continuity of care and made their foster homes their families for life.

The young people we spoke to similarly felt there was a qualitative difference between the two forms of family life:

A foster home is in between and I wanted a safe home.

You don't need to worry as an adopted child.

You can stay in the home.

In adoption you have a real mum, not in foster care.

As a foster child you can still worry about what is going to happen to you.

Although the children were confident of having had their foster parents' love, they were conscious that their full family membership was also brought into question by outsiders, including such matters as their different surnames, social work visits, undergoing statutory medicals and having enquiries made about them through teachers. All these are situations to which other children are not exposed. One even remarked that adoption removed 'the stigma of fostering'. The following quotation sums up these points:

Being adopted means it's your real mum; no more meetings and check-ups getting done on you all the time with doctors, social workers . . . People won't also bother thinking who is that going into the house, why they (the social workers) are going there all the time.

Many of the children and young people were greatly relieved that they no longer had to explain to friends and teachers why they had a different surname from that of their foster (now adoptive) parents. Yet Goffman (1963) rightly argues that whenever a change in name occurs, 'an important breach is involved between the individual and his old world'. This may be true where the change is against the child's wishes. Undoubtedly, carers may sometimes exercise direct or unspoken pressures on children to have their name or surname changed in an attempt to divorce them from their past; this should be resisted. In the case of our respondents, the initiative usually came from the children and they were glad to take on the new name because it removed the "difference" between themselves and their new families. One adolescent made the comment that he had to change his surname to that of his "parents" because he had not known any other family. Another one added: 'I wasn't pressurised, it was my own decision . . . I was delighted, I wanted to start a new life.' A young girl felt that her new surname made her 'somebody, a person'.

The majority of the children had not experienced negative discrimination but where this had occurred it had usually happened at school. It took the form of being called "a foster child" in an abusive manner, or "a bastard", implying second-class citizenship.

Although adoption was perceived by the children as a reason to feel pleased, nevertheless they were generally cautious as to whom they disclosed the fact. Those who had been called names preferred to share it only with close friends and acquaintances. Others felt that this was a personal matter and that it was their choice who they wanted to tell:

Tell people who take it seriously.

I talk about it sometimes to my best friends.

It depends who I am telling.

I don't think they will understand, why tell?

While the majority seemed discriminating about whom to tell about being adopted, some would add that they would tell openly 'if asked' or 'if the subject came up'. Some children, aware of the possibility of being taunted, tried to keep their status to themselves until their teacher asked the class, 'Is anyone here adopted?'

Feelings about being adopted

Among the written "exercises" we used to obtain data was a word exercise that asked children to circle words or phrases from a list to show which ones coincided with their feelings about being an adopted person. This was particularly aimed to help those who found it hard to describe their own emotions. Phrases were derived from our early pilot interviews with children and also from the rest of the research. (To avoid socialising the children in the use of certain language, the words and phrases used in the exercise were not shown to them until after the oral part of the interview was over.) Of course, we cannot be sure that these words meant the same to all the children but they mostly described either positive feelings such as "love", "happiness", "I belong", "normal", or negative feelings like "strange", "the odd one out", "a secret". Children were free to circle as many words as they wished.

A total of 37 children completed this exercise and usually they chose predominantly positive words or phrases. The ones most commonly circled were "happiness" (32), then "love" (26), "staying for ever" (25), "safe" (23), "I belong" (22). The ones least circled were "the odd one out" (2), "something to hide" (3), "feeling shy" (4), "strange" (6), "secret" (7). One child chose all five negative words and another chose four of them, but they both circled a number of positive words too. As well as choosing some of the positive words, 25 per cent of the children included at least one negative word such as "secret" or "strange". At least six children avoided the most positive words such as "happiness" and "love".

This shows how the children indicated their delight, security and sense of belonging, but this was accompanied by some unease and secrecy in a minority of cases. The children who chose the negative words were not obviously different from the rest except that more of them were seen by their parents to have moderate or serious behavioural/emotional difficulties.

Children's happiness
The next step was to ask the children to estimate their level of "happiness" when fostered and do the same now that they were adopted. They were asked to tick a 10-point scale with the lower two numbers indicating highest satisfaction and gradually decreasing until reaching 10, the lowest point on the scale. It is recognised that self-

rating may be influenced by how a respondent may be feeling at the time of the interview, or by a recent event or crisis, rather than convey the predominant feeling. Nevertheless, this was only one of a number of qualitative and quantitative ways used to ascertain the children's general disposition, so that each method acted as a check on the others.

In spite of their comments about the permanence of adoption and how they welcomed being adopted, half of the children indicated no change in their level of "happiness" between being fostered and being adopted. With only three exceptions, these feelings were at the two highest points in the scale during both the fostering and adoption experience. The rest of the children indicated increased "happiness" by an average 2.5 grades in the scale. Those who recorded gains could not be distinguished from the rest in terms of current and background characteristics.

Looking at the gradings in a different way, 80 per cent of children rated their current level of "happiness" as adopted at the three highest grades on the scale. Most of the remaining 20 per cent indicated a middling state of "happiness".

The children who indicated lower levels of "happiness" also featured largely among the group who chose negative words and phrases as being associated with adoption. Three of them had also shown unhappiness at being deprived of contact with a biological parent. The 20 per cent of the children who rated their level of "happiness" as low or moderate nevertheless had no wish to leave their adoptive families. In fact, some had also selected words such as "love" and "happiness" as associated with adoption and expressed pleasure at the fact of being adopted.

The children's self-images

We tried to approach the issue of how these young people saw themselves in another way, by asking them what they liked most or least about themselves and what was the best and worst thing in their life so far. On the positive side, most children felt good about being healthy, happy, friendly and honest. Over half of them singled out their adoption as the best thing that had happened to them in life. Outings and holidays were the next most common happy events. On the negative side, most children were concerned about their temper and bad behaviour, with four expressing concern about their appearance. No clear picture emerged of the worst things that happened in their lives. Several mentioned accidents and a considerable number referred to their earlier insecure life and memories of ill-treatment, the loss of an adoptive parent through death or being separated from a birth parent to live in a children's home.

When the children were asked to say what they would ask if they had three wishes, most of their replies (31) were about concrete things, such as money, clothes, cars, toys and a nice home. Another 24 wishes were about their personal well-being and that of the adoptive family. Altruistic feelings concerning others or the world were mentioned six times, and five wishes concerned meeting one or more members of the biological family. These replies give us some idea of what was important to them about themselves and their lives. Nevertheless, their preoccupations appeared to be what one might expect from a group of individuals of their age, although we do not have any comparative information to show whether the responses fall within the norm. Most referred to ordinary events and to their adoptive family, as, we suspect, would any child.

Behavioural and emotional problems

Another way to look at the children was to examine the presence or absence of behavioural/emotional problems as seen through the eyes of their adoptive parents, and sometimes confirmed by the children's own accounts. Sixty per cent of the children in this sub-sample were seen by their parents as having no problems at all or very minor ones, e.g. slightly shy. However, approximately 20 per cent were described as having serious problems, and almost a similar number as having moderate ones. But some children, who were seen as displaying moderate problems in some areas of their lives, such as shyness or bad temper, displayed no other problems. Only a minority of children (five displayed serious acting out behaviour, such as stealing, lying or aggression towards others which gave rise to serious concerns. The problems of most of the rest were of an emotional nature such as bed-wetting, sleeping difficulties, lack of concentration, clinging and attention-seeking behaviour, with approximately 25 per cent of all the children being described as moderately or seriously "shy". Three children had received psychiatric help in the past but the problems persisted. Girls were less likely than boys to feature in the problematic group.

According to the parents, almost 40 per cent of the children displayed no difficulties either before they joined them or at the time of the interview. Another 25 per cent who were displaying serious to moderate difficulties before joining their new families showed moderate or significant improvements, but approximately 10 per cent deteriorated. Five children were still causing serious concern to their families. Despite these serious difficulties, the families who had all taken in the children comparatively recently, with a view to adoption, nevertheless went through with it.

When considering all the children together, those displaying problems had only experienced slightly more moves than the others before joining their new families. However, children who had joined their foster families in the last two years before the adoption order was granted were more likely to display difficulties compared to the rest because they were placed as "special needs". As also already pointed out, children displaying problems indicated somewhat lower levels of "happiness" and chose more negative words as associated with adoption, and a higher percentage from this group had not been told about the adoption allowance. None of these differences reached a point of statistical significance, except for the last one, confirming perhaps previous studies (Triseliotis, 1973; Triseliotis and Russell, 1984) about the importance of open communication within families.

In summary, approximately 10 per cent of all children could be described as suffering some personal anguish or causing their parents serious concern. The stability of a few of these adoptions was rather precarious, although a breakdown would have caused considerable pain to both children and parents. Even among some of the children displaying serious difficulties, there was no diminished commitment

89

to the placement and they had no doubt about the mutuality of positive feelings between themselves and their parents. To put this in perspective, it needs to be remembered that we interviewed only older children and our overall data showed that major emotional or behavioural problems were less common among younger ones. The full survey also revealed that a considerable number of children who were now apparently well settled had experienced difficulties or needed specialist help earlier in their lives. The love and care of their foster and adoptive families presumably played a big part in their eventual good progress.

The children's attitude to payments

The possible impact on the children's identity and self-concept has been a major preoccupation of those interested in allowances. In other words, someone adopted with an allowance will have to resolve not only possible emotions about having been "rejected" by his or her birth family, but also feelings around being "paid for". A fundamental question we wished to pursue was whether children mind that their carers receive money to look after them.

Triseliotis (1980) found no evidence from his interviews of young people who grew up as fostered that they minded about their foster parents being paid. Indeed, they were critical of the authorities for being rather miserly in the amount of the allowance provided. Southon (1986), on the other hand, claims from anecdotal comments made to her by individual young people who had experienced fostering in Denmark, that fostering payments presented them with a dilemma: 'If there is payment', they said, 'you wonder if that's why they have you; and if not, there's a sense of being under obligation.' Some social workers reported to us similar remarks by foster children.

The fostering allowance

The majority of the children in the sample were aware that their parents had been receiving a fostering allowance for looking after them but only exceptionally did they have any idea about the amount involved. It was not clear to them how they came to know about the allowance. Probably they picked it up from conversations made within the family or with social workers: 'I knew about the fostering allowance but not how much or anything like that.' About one-third of children in this sample either did not know or believed that their foster parents were not receiving an allowance. Almost all the children who had exhibited this ignorance had been fostered since before they were five years old and many of them were among those who were told or found out rather late that they were fostered.

The fostering allowance was seen mainly as helping out with the purchase of food and clothes for all the family and occasionally for holidays:

I was getting fed and helped and that was all that bothered me. I was cared for.

Just so they can afford to buy clothes and other things.

We do cost money for clothes and other things.

There was a "matter of fact" approach in the way the children viewed the fostering allowance, with the emphasis on its practical value. Other remarks were: 'very good'; 'do not mind'; 'it's needed' or 'it's like a family allowance'. One teenager conveyed the general trend by saying:

I knew that they were getting an allowance for it because you cannot ask two people to bring another child or maybe even two into a house without giving them some sort of money for clothes and food. It came as no shock to me or nothing like that . . . I do not mind.

Even those who said that they had not known about the fostering allowance before were happy about it. Only a tiny group of children either said that they could not comment, or expressed some surprise. One 13-year-old declared:

I never thought that they could get money for looking after me, but now I think that it is just their work really to look after me.

This boy was very supportive of the idea of adoption allowances. None of the responses indicated any sense of stigma about the payments. They showed that the children's strong attachments were unaffected by the fact that their foster parents were paid to look after them.

Adoption allowances

There have been public misgivings about the payment of fostering allowances and their impact on children, but this was even more so in the case of adoption allowances. Many social workers we spoke with were worried that the introduction of adoption payments might lead in time to the children posing the question: 'Why am I being paid for?' Fears were also expressed that allowances would lead to two classes of adopted children – those whose parents were paid to look after them and those who were not, with possible adverse effects on the former's feelings of self-worth. In contrast to this, Southon (1986) quotes a ministry representative from the State of New York as saying on the matter: 'The children are usually delighted to be adopted and seem to have no qualms about the payment.'

Most of the children interviewed who knew about the allowance were told by their parents and only a few by their respective social workers. This kind of preparatory work was apparently left by social workers for the adoptive parents to carry out. Why social workers avoided this task is not entirely clear, although our contacts with social workers indicated that it had not occurred to many of them. Others said that it was up to the family, but they discussed with almost all the children the idea of adoption and they tried to elicit their feelings and views on the matter. That conforms with the legal obligation for children in care to be consulted about the future, insofar as they can understand. If the social workers thought the allowance was a domestic matter between the child and his adopting parents, they certainly underestimated the possible emotional difficulties on the parents' part of explaining.

Parents who shared the fact of the allowance with the children did not necessarily make it part of a process to ensure that the children had grasped what the allowance meant. Although many children were clear, some could either not remember being told or had a hazy idea.

Among the children we spoke with, five appeared not to know about the adoption allowance, although their parents maintained that they had been told about it. On the whole, the children who did know that an allowance was being paid had little or no idea how much money was involved. The most frequent explanation given by the parents to the children was that it was like a continuation of the fostering allowance. Many children also saw no difference between an adoption allowance and a fostering payment or even sometimes a family allowance. As with explanations of adoption, discussion of allowances may well need to be part of a continuing and repeated process taking account of age, place and circumstances (see also Brodzinsky, 1984). We know from our discussions with the adopters that, in many families, there is no tradition of discussing financial matters with children. There have been no systematic studies about communication over money between parents and children in the general population.

With very few exceptions, the children were positive or very positive about the payments. Apart from a few children who were generally shy or unforthcoming, there was no hesitation in what they said, nor traces of embarrassment or shame. Their comments ranged from those who saw allowances as definitely good and necessary, to those who regarded it as making no difference to their parents' feelings about them and vice versa. Some children also saw payments in terms of "fairness" towards those who do not earn enough but who like children and would still like to adopt.

Some people do need to be paid; those quite well off are all right.

I think it is quite right because a lot of people who like children might not be able to cope with the keeping without the extra money.

[The allowance should be for people that] ... cannot afford to adopt ... but they would still like to adopt.

A few children said that all adoptive parents should receive an allowance, and one added: 'it helps children to start another life'.

Others remarked that it would probably encourage more people to adopt. David Brown commented:

> *It is not going to be very good if two caring people want to adopt but they cannot do it because they have not the cash behind them.*

As with fostering, there was almost overwhelming support for the usefulness of the allowance. Most children put the emphasis on the practical value of the allowance to their families and to themselves, rather than on its possible psychological impact. The majority viewed it as income for the whole family, not for themselves alone:

> *Such as to buy clothes and the like . . .*

> *To buy clothes, just for food and things like that and toys and for the house.*

> *To keep us going.*

> *To buy things, food and that.*

A few talked about what the allowance would buy for them. Some referred to possible future adversities which the allowance could help to cushion, for example: '. . . if they were just sort of part-time working or something, they might not manage to cope', or 'in a way it is good because, like, if your dad is off work or something, you get money and it keeps the family going'. Asked to say what might have happened if no allowance was available, all the children seemed certain that they would still have been adopted, but there would be more hardship in the family. For example, the parents would find it harder to manage, go without things and have no holidays.

    The next questions were aimed at trying to get behind the children's feelings in another way, this time by asking them to say whether they perceived any difference between themselves and those adopted children whose parents were not receiving an allowance. Almost all the children who knew about allowances could see no difference and a few suggested that it was those families not drawing an allowance who were being deprived. Here are some of their replies on this point:

No difference at all.

None.

Nothing.

The money bit doesn't matter.

It makes no difference, you are still 100 per cent adopted if there is an allowance or not.

Thus, the children we interviewed did not convey any undue sensitivity about the fact that their parents were paid to adopt them. In this respect, their views differ considerably from the assumptions made by adults on their behalf. To them, money was apparently not very salient when compared with their feelings about their adoptive family; it did not detract from those feelings. Perhaps widespread acceptance of child benefit paid to all families has helped to reduce or even abolish possible differences between receivers and non-receivers. It is also possible that the preoccupation with the impact of payments on the children's identity is that of people speaking from a more economically comfortable position. On the other hand, when the children were asked whether they would tell friends or other outsiders about the allowance, their most common response was that they would not, because it had nothing to do with outsiders. They gave broadly the same kind of answers as their parents. This may reflect a sense of shame or more simply a culturally accepted tradition that money matters are not discussed outside the family. Characteristic responses were:

I don't think it is anybody else's business . . . it is up to Mum and Dad.

If Mum and Dad want to tell people, they can go ahead and do it, it is none of our business.

It has nothing to do with outside the family.

Only four children expressed surprise or doubts about adoption allowances but they were not necessarily opposed to them. Sixteen-year-old Donald did not expect that allowances accompanied adoption. He thought that, once adopted, 'that was it'.

Similar views were expressed by an 11-year-old, who said: 'I never thought that they would get money for looking after me.' Another child said that: 'families who adopt a child should be able to afford to keep it without an allowance'. One young person, who was feeling bitter about the lost links with his natural father, felt more hostile. He approved the idea of allowances for those not able to afford the additional expense involved but nevertheless likened allowances to 'an auction' or 'ransom money'. He was more uncertain about fostering allowances.

To check further the children's views on payments, they were presented with a number of statements about adoption allowances. Some were positive, some negative and these were intermixed (see Table 3.2). The children were then asked to tick the ones they agreed with (this exercise was not given to those children who were not told about the allowance). Not surprisingly, in view of what has been said so far, about 85 per cent of the statements ticked were positive. The only "negative" one which received much support concerned un-willingness for other people to know about the allowance, rather than any expression of personal misgiving. In this way, the children's views paralleled those of their parents.

In summary, of the children who knew about the allowance, only three had mixed views or were rather hostile to the idea. The rest welcomed the allowance, viewing it as necessary and as a commonsense arrangement. Equally, they could see no difference between themselves and other children whose parents were not receiving similar payments. Perhaps children of this age concentrate far more on what money can buy rather than articulate feelings about its intangible impact. It is possible when they are older they may come to feel differently. Yet the same group of children were able to put into words other important feelings about their transition from fostering to adoption and about their current position within the adoptive family.

Table 3.2
Statements about adoption allowances

A. Favourable statements	Number of children (N = 28)
Receiving an allowance makes no difference to how my parents feel about me	23
More children can be adopted if families can receive help with money	18
The adoption allowance helps all the family	16
All adopted children should have an allowance	12
The adoption allowance makes life much better for me	10
I do not mind most people knowing about the allowance	6
Without an adoption allowance life would be very hard	5

B. Unfavourable/qualified	Number of children (N = 28)
I prefer most people not to know about the allowance	12
Families who adopt a child should be able to afford to keep that child without an allowance	2
I am not happy with the idea that my parents receive an adoption payment	1
I wish we did not have an adoption allowance	0

Conclusions

In their comments the children demonstrated considerable clarity and perceptiveness about the nature of foster care and that of adoption. They perceived significant qualitative differences between the two in favour of the latter. Adoption was identified with continuity of care, permanence and security. In this respect it did matter to them whether or not they were adopted. The legality of adoption also formalised their presence within the family, putting an end to their "ambiguous" and uncertain position. In their words, they now had a family to call their own by right and without the fear of further moves. For many children in the sample, this would not have been achieved without the allowance. Those children who knew that their parents were receiving an allowance for adopting them saw nothing unusual in the arrangement, viewing it either as a continuation of the fostering allowance or as similar to child benefit. Whether they will continue to feel like this as they grow up may depend on whether society itself comes to associate such payments with stigma and discriminates against children whose parents draw an allowance.

If, as we have found, there are qualitative differences between long-term foster care and adoption in favour of the latter, then it is important that children who are free for adoption are not unnecessarily consigned to long-term fostering or to custodianship. Legitimate questions could, therefore, be raised about Sir Roger Ormond's judgment in re M (Minors), who said that, in his opinion, adoption was not designed to cater for children in long-term foster care and custodianship was better (Court of Appeal, 11 October, 1984). Another argument put forward by courts in subsequent cases for refusing an adoption order to foster parents and granting a custodianship instead, was the need to safeguard access by natural parents to their offspring. As we have found from a minority of children in this study, their meaningful links with people from the past need to be preserved. However, where the parents do not even plan or wish to provide a home for the child, then adoption with access safeguards security and continuity of care for the child without breaking important links. Certainly the very few children in our sample who were grieving for the loss of meaningful links from the past did not necessarily wish to go back to their original parents or relatives but simply to preserve that link through occasional contacts.

References

Brodzinsky D.M. (1984) 'New perspectives in adoption relations', *Adoption & Fostering* 8:2, pp. 27–32

Fanshel D. and Shinn E.B. (1978) *Children in Foster Care: A longitudinal investigation*, New York: Columbia University Press

Goffman E. (1963; reprinted 1986) *Stigma: Notes on the management of spoiled identity*, London: Penguin

Hill M. and Triseliotis J. (1988) 'Who do you think you are? Towards understanding adopted children's sense of identity', in Ross J. and Bergum V. (eds) *Children and Health Promotion*, Ottawa: Canadian Public Health Association

Jaffee B. and Fanshel D. (1970) *How they Fared in Adoption: A follow-up study*, New York: Columbia University Press

Raynor L. (1980) *The Adopted Child Comes of Age*, London: Allen & Unwin

Rowe J, Cain H., Hundleby M. and Keane A. (1984) *Long-term Foster Care*, London: Batsford/BAAF

Southon V. (1986) *Children in Care: Paying their new families*, London: DHSS

Thoburn J., Murdoch A. and O'Brien A. (1986) *Permanence in Child Care*, Oxford: Blackwell

Thorpe R. (1974) *The Social and Psychological Situation of the Long-term Foster Child with Regard to his Natural Parents*, University of Nottingham, Ph.D. thesis

Thorpe R. (1980) 'The experience of children and parents living apart', in Triseliotis J. (ed.) *New Developments in Foster Care and Adoption*, London: Routledge & Kegan Paul

Triseliotis J. (1973) *In Search of Origins*, London: Routledge & Kegan Paul

Triseliotis J. (ed.) (1980) *New Developments in Foster Care and Adoption*, London: Routledge & Kegan Paul

Triseliotis J. (1983) 'Identity and security in adoption and long-term fostering', *Adoption & Fostering* 7:1, pp. 22–31

Triseliotis J. and Russell J. (1984) *Hard to Place: The outcome of adoption and residential care*, London: Heinemann/Gower

Waldinger G.L. (1979) *Subsidised Adoption: A special case of paying people to parent*, University of Los Angeles, Dissertation for D.S.W.

Waldinger G.L. (1982) 'Subsidised adoption: how parents view it', *Social Work* 27:6, pp. 516–527

4 Perceptions of permanence

At a conference in 1990 John reviewed the permanence movement in Britain, which had become very influential in the 1980s. His paper was adapted for publication in Adoption & Fostering *(15:4, pp. 6–15, 1991) from which it is reproduced here. It asserted the importance for children to have a family base for life. Research evidence was reviewed showing that good successes could come from the growing number of adoptions from care, while the increased support for adopters was welcome. However, the paper criticised the "clean break" assumption – that meaningful birth family ties might need to be severed to facilitate adoption. Concern was expressed about the disruption rate for older children.*

It is tempting to start by saying that permanency through adoption for children with special needs is on the defensive, and that adoption policy and practice are at the crossroads because of the challenges they face. The fact is that adoption, as an institution, has always been at the crossroads, as it mirrors the society within which it is practised. Because society is not static but changes all the time, so adoption changes and adapts to new needs and challenges. For example, over the last 20 or so years there have been radical changes in patterns of living, including changes in personal, sexual, couple and family relationships. What is understood by the concept of family has been redefined to take account of diverse lifestyles, divorce, reconstitution and single parenthood. These changes are here to stay and adoption has had to respond to them.

In considering the various ways in which families are constituted now, and how atypical they are of our traditional image of the family, it is hard not to claim that adoptive parenthood has been a pace-setter in this direction. Psychological parenting is no longer confined largely to adoption but is becoming far more common, along with step-parenting and parenting through various forms of assisted reproduction.

Changes in personal and social relationships have always been the main dynamic underlining the evolution of the practice of adoption throughout history. Had I been writing on this topic five years ago, I might have been tempted to say that, for reasons that have not escaped you, adoption as an institution was moving towards its sunset. Permanence through adoption, for children with special needs, was then seen as the final remnant of what was once a big field of social work policy and practice. The end of this final form of adoption was expected to come with the provision of better preventive and supportive services to families to ensure permanence for children within their own families.

Two new issues have surfaced in the meantime, however, to give adoption a new dimension. Open adoption, which was previously characteristic of mainly non-European cultures, is gradually coming into prominence, along with intercountry adoption which Britain, compared to some other countries, resisted for a long time. Concepts of permanence cannot be examined in isolation from these other recent developments.

The concept of permanence

There is no agreed definition of the concept of permanence. Perceptions, therefore, are bound to vary. Different protagonists, depending on the ideologies and value positions they hold about the place of the family and the role of the state in relation to families and children, place different emphases on what is good for families and children. Polarised positions between the so-called "defenders of the family" and those who are perceived as "savers of children" can only delay the development of an agreed and coherent theoretical framework, based mainly on what empirically is known to be good for children. Insights gained from empirical studies can only illuminate part of the debate, because research is still lacking in many areas of practice. Some things we will also never know about because of the ethical objections to certain types of research involving human beings. Neither can the ethical dilemmas surrounding some of the issues be resolved totally by empiricism. For example, can permanence outside the family of origin be justified solely on the ground that it works? Or would, for example, the moral issues surrounding intercountry adoptions disappear, if research were to show that the children eventually do well or even very well?

It could be reasonably argued that in a world of instability with high divorce rates, marital reconstitution, step-parenting and a large number of single-parent families, it is somewhat paradoxical to talk of permanence for children coming into public care. Thus the concept of permanence can only be examined in relative terms and in the context of the society within which it is being pursued. At the same time, when planning for children who have already experienced a chequered background, there is perhaps an extra responsibility to ensure, if not guarantee, an added form of stability in their lives.

My own studies have led me to define permanency in practical terms, these being to provide each child with a base in life or a family they can call their own, and more hopefully a family for life (Triseliotis, 1983; Triseliotis and Russell, 1984).

Studies have been showing that the difference between those who manage to cope in adult life and those who don't is closely related to the kind of support systems they continue to enjoy and whether or not they have a base in life they can call their own and turn to for practical and emotional support when needed. This applies even more so to individuals who have spent a large part of their childhood in public care. Our own studies have shown that those who had no birth families to return to, but were fortunate to secure relative permanence within foster or adoptive homes, fared infinitely better in adult life, compared to those who left the care system with no such base. This empirical reality is one of the concepts which underpins the policy to secure permanence for children with special needs.

Few would disagree that it is in every child's interests that a strenuous effort is made to achieve permanence first and foremost within the child's own family and country of origin, where biological and psychological parenting, including ethnic identification, can occur simultaneously. Where this is not possible, and in the light of what has been said earlier, permanence may have to be pursued outside the family of origin. It would be hard to argue that everything possible was done to achieve permanence within their own families for all the children with special needs who have been adopted over the last two decades. For many though, adoption has provided the base which was missing from their lives.

Whether permanence for special needs children is on the defensive or not it is difficult to say. It is proper, though, that after 20 or so years we take stock and look at both the successes and blemishes. In the following pages an attempt will be made to: identify the various forces that gave the impetus to the adoption of children with special needs; examine the permanency movement's achievements and challenges; and briefly look at outcomes and the future.

The forces which gave the impetus to the adoption of children with special needs

A number of events seem to have coincided in the early 1970s to stimulate interest in permanence through adoption for children with special needs. First, the dwindling number of babies being available for adoption and, second, the realisation that there were large numbers of children in public care whose families were unable to have them back or who had no families to return to. Neither were there any realistic plans for the future of these children. Attention then was drawn to the needs of these children for continuity of care and for a family to call their own. It is doubtful, though, whether this new "move" would have taken place if it wasn't for the declining number of baby adoptions.

The third factor was an empirical one. Besides research, already referred to, concerning the plight in adult life of those who were formerly in public care, and who grew up in unstable arrangements, two other types of studies provided added impetus and optimism. First, a small but increasing number of studies were beginning to demonstrate the reversibility of early psychological trauma which came about through separations and deprivations. In other words, that children could overcome early adversities, provided suitable new conditions could be ensured (Kadushin, 1970; Clarke and Clarke,

1976; Bohman and Sigvardsson, 1980; Triseliotis and Russell, 1984). Second, that psychological parenting such as adoption and long-term fostering were a reality. Those who matter to children are generally the people who bring them up and not necessarily those who give birth to them (Triseliotis and Russell, 1984; Hill *et al*, 1989).

In this new type of adoption, the future psychological well-being of these children was dependent, not only on the accomplishment by adoptive parents of the traditional tasks associated with adoption, but adoptive parents were now expected to take on a treatment type role with many of the children.

If Britain responded to the decline in baby adoption by going all out for securing adoptive families for older children and children with disabilities who were previously thought unadoptable, a number of countries on the continent of Europe responded by turning mainly towards intercountry adoptions. It can be assumed that older children and those with disabilities or learning difficulties with no birth families to return to were either found long-term foster homes or kept in residential homes. This may be a somewhat simplified picture, but if the adoption statistics coming out of these countries are correct, then the adoption of own country children with special needs has hardly featured in recent years. One explanation why intercountry adoption did not develop in similar numbers in Britain, as on the continent, was possibly the stance taken by many black and white social work practitioners, the prohibition of non-agency adoptions and stricter immigration laws. A second explanation is the close links maintained by researchers, trainers and practitioners in Britain with the USA. It was the USA where the first ideas and service programmes for children with special needs were developed and these quickly crossed the Atlantic. Though the United States were pioneers in this field, eventually they followed a middle path to that of Britain and the continent of Europe by paying attention to both children with special needs and to intercountry adoptions.

Achievements and challenges

After more than a decade of pursuing a policy of permanency through adoption for children with special needs, there have been some astounding successes, but equally challenges and blemishes.

1 Achievements

• *Families for life*

The policies formulated and the practices developed seem to have had considerable success. If studies are right, within a period of three to five years following placement, something like eight out of every 10 children with special needs seem to stabilise with their new families (Thoburn and Rowe, 1988; Borland *et al*, 1991). This may not be a long enough period to judge outcomes. As we shall also see later, these figures hide significant variations in outcome, depending on age at placement, and sometimes on the agency making the placement. On the earlier definition of permanency, these children were provided with a possible base in life. This has not been achieved easily and the cost to some families has been considerable. We are not talking about older children only, but children displaying serious emotional and behavioural problems, children who have been physically or sexually abused, children with learning and physical disabilities and children who are HIV positive. For a variety of reasons, today's "special needs" displayed by children who need new families appear more intense and intractable compared to those of 10 or 15 years ago. The question arises as to whether we have reached the limits of what can reasonably be expected of permanent new families, without a much more comprehensive network of supportive treatment-oriented services being made available.

• *A body of new knowledge and expertise*

As a result of the challenge to place children with special needs with new families, child care practitioners have developed a large body of knowledge and expertise covering the preparation, assessment and post-placement support of new families and of the children involved,

105

using both individual and group methods. This body of knowledge and expertise is now being recognised more widely and is being transferred to other areas of child care work. The permanency movement has also demonstrated what can be achieved by agencies who develop coherent policies with accompanying services in this area.

• Empowerment and partnership

A less recognised achievement is the realisation that through organised, explicit and collaborative forms of preparation and assessment, adoption workers have provided 'the script for the expected behaviour for adoptive parenthood' (see also Kirk, 1987). The role of adoptive parents and the parenthood tasks to be carried out were not only better defined, but an explanation for the rationale behind them was also offered. This has included information and help to adoptive parents to understand and use child development theory, particularly as it emerged from the studies of separated children. This was an empowering approach and far removed from the "all powerful" adoption social worker image. Adoptive parents were being prepared, trained and supported to become their own experts within realistic limits. As a result, a climate of increased partnership began to develop between adoption workers and adoptive parents well before the word "partnership" became fashionable in social work. This type of relationship formed the background against which post-placement support was provided. I am aware that this shift in practice is not yet uniform across the country. Far from being complacent, we have to be reminded that some applicants still complain of long waits to obtain a response or to be prepared/assessed. Worse is the way that non-accepted applicants are left with little or no support following a long period of preparation/assessment.

• Intensified rehabilitation efforts

Because of the need to make the case before the courts to free some children for adoption, studies suggest that after about the mid-1980s the pursuit of permanence sharpened, and efforts for the rehabilitation of children with their own families intensified (Lambert et al, 1990).

Challenges

A number of recent challenges seem also to have put the pursuit of permanency outside the family of origin on the defensive. These challenges have to do with the legitimacy of adoption, the setting of time limits and the clean break approach, and the role of the birth parents.

• *The legitimacy of adoption*

The first challenge concerns the legitimacy of adoption for children who enter public care without their parents having originally asked for adoption. As an example, approximately 40 per cent of children adopted each year in Scotland, England and Wales have been in public care. In England the percentage leaving care through adoption has been rising since the late 1970s. The critics of adoption argue that this is because not enough is being done to enable children to stay or return to their families of birth.

Some critics also contrast the attention being paid to children with special needs for new families, including the pre-placement and post-placement support offered, with the negligible help offered to children and their families before and during admission to care or following return home from public care. The payment of adoption allowances, to secure permanence for children with "special needs", is also quoted as an example which has exposed the weakness of general social provision for ordinary families and children. If similar allowances and attention were paid to birth families, it is argued, these might have helped to keep families and children together.

The legitimacy of adoption will continue to be challenged so long as much of child care need is generated as a result of extremes of poverty and homelessness in relation to the rest of the population. The lack of adequate provision and of supportive services undermines the coping resources of many parents. An acceptable policy of child care, and therefore of adoption, has to include adequate resources at the general, the preventive and tertiary levels to enable families to raise their own children, before permanency through adoption can be legitimised. While Teague's (1990) argument that adoption represents a deliberate child care policy for "ideological mastery" or "social control" is extreme, the critics of adoption have to be taken seriously. Ideological domination are the words used by opposing sides to accuse each other either of excesses in the separation of children from their families or in unfounded professional optimism about the chances of rehabilitation.

The close relationship that exists, though, between poverty and the relinquishment of a child for adoption, whether voluntarily or involuntarily, cannot be dismissed easily. It is mainly improved social conditions that have reduced own country adoption to almost nil in some northern European countries such as Scandinavia and Holland. It is, equally, the extremes of poverty in some "third world" countries that force parents to part with or sell their children. If we are serious about children's best interests, then concepts of permanence have to start with permanency in family of origin and country of origin, moving away from a position of viewing all children admitted to care as potentially free for adoption.

The provisions in the Children Act 1989 for support to families are to be welcomed, but the test will be its implementation and how the resourcing of preventive and rehabilitative services will be achieved. It is also the view that, with "child protection" capturing the headlines and resources, little is left for mainstream child care work. Is it not a paradox that a few dramatic cases of child abuse capture the attention of both the profession and the media, but not the extreme conditions of poverty and homelessness affecting thousands of children?

We have to accept, however, that even in the best regulated societies, of which we are not one, there will always be situations where, irrespective of how much provision there is and how well services are delivered, some parents for personal or social reasons, or most likely for both, will be unable to continue or resume the care of their children. Worse still is the fact that where children are concerned, social workers have to act from how the situation stands now, instead of how it might have been if past mistakes had not been made. The dilemma is how to respond to an existing situation, knowing that to be able to grow up and face the demands of adult life, children require stability, security and continuity of care with a base in life to call their own. They should obviously have the right to attain these conditions within their own families, but in my view they also have a right to achieve permanence with new families, when everything else has failed. The example of the harsh circumstances of children who leave public care without a base in life has already been referred to and does not offer an attractive alternative.

Farmer and Parker (1991) found that one in five children in care were unlikely to return home and long-term arrangements seemed desirable. Furthermore, they found that for 38 per cent of the children return home broke down and the outlook for second and third attempts was not good.

Obviously we have to satisfy ourselves that the children and their families had the best possible help to resume the care of their children, and had adequate support following the children's return home. We have not yet used with birth families the experience gained from supporting new families to maintain placements. Dingwall *et al* (1983), though, observe that it is right and reassuring that social workers think the best of parents but wonder if sometimes they are over-optimistic about achieving rehabilitation.

It is a sad fact that we lack a shared philosophy of child care policy and practice which explicitly, rather than implicitly, also includes permanence through adoption. This can result, as McMilland and Wiener (1988) argue, in 'resistance, often mute, to permanent care plans (outside the family of origin). At worst, this will show in deliberate sabotage of the plan . . .'. As a result, in their view, plans to move children on to permanent homes are often not realised and they continue to drift through the care system and placement. Information is also emerging that with devolved and tight budgets in some social services departments, adoption allowances receive less sympathetic attention than before.

• *Time limits and the "clean break" approach*
Rigid time limits and the "clean break" policy, which went alongside permanency planning through adoption and possibly still do, have

been one of the big blemishes in the permanency movement's short history. While many children moved into new families without leaving behind important links, others had meaningful ties severed before joining their new families. The significance of the emotional links between especially an older child and a mother or father or grandparent were often underestimated and some children were cut off from emotional lifelines before they had established new ones. Some of the examples are too painful to relate here. Margaret Forster's recent book, *The Battle for Christabel*, should become compulsory reading for all adoption workers with regard to this topic.

I challenged this policy in 1985 and I would like to think that each child's meaningful ties to past figures are assessed and maintained in a form of open adoption. A range of studies suggest that contact does not threaten the stability of the placement, provided the new family have agreed to it. On the contrary, contact seems to help stabilise the arrangements. I am not saying that all contacts are worth preserving, but as Fratter (1989) has also shown, it is possible to provide legal and emotional security to children through adoption without cutting them off from earlier important links.

Why and how such a situation came about is difficult to explain. There are those who attribute it to the legacy of the Poor Law with a strong desire to "save children" from what are seen as neglectful parents. Like a hundred or more years ago, the importance and meaning of parents to their children has again been underestimated. Older children, particularly, quickly lose their sense of identity and self-concept when communication with their biological parents is suddenly altered or terminated (Gibson and Noble, 1991). Jenson and Whitaker (1987) add that the bond that unites parent and child does not totally dissolve when a child is placed with another family. This does not mean that children cannot develop psychological bonds with a new family, but they can do this more easily when their earlier attachments are recognised, and where necessary maintained. Not surprisingly, arranging adoption with contact is a far more complex process compared to closed adoption.

Both the concept of adoption with contact and open adoption, used appropriately, should help to expand the boundaries of adoption.

With few exceptions, such as where the law has to protect children, parting with a child through adoption should be a voluntary act and free of pressures. Tentative research findings suggest that some parents of both younger and older children within the public care system who are unable to care for their own children would not be unwilling to agree to adoption, provided the links were maintained. When it comes to baby adoption, openness could give rise to increased altruism. Altruism, as a motivating factor in adoption, already operates in some societies where adoption is seen as a donation without severing contact. However, altruism, openness and contact have also to be shown to be in a child's interests, irrespective of the adults' intentions and preferences.

A sense of altruism, though, can only develop if birth parents come to feel equal, have a choice, are in control and own the adoption decision. It could be rightly argued that there is no such thing as pure altruism – without some self-interest. In this case the satisfaction for the birth parent comes not only from the knowledge that she/he can be of service to other human beings, but also from safeguarding the well-being of her child without the feeling of total loss if it includes contact or continued updating. No doubt there is still much more that needs to be learned about the long-term impact of open adoption. In the meantime, social workers are not only facing the emotional challenge of finding families for children with special needs, but also families that can accept contact and openness.

• The role of birth parents
One shift in attitude that seeking new families for children with special needs has brought about has been the recognition that such families offer a service. This has helped to lower the barriers between professionals and adoptive families and contribute to a climate of greater collaboration and partnership. Sadly, this has not been matched with a similar change in relationships between many birth parents and social workers. Increasingly we are faced with angry birth parents and stressed social workers experiencing a gap in communication and in constructive relationships.

During the early part of the permanency movement, conflict featured very little, if at all, because many of the children had been in public care for a long time and most parents had disappeared or lost interest in their children. As those children moved on, a new generation of parents and children emerged, but with different needs and expectations. More parents are readier now to challenge social work decisions, including the use of the courts. At the same time, social workers' awareness of the need to plan early to prevent drift in children's lives has increased the likelihood of conflict with parents, resulting sometimes in bad feeling, acrimony and stress. The handling of the increasingly conflict-ridden nature of adoption work seems to have contributed to some of the disillusionment towards permanency planning currently found among practitioners. Around 600 parental consents to adoption are dispensed annually by the courts in England and Wales as having been *'unreasonably withheld'*. [Source: Report to Parliament on the operation of the Children Act 1975 (1979).]

Like other users of services, parents of children in public care are readier now than before to challenge social work decisions at every stage and especially when adoption is being considered, and this is likely to increase under the concept of "parental responsibility" provided for in the Children Act of 1989. Social workers are rightly encouraged to look upon parents as partners and to try to plan jointly with them, but partnership does not always stand the strain arising from different perceptions of what is good for a child and especially as the parents' power does not match that of the worker. As an example, conflict is inevitably generated when freeing procedures are used which give parents the right to defend themselves before a court of law, and some have successfully done so. Yet social workers mirror in some ways the parents' agony and stress in their experience of protracted and stressful court procedures – something for which they have little preparation or support. There are no clear criteria for decision-making when the children are not free for adoption. In addition, the adversarial aspects of many proceedings before the courts often exacerbate rather than reduce conflict.

Outcomes

Do the outcomes achieved so far justify the pursuit of permanency through adoption for children with special needs, or do the challenges referred to earlier call for a much more cautious approach? Similarly, are the breakdowns experienced unacceptably high or within acceptable limits? To answer some of these questions we have to turn to outcome studies. The studies themselves are far from unproblematic. Inconsistencies and contradictions abound, but some agreement is also beginning to emerge about specific issues and circumstances.

I am not alone in recognising the complexities and hazards of trying to assess and compare outcome studies involving children placed for adoption or foster care. This is not the place to discuss in detail the methodological complexities but some of these include: not comparing like with like; failure to establish children's baselines on entering the system; questions of definition and measurement about such concepts as "satisfaction", "well-being" and "self-esteem"; and variations in the length of time between placement and the studies taking place. Where long-term criteria are used to assess outcome, the intervening variables can distort the picture. Finally, long-term or follow-up retrospective studies have not yet emerged.

A simple example of how outcomes for older children can be distorted is whether those children who are adopted by their long-term foster parents are included in the sample. Foster parents don't usually proceed to adoption before considerable stability in the placement has been achieved. An additional point to be borne in mind is that an increasing number of British studies now refer in their findings to both permanent family foster care and to adoption because of the many overlaps between these two types of substitute parenting. A further complication with adoption studies is that some have concentrated on disruption before and after the adoption order was granted, while others focus only on what happened following the granting of the adoption order.

In assessing satisfactory or unsatisfactory outcomes, studies have used the rather crude criterion of the placement continuing or breaking down following a certain period of time after the arrangement is made. Of course continuity of a placement is not always synonymous with success. Nor is a disruption or breakdown always disastrous for the child.

Highlighting the dangers of comparing outcome studies is not meant to paralyse thinking and action but it serves to add caution to the making of too definitive statements. We have to start somewhere though, if we are ever to be able to build more sophisticated and sensitive measures.

Children with special needs

A spate of studies which have been monitoring and evaluating perm-anency through adoption for children with 'special needs' began to emerge in the 1980s, and are still doing so. These have been appearing, mainly in the USA and Britain, where such policies and practices have been pursued. While in the case of baby adoptions the characteristics of the adopters were found by earlier studies to be the most crucial factor, when it comes to children with special needs, the picture is much more complex. In this instance both the characteristics of the child and of the adopting family seem crucial to outcome, including what Belsky (1981) calls 'the context within which parenting takes place'.

On average, something like eight out of every 10 children seem to settle down with their new families reasonably well. Looking at the figures, though, in greater detail, they show that children placed when under about the age of 10 have a consistently lower rate of breakdown than those who are placed when older. For the under 10-year-olds the rate may be as low as 10 per cent, but it rises to between 15 and 50 per cent for those who are older, depending on which study is examined. The breakdown rate for the age group of 10 and over is not monolithic but varies, usually rising with increased age and increased difficulties displayed by the child. A breakdown rate of between 25 and 40 per cent may, therefore, be accepted as usual. What happens to those who are adopted in adolescence presents a complex tableau of benefits and losses with breakdowns reaching sometimes 50 per cent and over. Older age is not infrequently accompanied by emotional and behavioural difficulties which many carers find difficult to handle. The child's ambivalence about commitment to the placement is often a further factor posing a threat to it.

Other pointers from the studies are that adoption with contact does not seem to threaten the stability of the placement, provided the adoptive family have agreed and have been prepared for this. Similarly, siblings placed together seem to experience fewer disruptions than when they are split, though other factors may be more important than the sheer fact of being a member of a sibling group, such as the quality of relationships between siblings. Children with learning difficulties and physical disabilities have been found to do very well by more than one study and they demonstrate consistently low breakdown rates. The main explanation for this is that such children are mostly adopted by people with previous experience of caring for children or adults with some disability.

Placing young children with families who have other children near the new child's age continues to carry a high risk for the placement. While childless couples were found in our recent study to be more successful in parenting young children, experienced parents were more successful in parenting older children who were disturbed (Borland *et al*, 1991).

Who can successfully parent a child and which children can be parented by new families is still far from clear, but a crucial variable contributing to disruptions, and mentioned by several studies, is the failure of the child to bond or attach itself. This is not always a one-way process, but can relate to characteristics in both the child and the carer. Without some form of attachment to provide a degree of mutuality and satisfaction in the relationship, the arrangement usually breaks down from between 12 and 18 months. In other words, when no rewards begin to emerge after a period of time, carers tend to give up. As in marital relationships, and in line with "exchange" theory, something is expected back at some point. Similarly, breakdown is more likely if carers find that the adjustment and well-being of other children in the family is threatened as a result of the new child's behaviour. Estimating, however, the possibilities of attachment when matching family and child is far from easy. It is an area where much more refinement in assessment processes is required. Though commitment and perseverance by the new parents is essential for successful outcome, a realistic view from the start of what the parents are taking on can also be decisive. Combining temporary optimism with realism from the outset is not always easy.

It remains difficult to predict which individual children will settle well with their new families, but certain features of the social work service increase the likelihood of stability for children of all ages. These are: more accurate assessment; better planning and preparation; the provision of adoption allowances; and a wide range of post-placement support services with specialist staff being available for use and consultation by families as the need arises. Staff who are knowledgeable and experienced in the field of child care seem to be more successful in making stable arrangements compared with others.

The adoption of adolescents

As already pointed out, permanency through adoption for adolescents carries many risks, with breakdown ranging between 30 and 50 per cent. A number of agencies, possibly discouraged by the high rate of breakdowns among older children, including the high investment demanded in human and physical resources and the distress that usually follows from breakdowns, are either far more cautious and discriminating, or have given up altogether considering adolescents. Yet a blanket approach is not in the children's best interests. After all, even among the most difficult to place groups, at least half the children settle down in their new families.

How do practitioners distinguish between those who are going to succeed from the rest? Good assessment and good preparation of both children and families are again emerging as important variables that contribute towards placement stability. Above all, especially with adolescents, it is important to listen to them, obtain their views and establish their wishes and feelings. In the past, we have perhaps not always listened carefully and enough to what they had to say, or failed to involve them more fully in planning and decision-making. Some of them may not want adoption, but something different; others may want security through adoption but without severing links with their birth families; others still may want to commit themselves fully to an adoptive family.

It is too early to predict how the concept of "parental responsibility" built into the Children Act 1989 is going to affect adoption, but a possible unwelcome outcome would be to deprive, especially older children, of a badly needed secure base in life through adoption. Based on our studies here, adoption as an option should not be ruled out for older children and for those who wish to retain links with members of their birth families. Possibly the best chance for older children entering care, and who cannot return to their families, is fostering with a view to adoption, even if it takes some time. Otherwise such children will be condemned to a life of rootlessness. Adoption through foster care has achieved considerable success in the past, but the move by many agencies towards contractual, time-limited placements could jeopardise this route unless more flexible placement policies are developed.

It is the legality of adoption and the emotional security that goes with it that sets it apart in the minds of the children and their adoptive parents from other forms of substitute parenting. A second tier of adoption order will only be perceived as a second-class type of adoption. A second-tier adoption may have worked, for example, in France, though I am not familiar with any French studies in this area, but the historical backgrounds and contexts between Britain and France are not the same. Other ways could be found to provide security for children who cannot return to their families and where adoption, as we understand it now, cannot be pursued.

The way forwards
The permanency movement has demonstrated what can be achieved in the placement of children with special needs. A small group of practitioners and managers can take a lot of credit for these achievements. Many of the children who found new families were emotionally damaged and often displayed behavioural difficulties. There is a lot of

evidence now which points to the capacity of many children to overcome deprivation and emotional damage. For some very damaged children we may be unable to undo all the earlier damage but we could provide a range of compensating experiences. Mistakes have also been made in the past – taking stock can only help to produce a more measured response. It would be a retrograde step, though, to relax the efforts and the impetus developed in finding new families for children who have no one to turn to. Social workers cannot be held responsible for the defects in social policy and for its failure to provide supportive and rehabilitative services to all families and children.

Caring for children with special needs has also proved stressful and painful. Besides offering care, many adoptive and foster parents are also expected to provide therapy to some very disturbed children without having been trained or equipped to do so. More attention must therefore be paid to how to furnish them with problem-solving skills and with a network of treatment services they can call upon without being labelled as dysfunctional. Permanence can be achieved through a number of routes and care arrangements. Joining a new family through adoption still remains the preferred option for some vulnerable children with no one else to turn to. There are strong pressures here and in other countries to see the abolition of adoption, especially for older children, for the wrong reasons. This should be resisted. Adoption will phase itself out only when every child can live with its own family and in its own country, thus maintaining continuity and stability. This position has not yet been reached. Its discouragement could prove detrimental to many children who would be condemned to a life of rootlessness for ideological reasons.

References

Belsky J. (1981) 'Early human experience: a family perspective', *Developmental Psychology* 17:1, pp. 3–23

Bohman M. and Sigvardsson S. (1980) 'Negative social heritage', *Adoption & Fostering* 101:3, pp. 25–31

Borland M., O'Hara G. and Triseliotis J. (1991) 'Placement outcomes for children with special needs', *Adoption & Fostering* 15:2, pp. 18–28

Clarke A.M. and Clarke A.D.B. (eds) (1976) *Early experience: myth and evidence*, London: Open Books

Dingwall R., Eekelar J. and Murray T. (1983) *The Protection of Children*, Oxford: Blackwell

Farmer R. and Parker R. (1991) *Trials and Tribulations*, London: HMSO

Fratter J. (1989) *Family Placement and Access*, Ilford: Barnardo's

Gibson D. and Noble D.N. (1991) 'Creative permanency planning: residential services for families', *Child Welfare*, 70:3, pp. 371–82

Jenson J. and Whitaker J. (1987) 'Parental involvement in children's residential treatment', *Children and Youth Services Review* 9:2, pp. 81–100

Kadushin A. (1970) *Adopting Older Children*, New York: Columbia University Press

Kirk D. (1981) *Adoptive Kinship*, Toronto: Butterworth

Lambert L., Triseliotis J. and Hill M. (1990) *Freeing Children for Adoption*, London: BAAF

McMillan I. and Wiener R. (1988) 'Preparing the caretaker for placement', *Adoption & Fostering* 12:1, pp. 20–22

Teague A. (1990) *Social Change, Social Work and the Adoption of Children*, Aldershot: Avebury/Gower

Thoburn J. and Rowe J. (1988) 'A snapshot of permanent family placement', *Adoption & Fostering* 12:3, pp. 29–34

Thoburn J. (1990) *Success and Failure in Permanent Family Placement*, London: Gower

Tizard B. (1977) *Adoption: A second chance*, London: Open Books

Triseliotis J. and Russell J. (1984) *Hard to Place*, London: Gower

Triseliotis J. (1983) 'Identity and security in adoption and long-term fostering', *Adoption & Fostering* 7:1, pp. 22–31

5 The theory continuum: prevention, restoration and permanence

This chapter from Prevention and Reunification in Child Care *by Marsh and Triseliotis (BAAF, 1993, Chapter 1) elaborated on points made in the previous one that children require current stability and a sense of permanence about the future, but this can be achieved for vulnerable and separated children in a variety of ways. A spectrum of care arrangements is considered, from living with birth family to adoption. The need for alternative care can be reduced by more general social policy provisions in areas such as poverty and drug misuse. Good targeted support services need to be available for each of prevention, post-placement support, reunification efforts and permanent substitute family care.*

Introduction

This chapter provides a framework for examining and applying the concept of permanence in children's lives, from prevention to restoration and permanence (where necessary) outside the family of origin. Though implicit in the Children Act 1948, nevertheless it was Maluccio *et al* (1986) who conceptualised permanence to include also policies and practices which contributed towards the achievement of stability of care within the child's own family rather than solely outwith. Building on this idea, permanence is defined here as a state which aims to promote the child's physical, social and psychological well-being through providing consistent care, stable relationships and a social base in life from which to face adulthood. Yet with separation, divorce, single parenthood and formal and informal reconstitution being characteristic of many families, care is needed not to set unrealistic expectations of families. For example, Farmer and Parker (1991) demonstrate that the majority of children who are returned to their families from care "on trial" achieve relative stability within continuing changing family circumstances.

It is recognised, however, that there will be occasions when it would be in a child's best interests for permanence to be sought and achieved outside the original family through permanent foster care or adoption. Such arrangements need not result in the child losing meaningful links with members of its original family. Not surprisingly, perhaps, the concept of "the family" conjures up different images, meanings and reactions in each of us and it is not the intention to debate these here. Suffice it to say that in this context "family" can mean any kind of stable arrangement, irrespective of how it has been arrived at, and which can provide for the needs of its members without exploitation or harassment. The preferred place for the achievement of permanence is the child's own immediate or wider family. The thrust of the Children Act 1989 is the achievement of permanency primarily within the child's own family, through a combination of measures ranging from supportive services to the provision of "accommodation" and of care services.

While acknowledging permanence as the ultimate objective, the concept is too global to make for easy operationalisation. It is necessary to partialise it into identifiable and manageable parts to aid specific policy, planning and practice considerations. Others, such as Hardiker *et al* (1989), have conceptualised all child care work as "preventive". Like "permanence", though, this concept too is broad, requiring to be separated into distinctive components. Different stages of family and child care work – including general support to families and children, the provision of accommodation, pre-admission work, reunification and post-placement work – all share many common-alities in terms of policy, planning and practice, but at the same time they also have a number of important and distinct differences. Failure to separate these could result in new confusions about means and ends and about roles and expectations. Fisher *et al* (1986) argue for prevention, rehabilitation and the provision of care to be all redefined as "assisted parenting", to allow for a spectrum of assistance and to maintain a focus on the welfare of the child. Again, like the terms "prevention" and "permanency", "assisted parenting" is equally too broad and not free from ambiguities.

The framework outlined here (Figure 5.1) separates approaches between permanence within own family and permanence outside the family of origin. Permanence within own family has a number of strands. It starts with the assumption that general social policies and the families' own efforts will contribute towards family stability in the vast majority of cases without external intervention. The framework then moves on to recognise that some families will need additional help, as a form of service, which can include the identification of child care need, the offer of family support services as set out in Part III of the Children Act 1989, the provision of accommodation or of relief care and the operation of diversion schemes. As a result of such action most of the children involved will never have to enter the formal care system. The third stage acknowledges that admission to temporary care may be necessary for some children for protection or containment. The eventual aim is for all children to be reunited with their immediate or wider families or be helped towards independent living. These steps are not meant to be linear, but should allow for moves between the various stages and forms of care.

Finally, permanence outside the family of origin is meant for those children who are unable or unwilling to return home. This form of permanence may be planned from the start or following the failure of restoration plans. Though the Children Act 1989 makes little reference to permanence with new families, it would be retrograde if it were interpreted as discouraging such moves where appropriate. In spite of some past mistakes, considerable achievements have been attained in this field.

Permanence within own family

Degrees of permanence within one's own family are achieved by most families without social work intervention. Some families who may need assistance will also ask for it and sometimes it will be available and at other times not. Other families will be reluctant to seek it or to accept it when offered or the right help may not be available. As others have pointed out, what is prevention of family breakdown or family support is unclear and ambiguous. Ambiguities surround such

Figure 5.1
Achieving permance in children's lives

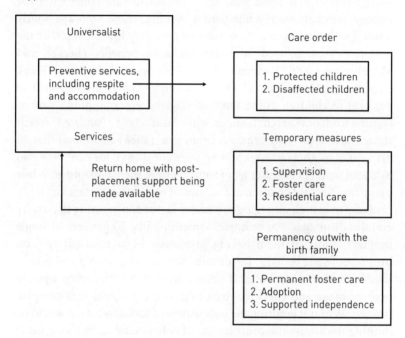

questions as: the nature of prevention and what it is about; on what knowledge it is based; how it can be best achieved and at which stage or stages; whether removal of a child amounts to failure; and how can programmes be monitored and measured. Some of the conceptual and methodological problems are well set out by Wells and Biegel (1991) and Whitaker *et al* (1990).

It is suggested that permanence within own family can be achieved through: (i) general social policy provision; (ii) the offer of targeted supportive services as outlined in Part III of the Children Act 1989, including the provision of accommodation; and (iii) temporary admission into care with restoration as the main aim, including the offer of post-restoration support services.

(i) Prevention achieved through general social policy provision

All studies are agreed that children who come to the notice of the social services and those who are admitted to care come from the poorest families, mainly one-parent families, those who are poorly housed or homeless and those who rely on very low incomes, or the long-term unemployed who are on state benefits (Becker and MacPherson, 1986; Packman *et al*, 1986; Strathclyde Social Work Department; Hardiker *et al*, 1989). Packman *et al* (1986) identified 40 per cent of children in the south of England entering public care as coming from one-parent families, while Strathclyde's (undated) recent study identified 70 per cent. Packman *et al* (1986) also found that 30 per cent of mothers whose children were considered for care were said by social workers to suffer from some form of mental disorder. While many families and children are victims of social circumstances, family breakdown is itself emerging as a major factor contributing to poverty and disadvantages. For example, something like 70 per cent of single mothers (most of them having previously been married) rely on insufficient state benefits. In addition, serious relationship and behavioural problems, alcohol and drug-related difficulties often operate both as cause and effect, contributing to the problem in a complex process. Without ignoring the seriousness of social factors, it would be limiting to dismiss the contribution of behavioural factors as generators of child care need.

The framework adopted here recognises the importance of universalistic services free of stigma or constraints made available to all families and children (Figure 5.1). In other words, a range of services has to be available to all families and not only those who are on the periphery of care. Poorer families also need access to the kind of resources and services that the majority of families now buy through the open market, because they command the means to do so. This would include locally-based services such as crèches, day nurseries, youth centres, out-of-school hours leisure facilities, appropriate income support, good quality housing and education. Social workers command very few of these resources and so are not in a position to influence outcomes in any significant way. It is therefore the job of politicians to confront the structural inequalities that underlie much of family and child care need. Failing that, we are left with only a residual model of child welfare. Parker (1992) also makes the point that, like public health, prevention could not be achieved entirely on an individual basis because child care need is strongly linked to poverty and inequality.

Parents' obligations to look after and protect their children are widely accepted, but the obligations of the state are subject to different interpretations, depending also on value and cultural dimensions. There are those, for example, who see it as the family's responsibility to rear its own children by its own efforts and resources and without outside interference, except in cases of serious neglect or abuse. Ideas about self-management and self-dependence with reliance on the private or voluntary sector fashion this approach. It was well expounded by Amiel (1990) who, commenting on Mrs Thatcher's apparent lack of certainty on which way to jump in fashioning a policy for the family, adds that Mrs Thatcher should deliver 'a plague on the house of anyone who wishes to design any policy at all. The best thing one can do for the family is to leave it alone' (p. 19). A state safety net, in her view, is all that is needed. In other words, if people choose to have children they should be prepared to shoulder the consequences.

On the basis of clinical experience, another group support the same approach i.e. that public provision should concentrate only on those families "whose need for it is greatest" and that social services intervention on how a family rears its own children be restricted to cases of serious physical or sexual abuse (Goldstein *et al*, 1980). Support for such an approach is based on the premise that children once separated from their families are psychologically irreparably damaged. Such a step, therefore, should only be contemplated as a last resort. Others equally argue for less coercive intervention in family life, but also for universalistic public welfare provision to be made available in the form of income support, day care, proper housing, etc. Their view is that universalistic provision will make unnecessary state intervention in the lives of families and children except in very few cases, e.g. cases of gross neglect (Holman, 1988). Yet another group are perceived as "child savers", who favour an active interventionist policy in family life. This approach often results in the removal of children with permanency outwith the family of origin as the main objective. Those described as "child liberationists" advocate that children should be free from all forms of adult oppression, including those masquerading as protection, and be granted full adult status. (For a detailed discussion of different ideological positions, see Harding, 1991.)

The Children Act 1989 tries to reconcile the different positions in ways that may be seen as irreconcilable. For example, it provides for the protection of children but with minimum interference in family life. It avoids structural policy issues by focusing instead on the micro-level of prevention, making explicit reference to support for families and children. Though it would be unrealistic to expect that the Act would tackle wider issues such as employment, income maintenance and housing, nevertheless it was these deficiencies that largely contributed to the failure of previous preventive efforts.

(ii) Prevention achieved through the offer of targeted supportive services

There is no shortage of writings making the case for interventive preventive work, in addition to the provision of general social services. Recent examples include the House of Commons Social Services Committee Report (1984), Cook (1985) and Holman (1988). As early as 1980, Parker urged that prevention should be an objective at all stages of child care intervention, adding that the overall aim was to prevent family breakdown rather than to prevent admission to care. However, he recognised that prevention of family breakdown as a result of temporary incapacities of the parents or of a temporary disturbance in the child would differ from the intervention needed when a child was 'at risk of physical injury, disturbed emotional development or death' (p. 44).

While acknowledging that the overall aim is the prevention of family breakdown and not simply admission to care, a distinction still has to be maintained between preventive work before and after admission through care proceedings. The Children Act 1989 puts the provision of accommodation firmly into the area of prevention. By doing so, it sharpens the difference between out-of-care and in-care provision, the latter through care proceedings.

The provision of accommodation and of respite care, while welcome, could have its own drawbacks if not properly managed. For example, empirical evidence suggests that children separated from their families suffer emotionally and though they can recover on restoration, the impact of repeated admissions could prove harmful. Worse still is the fact that many children do not return to the same carers. The other reservation is the knowledge that a sizeable minority of children, once moved away from home, fail to return. Short periods of accommodation will still require considerable planning and preparation of the children, parents and carers. Specific policies and services formulated on the basis of this part of the Act will have to be developed in a way that demonstrates what supportive work with families, including accommodation, are meant to achieve and how.

As already pointed out, the Children Act 1989 is specific about a range of supportive services that could be made available at this stage. In Scotland, much reliance has been placed on section 12 of the Social Work Act (Scotland, 1968) which refers to the promotion of social welfare. Though more facilitating than section 1 of the former Children Act 1980, it is still too vague to respond to the requirements of needy families and children. Research has already cast serious doubts on the preventive impact of these Acts (Heywood and Allen, 1971; Jackson and Valencia, 1979), with the House of Commons Social Services Committee Report (1984) acknowledging the failure of previous preventive efforts.

How far the preventive aspects of the Children Act 1989 will fulfil aspirations will depend on the resources made available, the kind of policies and programmes the local authorities develop and how the services are delivered to families. This part of the Act is neither mandatory nor entirely permissive. Consumer choice and access are likely to prove incompatible with budgetary restrictions, rationing of resources and "comparative monetary values". Gardner (1992), in a review of how the Children Act, 1989 is actually working, refers to the disbelief of social workers because 'these claims on behalf of families imply that there are more services because of the 1989 Act' (p. 17).

Holman (1992) observes on the matter that 'partnership will not prosper if local authorities cannot supply the kind of open, non-stigmatising services which facilitate rather than restrict family life'. He then gives the example of Newcastle Social Services Department which soon after the introduction of the Children Act 1989, had to cut the number of social workers and day care staff to avoid being rate-capped. A more cynical view is that the emphasis placed by the Act on the concept of "parental responsibility" is meant to detract attention from structural deficiencies. Similarly the concept of empowerment, suddenly so popular among practitioners, could be abused to rationalise failure to respond to reasonable dependency needs. Parton (1991) views the concepts of partnership, participation and of parental responsibility as consumerism under a different guise.

The underpinning of a policy of prevention with specific goals should ideally be influenced by knowledge of what is empirically known to be good for children and their development. Based on such a policy, culturally acceptable supportive service provision in the area of prevention could provide for services such as pre-school day care, out-of-school care, childminders, family centres, social work counsel-ling and support, diversion schemes such as voluntary supervision, counselling, intermediate treatment programmes, and respite services for young and older children. Assuming the resources are available, there is no reason why the social worker for the family could not generate packages of services to suit each family. Figure 5.2 highlights some of the services that could contribute towards assisted parenting and the offer of relief without removing the children other than on occasional days or weekends. This is not meant to be an exhaustive list. Of particular interest are the kind of self-help projects that could be set up to empower families and to encourage them to participate "in decisions affecting their own lives".

When it comes to direct intervention with the most needy families, it is perhaps no coincidence that a coherent model of intervention has yet to be developed and demonstrated to work. For example, is a highly intensive, short-term form of focused work which combines advocacy, empowerment, networking and counselling more appro-priate compared to more episodic, emergency responses or to open-

Figure 5.2
Achieving permanency for children

Focus of attention	Permanence within own family		Permanence outwith own family
	(a) *Prevention* ←	→ (b) *Admission into care* ← → (c) *Restoration*	
		Programmes	
1. Parents	Social work intensive support; counselling; services in cash or in kind; home-helps; family & marital counselling; utilisation of family & neighbourhood networks; self-help groups	(b) Preparation for child's admission + services under (a). Continue to prepare family for reunification (c) Preparation for restoration plus services under (a)	General support
2. Parents and child	Above plus family centre; day care; family work; respite accommodation for child and parents	(b) Preparation of parents and child for admission into care (c) Preparation of child & family for restoration. Post-restoration support	Keep links where these exist
3. Child	Day care; counselling/support; I.T./group work. Accommodation	(b) Prepare for admission to care. Residential care; foster care; counselling; group work (c) Post-restoration support; counselling; peer group. Independent living	Preparation for permanent foster care or adoption. Post-placement support in new family (individual or group processes)
4. Permanent substitute parent			Preparation for placement and post-placement support.

ended forms of intervention? Gibbons *et al* (1990) advocate a strategy of neighbourhood-based family support services delivered by independently run voluntary and informal groups. Local authorities would intervene in situations where serious problems had already been identified.

The most cogent argument perhaps against preventive work is that it is difficult to demonstrate its effectiveness and that in fact it does not work. Yet the picture that emerges from Wells and Biegel's (1991) edited reports on the subject, while not unequivocal, concludes that there was 'reason to believe that brief, intensive in-home services can effect measurable change in the environment, attitudes and behaviours of at least some severely stressed dysfunctioning families ...' (Nelson 1991, p. 207). The reviewer goes on to admit that it is not clear how exactly the various interventions produced the evidenced changes or what characteristics of interventions and families best correlate with "success" or "failure" of how durable the improvements are. Some gains from a somewhat similar form of intervention were identified by Benbenishty *et al* (1991) in Israel. These researchers suggest that staff should be given more power to allocate resources, especially with younger families. Allocating monetary resources to users should be part of the strategy of prevention. In the case of teenagers, where the breakdown of relationships is often the key problem, resources could be used to provide early counselling opportunities, diversion schemes and support for independent living. Pecora *et al* (1992), reporting on the achievements demonstrated by an evaluation of intensive family prevention services, outlined the characteristics of the service as:

> ... respect for clients and serving families on an intensive basis in the home setting – with behaviourally oriented training, clinical services, concrete services, and advocacy – empowers parents with both the skills and resources necessary to create safer, more enriching home environments.

Irrespective of how well such measures are carried out, admission into formal care may still be necessary, either as a step to protect children who are victims of serious neglect or abuse, or who are seen as too troublesome, or where family relationships have become too strained. For example, a number of adolescents enter the care system as a result of conflict between them and their parents or step-parents. Chronic relationship difficulties, conflict arising from reconstituted relationships and chronic alcohol or drug problems are the kind of difficulties that are usually found to be resistant to change. More time may be required. Equally, some children who are victims of neglect or abuse may require time away from the family. Admission into care need not therefore be identified as a failure of social work or as a stigmatising process, provided explicit restoration and rehabilitation plans are built into both the policies and services provided.

(iii) Admission to care, restoration and post-restoration support

A key aim of the Children Act 1989 is to keep children away from the courts, but it recognises that this may be necessary in certain cases. Except for a very tiny proportion of children, where admission to care may signify permanent separation from the family of origin from the start, in all other circumstances such a step is viewed and planned as a temporary form of separation and with clear restoration plans. Temporary care can offer parents and children a period of time to sort themselves out, to recover from illness or to build around them a range of supportive services that will help towards rehabilitation. In this respect all admissions, with very few exceptions, have as their main goal reunification with the immediate or wider family of origin. In order to provide direction, the objectives of admission have to be clearly stated for each child, and under the Children Act 1989, demonstrated in court.

As part of the process of admission, restoration and post-restoration support, detailed policy and planning objectives are again necessary detailing: the preparation process; the actual admission; the period in care; the reunification and post-restoration support to be made available. Resources have to be earmarked, not only for the substitute forms of care, but for continued work with the family – while the child is away – to speed reunification. Stressing the importance of "positive" planning for children in care, the House of Commons' Report (1984) added that:

> . . . there are many ideas put forward of what should or could be involved, but there is widespread agreement that more positive planning would help ensure that children do not stay unnecessarily long in care and that fewer children once in care are inappropriately placed. The quality of such planning is a test of the quality of social work management.

Most of the drawbacks identified by studies have been about the relative absence of consistent work with families, whose children were looked after in care, to make restoration possible. The DHSS document, *Social Work Decisions in Child Care* (1985), noted how 'far less attention is given to what is to happen after admission than to whether to admit or not to admit and if children stay in care social work attention fades.' Many of the gains achieved by children when in foster or residential care are often lost by returning to circumstances not very different from the ones they originally left behind.

The Children Act 1989 places an obligation on social workers to consult with parents about a child's possible placement. The choices are basically between residential and community care in the form of foster care, including return home on trial. There can be a variety of residential care provision and equally foster care is not a single form of care but provides for different substitute family care arrangements. Both residential and foster care services have largely been looked upon until now as either/or and not as possible combinations of care, especially for teenagers. Existing rigid divisions between residential, foster care and even diversion schemes do not help to identify the best care combinations. Empirical evidence about successful packages of care is lacking, though apparently a short period in residential care followed by fostering seems to work (Parker, 1966; Berridge and Cleaver, 1987).

The move, since the middle 1970s, away from residential care provision towards foster care as the preferred option for temporary substitute care, has been questioned by the Wagner Report (1988). It concluded that:

> *... there are circumstances in which group living will be the preferred choice and that the appropriate provision, which is not necessarily in the form of large establishments, needs to be made available and developed.*

Others have also pointed out that, if for no other reason, residential care provision will be needed because of the inadequacies in other services or limitations in other choices (Berridge, 1985; SSI, 1985). More important still is the fact that residential care is the preferred form of care for some teenagers. Parker (1988), in his review of the literature on residential care, identified nine factors which contribute to the effectiveness of residential institutions for children. He also saw the reduction in the size of the residential sector as an opportunity to decide how it should develop and for what reason. Recent revelations about "pin-down" regimes put the spotlight again on residential establishments as the Cinderella of the social services.

The shift towards foster care has come about despite the fact that it is far from unproblematic. For example, breakdown rates range from about 25 to 30 per cent during the first two years, rising to around 40 and 50 per cent by the third year. (For a summary of foster care outcomes see Triseliotis, 1989.) Even the assertion that foster care is cheaper vis-à-vis residential care is challenged by Knapp (1983) who claims, following his studies, that for comparable groups of children, the apparently favourable cost differential between foster care and residential care is not as large as it was generally believed to have been. He adds that once the easy-to-place children have been boarded out, foster care becomes increasingly costly.

Services to families

Both American and British studies since the early 1970s have provided some clues on the type of services needed to hasten children's rehabilitation with their families (Jones *et al*, 1976; Fanshel and Shinn, 1978; Aldgate, 1980; Millham *et al*, 1986). Yet studies still find that most child care work is reactive, responding mainly to pressures from elsewhere, particularly the behaviour of the children in their placement and the attitudes of parents or their carers (Fisher *et al*, 1986).

According to these writers, plans for children were not, apparently, the outcome of a conscious planning process but emerged as ad hoc arrangements, following everyday contacts with children, parents and carers. Efforts, when initiated, were unsustained and post-placement support, in contrast to post-placement support to adoptive families, was almost totally lacking. What was usually missing was clear policies about restoration and post-restoration support, with definite resources set aside and with guidelines for practitioners to follow and implement. Such policies and programmes have to be explicit on how restoration and rehabilitation of children to their families is going to be achieved. Policies also need to specify how the links between parents and children in care are to be maintained, how to prepare parents to have their children back and the type of post-placement services to be made available.

Because few children return to their own families after a period of about 18 months or so in care, it is suggested that policies and services should be geared towards very intensive work, particularly in the early stages of care. However, rehabilitative efforts need not relax in the face of evidence, which suggests that a proportion of children can still be rehabilitated after long periods in care. For example, the Oregon Project (1977) and Trent (1989) demonstrated how a number of children were successfully restored to their own families as a last effort before permanency outwith the family of origin was undertaken. The study of *Freeing Children for Adoption* (Lambert *et al*, 1989) made similar observations. The latter study also found that because of the greater scrutiny exercised by courts before freeing a child, social workers were increasingly becoming more aware of the need to intensify rehabilitative work to satisfy the courts that every effort for restoration had been made. At the same time, it is useful to bear in mind Dingwall *et al*'s (1983) writings that warn against 'professional over-optimism' about the achievement of rehabilitation, which in some cases exposes children to repeated failures. This is supported by Farmer and Parker's recent study (1993). Each failure in rehabilitation makes a subsequent one more difficult to achieve.

Preparation and post-restoration services

Preparing children for returning home and parents for having their children back is a further necessary stage in the procedure but restoration by itself is not enough, as demonstrated again by Farmer (1993) and Atherton (1993). It implies a deliberate and well thought-out programme of supportive services to parents and children following the return home. Like the programmes used when moving children to new families, similar ones are indicated for children about to return home and following their return. The expertise required and the range of physical and human resources identified as being necessary, for example in maintaining the placements of "special needs" children with foster and adoptive families, can be usefully introduced in the case of children who return to their own families. The dearth of work in this direction is illustrated by the fact that although there are now a number of examples illustrating how groups can be used for both preparation and post-placement work with children and new families (Triseliotis, 1988), hardly any such projects have been developed for natural parents and children. As with some foster and adoptive families, permanency in own family may require, in some cases, support till the child reaches late teens and possibly beyond. If adoption allowances can be used to stabilise a child's position in a new family, why not do the same for own family placement? Support may also mean short periods of respite care following rehabilitation.

In spite of everything that has been said so far, and however well all the previous stages of prevention, admission, restoration and post-restoration work are carried out, there will still be a minority of parents who will be unable or unwilling to resume parenting. Some children may not wish to return home, and for some it would be inadvisable to return them. When such a stage is reached, the agency's responsibility is to consider the long-term welfare of the child with the aim of achieving permanency within the wider family or with strangers.

Permanency outside the family of origin

A holistic framework and theory of child care cannot sidestep the issue of permanency away from the family of origin. We have to accept that even in the best regulated societies, of which we are not one, there will always be situations where some children will be unable to grow up with their birth parent(s) or other relatives. As an example, Farmer and Parker (1991) found that one in five children in care were unlikely to return home and long-term arrangements seemed desirable. Similar observations are made by Dingwall *et al* (1983) and Bamford and Wolkind (1988). Yet empirical evidence available suggests that a sense of belonging and security are necessary for the well-being of children. Furthermore, these qualities are mostly to be found in a family-type environment. It is not my job to defend or bury the family. However, children who grow up without a social base in life are far more vulnerable to adversities and not infrequently run into similar problems to their parents (Triseliotis, 1980; 1983; Triseliotis and Russell, 1984; Stein and Carey, 1986).

The word "family" conjures up different images, meanings and reactions in each of us, depending largely on our own experiences or of those close to us. We may need a new word that conveys the experience of mutually supportive and nurturing relationships without exploitation. Something like "home" or the Greek word *spitiko*. It is a social base where even in older age an individual goes for a Sunday lunch or to spend Christmas. Roycroft (1992) quoted a study by Newcastle University on 1000 families over a 30-year period which found that 'family life enables children to thrive, reduces mental stress and the family is best able as a unit to adapt to disability' (p. 2). He went on to add, however, that according to the same study 'family structures would be an historical curiosity by the year 2030'. Whatever type of institution eventually evolves, the empirical evidence supports the need for a social base or home to which an individual can belong and is able to return to if and when necessary.

A number of questions follow from this, such as whether children have a right to a new family to achieve acceptable levels of stability, or whether it is right that they should wait in uncertain arrangements in the hope that the natural family will one day resume care; equally, whether parents have a right to have their children back, irrespective of how long they have not cared for them and/or not kept in touch with them. It should be possible, of course, for children to acquire greater permanence in their lives outside their families without necessarily having to sever meaningful links with members of their birth family (Triseliotis, 1985; Fratter, 1989; Triseliotis, 1991). Permanence could be with existing foster carers, with custodians or with new adoptive families.

The movement for permanency outside the family of origin is now underpinned with considerable empirical backing, which could be summarised as follows: Drift in care within unstable and changing care situations and relationships mostly results in damaged children who later become damaged adults (Wolkind, 1977; Triseliotis and Russell, 1984). Children require stability and security in their lives and though early adverse experiences can be reversed, this relies on the achievement of optimum conditions (Kadushin, 1970; Tizard, 1977; Triseliotis and Russell, 1984; Quinton and Rutter, 1988). A threat to an individual's well-being and to the formation of a secure identity can develop through the absence of consistent and continuous relationships, lack of attachment to people a child can call its own, and from not having people on whose support a child or young person can rely. In a recent survey, the Prison Reform Trust (1991) found that more than a third of young prisoners and nearly a quarter of adults in jail were previously in local authority care.

The search for permanency outwith the birth family is further reinforced by studies which show that adopted people on the whole do not fare any worse than the general population. These findings apply even to "high-risk" and "special needs" children adopted when under the age of 10 (Kadushin, 1970; Tizard, 1977; Triseliotis and Russell, 1984; Borland et al, 1989; Thoburn, 1990). Permanent foster care, though not providing the full security that goes with adoption, still provides many children with considerable security and with a social base in life (Triseliotis, 1980; Zimmerman, 1982). Rowe et al (1989) describe long-term foster care as "good enough", even if not being as good as adoption. It is worth noting that most adoption allowances in the first years since the introduction of the schemes were taken up by long-term foster parents choosing to adopt their foster children (Hill et al, 1989). The same publication also discusses the children's explanations for their preference of adoption compared to long-term fostering. Adoption, through foster care, may be the most successful way of achieving permanence in the lives of adolescents who are unable or do not wish to return to their own families.

It could be claimed that many families whose children have recently moved to new permanent families or are even moving now, have not had the benefit of the kind of total approach in policies and practices suggested and that adoption or long-term fostering happens by default. This is largely true and the situation is likely to continue until a more integrated child care policy is developed and implemented. In the meantime, children cannot be held back because of past mistakes and deficiencies in policies and practices.

The place of policies and service planning

All the stages outlined earlier have to be supported by an integrated approach which pays attention and demonstrates the interconnections between policy, service planning and service delivery and resources. Ideally, an integrative approach at local government level, where the child care services are located, would have to link and carry on where national policies leave off. This can be difficult in Britain where, as already pointed out, official policy on the family, besides pious statements, is either non-existent or based on a largely residual model.

Wider social policies on services such as housing and income benefits which are outside the control of the social work services can seriously limit and constrain what can be achieved by local government through the provision of personal social services. In fact, it is the presence of the personal social services that continuously expose the weaknesses and gaps of national policies. In the aftermath of the publication of the DHSS Studies (1985), most of the debate was conducted in a climate of unreality, as if resources were there to be used rather than being strictly rationed commodities. *Social Work Decisions in Child Care* failed to examine in any detail the implications of resource constraints on social work activity and decisions. It concentrated instead on micro issues such as absence of policies, the need for better knowledge of law by social workers or lack of skills for direct work with children. These needed to be emphasised but the inescapable conclusion is that general social policies that sustain big inequalities often define the need for external resources.

Policy-making is about the identification of need, the setting of priorities in terms of objectives and the allocation of resources to meet these objectives. It is also part of the policy-making to decide on the kind of resources to be set aside to finance local organisations and local initiatives that could help foster networks through the setting up of neighbourhood and other self-help groups. Within social service departments the responsibility for policy-making lies with the elected representatives aided by managers, planners and hopefully by research findings. Yet, like at the national level, studies claim to have found no evidence of co-ordinated policies in this area. The studies summarised in the DHSS (1985) document referred to the absence of coherent policies and planning, to vague goals, to crisis-orientated and unsustained forms of intervention. In summary, no overall shared philosophy and strategies of child care emerged from the studies. Packman *et al* (1986) add that ' "grasping policy", like grasping "decisions", was a matter of trying to capture something that was multi-dimensional, constantly moving and, furthermore, something that often appeared ghostly and insubstantial in outline and detail' (p. 13). No policies could be identified all along the line from prevention to admission and restoration. Packman *et al* also observed that admission policies were too general, confused, ambiguous and contradictory in terms of their status and acceptability.

A more recent report by the Social Services Inspectorate (SSI, 1990) paints a somewhat more optimistic picture, demonstrating 'a steady trend' in the development of policy and strategy documents and of professional support for 'putting policy in writing'. Areas that were still relatively under-developed in terms of policy issues included children with disabilities and the health and educational needs of children in care – and we would like to add policies and services to teenagers. Where the SSI report was particularly critical was on the rare reference to policy implementation. The report rightly asks how far aspects of written policies are followed through in practice. It is too early yet to say how far the Children Act 1989 and the Community Care Act have fostered a different approach to policy-making and implementation.

If policy-making is about the identification of need, and the setting of objectives and about resourcing, then planning is about achieving policy intentions within set budgets and through service development such as the provision of accommodation, family support services and the setting up of diversion schemes. Parker (1971) also adds that it involves '… [a] reasonably clear practical vision of the future and more specifically, taking a sequence of steps which are instrumentally relevant to that end'. Finally, planning has to assure quality and to indicate who is meant to be reached by a specific service, and what it is expected to achieve in terms of measurable goals. Clarity and specificity about means and ends make easier also the subsequent monitoring and evaluation of the service offered.

The relationship between policy-making, planning, service delivery and monitoring can be demonstrated in Figure 5.3. Policy determines objectives and resources; planning implements policy through pro- gramme building; practice operationalises the programmes; and monitoring tries to establish how well policies are being implemented and how well or otherwise specifications are being followed, such as types of counselling offered or who is being reached. Finally, the impact and quality of the service could be evaluated in terms of outcomes.

The processes set out in the diagram opposite recognise the complexity of interactions taking place and therefore the influence they have on each other. For example, while policy determines planning and programme-building, the latter influences policy, pointing to necessary adaptations or to new directions. Similarly, the monitoring of programmes and service delivery can influence policy, planning and practice. Practitioners themselves, as Packman *et al* (1986) also point out, while implementing policy can also help to make it.

Services developed have to cover all the possible stages of provision from prevention to preparation, accommodation, reunification and finally permanence, where necessary, outside the family of origin. Figure 5.2, which outlines the main range of services, does not distinguish by how the child comes to the attention of the social services but by need and by whether the focus is on the parents, the

Figure 5.3

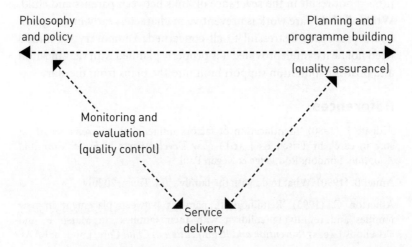

Philosophy and policy

Planning and programme building (quality assurance)

Monitoring and evaluation (quality control)

Service delivery

parents and the child, or the child alone. Planners devising services could build greater detail into this framework by, for example, separating needs and responses by age groups, e.g. 0–4, 5–8, 9–13 and 14 onwards. These groups represent different developmental stages, with some similar and some different needs for each age group which require separate attention. (Attention is drawn to Parker *et al*'s report (1991) on behalf of the Department of Health's Working Group, which devised schedules with dimensions reflecting the needs of the different age groups identified above. The guidelines outlined in the report can be used both as a developmental and as a self-monitoring tool, and also as a monitoring device.) A more detailed diagram could also identify the knowledge and skills required by social workers for each specified activity.

Concluding remarks

This chapter advocates a framework for child care policy, planning and practice which aims to achieve permanency of care within the child's immediate or wider family, thus reducing significantly the need for any child to be placed permanently outwith his or her own network. Permanency outside the family of origin is not ruled out but it need not result in the severance of links between parents and child. While all child care work is preventive in character, early intervention could prove less distressful to all concerned. Temporary separation need not be harmful, provided it is properly planned with reunification and post-rehabilitation support built into the plans from the start.

References

Aldgate J. (1980) 'Identification of factors influencing children's length of stay in care', in Triseliotis J. (ed.) *New Developments in Foster Care and Adoption*, London: Routledge & Kegan Paul

Amiel B. (1990) 'What to do with the family', *The Times*, 20 July

Atherton C. (1993) 'Reunification: parallels between placement in new families and reunifying children with their families', in Marsh P. and Triseliotis J. (eds) *Prevention and Reunification in Child Care*, London: BAAF

Bamford F. and Wolkind S.N. (1988) *The Mental Health of Children in Care: Research needs*, London: ESRC

Becker S. and MacPherson S. (1986) *Poor Clients: The extent, nature and implications of poverty among users of social work services*, University of Nottingham

Benbenishty R., Ben-Zaken A. and Yekel H. (1991) 'Monitoring interventions with young Israeli families', *British Journal of Social Work* 21:2, pp. 143–55

Berridge D. (1985) *Children's Homes*, Oxford: Blackwell

Berridge D. and Cleaver H. (1987) *Foster Home Breakdown*, Oxford: Blackwell

Borland M., O'Hara G. and Triseliotis J. (1989) 'Permanency planning for children in Lothian Region', Department of Social Policy and Social Work, University of Edinburgh

Cannon C. (1991) 'Seine policies', *Social Work Today*, 14 March pp. 25–26

Cook T. (1985) 'Fine in theory, hard in practice?', in Family Rights Group (ed.) *The Link Between Prevention and Care*, London: Family Rights Group

Cook T. and Miller J. (1981) *Direct Work with Families*, Family Service Units

Department of Health and Social Security (1985) *Social Work Decisions in Child Care*, London: HMSO

Dingwall R., Eekelaar J. and Murray T. (1983) *The Protection of Children*, Oxford: Blackwell

Fanshel D. and Shinn E.B. (1978) *Children in Foster Care*, New York: Columbia University Press

Farmer E. (1993) 'Going home: what makes reunification work?', in Marsh P. and Triseliotis J. (eds) *Prevention and Reunification in Child Care*, London: BAAF

Farmer E. and Parker R. (1991) *Trials and Tribulations: Returning children from local authority care to their families*, London: HMSO

Fisher M., Marsh P. and Phillips D. (1986) *In and Out of Care: The experiences of children, parents and social workers*, London: Batsford

Fratter J. (1989) *Placement and Access*, Ilford: Barnardo's

Gardner R. (1992) 'Court in the Act', *Community Care*, 25 June

Gibbons J., Thorpe S. and Wilkinson P. (1990) *Family Support and Prevention*, London: HMSO

Goldstein J., Freud A. and Solnit J. (1980) *Before the Best Interests of the Child*, US: Burnett Books

Hardiker P., Exton K. and Barker M. (1989) *Policies and Preventive Child Care*, Report to the Department of Health

Harding L.F. (1991) *Perspectives in Child Care Policy*, Harlow: Longman

Heywood J. and Allen B. (1971) *Financial Help in Social Work*, Manchester: Manchester University Press

Hill M., Lambert L. and Triseliotis J. (1989) *Achieving Adoption with Love and Money*, London: National Children's Bureau

Holman R. (1988) *Putting Families First*, Basingstoke: Macmillan

Holman R. (1992) 'Flaws in partnership', *Social Work Today*, 20 February

House of Commons (1984) *Social Services Committee Report: Children in care* (Short Report), London: HMSO

Jackson M.P. and Valencia B.M. (1979) *Financial Aid through Social Work*, London: Routledge & Kegan Paul

Jones M.A., Neuman R. and Shyne A. (1976) *A Second Chance for Families*, Washington D.C.: Child Welfare League of America

Kadushin A. (1970) *Adopting Older Children*, New York: Columbia University Press

Knapp M. (1983) *Evidence to the House of Commons Committee on Child Care*, Personal Social Services Research Unit

Lambert L., Buist M., Hill M. and Triseliotis J. (1989) *Freeing Children for Adoption*, London: BAAF

Maluccio A., Fein E. and Olmstead K.A. (1986) *Permanency Planning for Children*, London: Tavistock

Millham S., Bullock R., Hosie K. and Haak M. (1986) *Lost in Care*, Aldershot: Gower

Nelson D.W. (1991) 'The public policy implications of family preservation', in Wells K. and Biegel D.E. (eds) *Family Preservation Services*, Thousand Oaks, C.A.: Sage

Oregon Project (1977) *Overcoming Barriers to Planning for Children in Foster Care*, U.S. Department of Health, Education and Welfare

Packman J., Randall J. and Jacques N. (1986) *Who Needs Care?*, Oxford: Blackwell

Parker R. (1966) *Decision in Child Care*, London: Allen & Unwin

Parker R. (1971) *Planning for Deprived Children*, London: National Children's Home

Parker R. (1980) *Caring for Separated Children*, Basingstoke: Macmillan

Parker R. (1988) 'Children', in Sinclair I. (ed.) *The Research Reviewed*, London: National Institute for Social Work

Parker R., Ward J., Jackson S., Aldgate J. and Wedge P. (1991) *Assessing Outcomes in Child Care*, London: HMSO

Parker R. (1992) *Away from Home*, Ilford: Barnardo's

Parton N. (1991) *Governing the Family*, Basingstoke: Macmillan

Prison Reform Trust (1991) *The Identikit Prisoner*, Prison Reform Trust

Quinton D. and Rutter M. (1988) *Parental Breakdown*, Aldershot: Gower

Rowe J., Hundleby M. and Garnett L. (1989) *Child Care Now*, London: BAAF

Roycroft B. (1992) 'Traditional family facing extinction', *Community Care*, 14 May

Social Services Inspectorate (1990) *Child Care Policy: Putting it in writing*, London: HMSO

Stein M. and Carey M. (1986) *Leaving Care*, Oxford: Blackwell

Strathclyde Social Work Department (undated), *Who are They?*, Strathclyde Social Work Department

Thoburn J. (1990) *Success or Failure in Permanent Family Placement*, Aldershot: Avebury

Tizard B. (1977) *Adoption: A second chance*, London: Open Books

Trent J. (1989) *The Rehabilitation of Children to their Birth Parents*, Ilford: Barnardo's

Triseliotis J. (1980) 'Growing up in foster care and after', in Triseliotis J. (ed.) *New Developments in Adoption and Foster Care*, London: Routledge & Kegan Paul

Triseliotis J. (1985) 'Adoption with contact', *Adoption & Fostering* 9:4, pp. 19–24

Triseliotis J. (ed.) (1988) *Group Work in Adoption and Fostering*, London: Batsford

Triseliotis J. (1989) 'Foster care outcomes', *Adoption & Fostering* 13:3, pp. 5–16.

Triseliotis J. (1991) 'Maintaining the links in adoption', *British Journal of Social Work* 21:4, pp. 401–14

Triseliotis J. and Russell J. (1984) *Hard to Place*, Aldershot: Gower

Wagner Report (1988) *Residential Care: A positive response*, London: HMSO

Wells K. and Biegel D.E. (eds) (1991) *Family Preservation Services: Research and evaluation*, Thousand Oaks, C.A.: Sage

Wolkind S.N. (1977) 'Women who have been "in care": an epidemiological study', *Journal of Child Psychology and Psychiatry* 18:2, pp. 179–82

Zimmerman R.B. (1982) *Foster Care in Retrospect*, New Orleans: Tulane University

6 Social work supervision of young people

While most chapters are concerned with children growing up apart from their birth families or adults who grew up separated, this one considers support to young people living with their birth families. Drawing on a study that examined service packages for teenagers in difficulties, it focuses on formal and informal supervision. Most often young people and their parents were assisted separately rather than through family work. Results were mixed, but some young people reported changing as a result of advice or challenge, when this was combined with a willingness to listen and a relationship of trust. The chapter is co-authored by Borland, Hill and Lambert and was originally published in Child & Family Social Work *(3:1, pp. 27–36, 1998).*

Introduction

This paper reports on social services (social work) involvement with teenagers on formal or informal supervision. In either case, the main premise is that the local authority will deploy community resources to divert young people from anti-social behaviours or to relieve them from family and peer pressures. The findings presented here are drawn from a much wider study focusing also on care measures for this group (see Triseliotis *et al*, 1995). We recognise that evaluating outcomes of social work intervention is "contentious and complex" but we have to start somewhere. Unlike the nature of probation supervision, which has received extensive coverage in the social work theoretical literature over the years, that of children and young people has received only scanty attention (see Giller and Morris, 1978; Harris and Webb, 1987; Singer, 1989).

As we have also found from an examination of local authority child care policies, most attention has gone to younger children and their families. This bias has resulted in a failure to develop consistent and coherent policies and services for older children and their families. Yet a key demographic feature of recent years has been the fact that not only has the number of children looked after been falling, but also the average age of those admitted has risen (Department of Health, 1996). A further explanation, in our view, for the failure to develop policies has been the division of responsibility for young people in England and Wales between the Department of Health and the Home Office. With neither service fully responsible for adolescents and teenagers, theoretical, professional and outcome issues surrounding supervision have largely been ignored. Parsloe's (1976) comment some 20 years ago that supervision 'can mean anything or nothing' is as true today as it was then. Scull (1983), too, did not think supervision achieved anything.

While Hardiker *et al* (1991) view all forms of intervention with children and families, including care, as part of preventive work, others tend to distinguish between different levels (Marsh and Triseliotis, 1993). Preventive work is usually associated with informal measures of support and supervision following a request by parents, referral agencies or, more unusually, a young person. Voluntary supervision is also offered as an alternative to a formal disposition when the young person appears before a Hearing in Scotland or juvenile court (now youth court) in England and Wales. Finally, a formal supervision order can be made by a Hearing or a youth court. If we dwell in some detail in this paper on issues of care and control, it is because we found that much of formal or informal supervision is offered to young people who have been involved in offending behaviour. Irrespective of the way a child or young person comes to be supervised, however, the same range of services and resources is meant to be deployed to help resolve difficulties or reduce troublesome behaviour.

Justice or welfare?

The general treatment by the courts and other statutory bodies of children who are troublesome has often been examined mainly in relation to the so-called "welfare" and "justice" models. A dominant view in the 1970s was that welfare, rather than punishment, considerations should prevail by concentrating on needs rather than deeds.

Parsloe (1976), among others, argued for a welfare orientation because of what she called the juveniles' 'developing and immature state'. Jones (1983) supported a welfare model on the basis that children are less autonomous than adults and require, as a result, more guidance. Over the years, notions of control have come to be associated with the justice model, while care is seen as closer to welfare. Furthermore, the "welfare" approach came to be narrowly associated with "treatment" models, though it need not be. Harris (1980) wanted to see a separation of "caring" and "controlling" functions on the grounds that supervision makes no difference to re-offending anyway, and yet the controlling aspect limits the assistance made available to those on supervision.

In Scotland a compulsory supervision requirement by the Hearing system is part of a non-judicial process, but in England it is the result of a judicial one. The Children Act (England and Wales) 1989 reduced the welfare/control link implicit in the 1969 Children and Young Persons Act, and while emphasising the "non"-criminal side of child care, it distinguished children who offend from those in need of protection. Many of the teenagers who come into the first category will now be treated by the Criminal Justice Act 1991. The latter Act, apparently because of the success of social services community responses, brought greater social services involvement with 17-year-olds through Youth Justice schemes and a consequent need for closer collaboration between the social services, the probation service and the police. The same Act also supported the increased use of community-based sentences. These measures in part reflected the thinking in a Home Office report (Home Office, 1988) acknowledging that most young offenders grow out of crime as they become more mature and responsible.

Not long after, and as a result of widespread public concern about juvenile crime, such as the killing of James Bulger, or serious persistent offending, a different approach was being signalled by the Criminal Justice and Public Order Act 1994. Among other things, the Act provided for a secure training order in secure training centres, for 12-, 13- and 14-year-olds, though this part of the Act will not be implemented until the centres have been built.

The positions taken by those championing either a welfare or justice model seem to reflect ideological or empirically based arguments. For example, those arguing for a justice approach claim that, for a number of reasons, children's rights receive insufficient protection in systems based on "welfarism" (see contributions to Morris and Giller, 1983). Asquith (1983), though, distinguishes between establishing the facts and disposition, and argues that justice for children need not be seen as synonymous with asking for punishment or retribution. Writing later, Harris (1991) claimed, possibly justifiably, that juvenile justice is now a less central issue for social workers than once it was.

These debates, along with other writings, such as those of Bottoms and McWilliams (1979), also shifted the emphasis of supervision in general, not just for children, away from notions of "treatment" and notions of welfare. These writers argued instead for maximising client choice 'within limits set by the courts or any other statutory body concentrating help, and not treatment, in relation to client defined problems'. The emphasis here is on help, not control, and on shared assessment and joint definition of tasks as the basis for social work action.

The critics of this view have singled out the impracticality of separating the two functions and often the difficulty of distinguishing between them. For example, Singer (1989), from an analysis of interviews with older teenagers, supervisors and probation officers, could find no evidence for the existence of incompatibility between notions of 'support and surveillance' (p. 38). In fact, he found that both probationers and supervisors had difficulty in distinguishing when a response was "care" and when it was "control". His conclusions find theoretical support from Spicker (1990) who argues that social workers should reconcile themselves to the use of authority on the grounds that, as they act to change the client's situation, it means that at least in part they are there to affect the behaviours and responses of their client and therefore exercise some control. He comments that 'the social work relationship is often formed in a context of authority and approaches which seem to be non-directive are realised within this context' (p. 227). Jones (1983) too, sees no incompatibility between notions of welfare and control and argues that to make supervision credible 'requires an acceptance of the demand for control as well as care and the need to consider both natural and social justice' (p. 106). The Audit Commission (1996) urges 'youth justice services to give the young offender support and encouragement in addressing their behaviour' (p. 41). Finally, Pratt (1985) views the avoidance of further trouble, provision for constructive use of enforced leisure, understanding of the social damage caused by crime and other similar situations as reasonable social work and probation objectives.

The research study: sample and methods

The main part of the research was an intensive study of a sample of 116 young people aged 13–17 from five agencies, three English and two Scottish, between 1991 and 1993. The young people were followed for a period of approximately 12 months from the point at which decisions were made about the need for care or supervision or when major changes to existing arrangements became necessary. At the start of the measures of intervention, 55 of the 116 young people were on statutory or voluntary supervision. Here we concentrate on the views of 50 of the young people's social workers, 47 of the young people interviewed (33 male and 14 female) and the 32 parents who were seen both at the start of the measures and a year later.

Our questions to each of the three parties aimed to elicit inform-ation on the process, content and outcome of supervision from the perspective of the three actors, including whether the young person had benefited or not and how far the problems that originally led to supervision had been reduced or disappeared. The semi-structured interview schedules contained a mixture of pre-coded and open-ended questions. Some self-completion charts and lists, including the Coopersmith Self-esteem Inventory (1990), were used with the young people. Finally each party was asked to complete a modified version of the Rutter behaviour scale.

Findings

The main reasons for the young people being on supervision had to do with behaviour outside the home, mainly offending and drug-taking, school-related problems and relationship difficulties at home. An unusually high proportion came from single-parent households and reconstituted ones. Child protection issues, though, featured very little. Social workers and young people agreed in 61 per cent of the cases that offending/drugs contributed to the need for supervision measures. In the remaining 39 per cent, one of the two parties made no reference to offending/drugs as being a contributory factor. School and domestic difficulties predominated in these cases, though these were also present in some form with those engaged in offending behaviour and/or drug-taking. Graham and Bowling (1995, p. 3) comment from their study that 'both males and females who were less attached to their families were more likely to offend than those who were relatively content at home'. They go on to attribute most offending behaviour to delinquent peers, truancy and low parental supervision.

We found no evidence to suggest that these young people were alienated from their communities or that they had developed an alternative lifestyle or value system. We were rather struck by their aspirations for what are seen to be ordinary adult expectations, that is the wish to have reliable friends, good education, a job, a home and keep out of trouble. They were not a class apart from the rest of the community. Neither did they see themselves as behaving in an extraordinarily different way. The majority viewed supervision as the price paid for misdemeanours and as a result they did not resent it.

Just over one-third of the young people were on informal supervision and the rest were on formal supervision. While those who were on informal supervision came mainly to the attention of the social services (work) directly, those on formal measures came through the English juvenile youth court system or the Scottish children's panels.

Expectations

There was considerable uncertainty among a sizeable percentage of young people about the objectives of supervision, what to expect from it or how to use it, which appeared to reflect that of their supervisors. Our data suggested an absence of discussion with young people about the purpose of supervision, and a lack of jointness in planning and in the setting of goals. Giller and Morris (1978) also identified that young people on supervision did not know what to expect from it. The social workers' uncertainty of what to do with supervision orders is also reflected in the analysis of social work records carried out by Harris and Webb (1987).

Social workers put a lot of effort into developing a personal relationship with the young person and, on the whole, set long-term goals around offending, the young person's developmental needs (that is self-esteem, greater maturity or increased confidence), improved family functioning, schooling and independence. In contrast to social workers, young people would set single expectations focusing on "here and now" concerns. They also put the emphasis on better family relationships, the reduction or stopping of offending/drugs, not going into "care" and better schooling, followed by the wish to move towards greater independence. In their turn, parents stressed the need for a cessation of offending/drugs, less family conflict and improved education. Unlike social workers, young people and parents put little or no emphasis on personal development.

Contracts were rarely used, leading also to a failure to review goals regularly, especially as young people's wishes arose mainly out of immediate concerns which shifted with time.

The methods used in supervision

When supervising young people in the community social workers referred to five main methods being deployed: individual counselling; family work and advocacy; the co-ordination of services; linking the young person to groups; and outreach-type activities.

Many social workers used a combination of these methods, under-pinned by general support. At other times, some of the resources such as groups/activities were used instead of individual or family contacts. Though none of the young people used the word "counselling" to describe what went on between themselves and their social worker, nevertheless their descriptions referred to a type of counselling that involved talking and examining behaviours and relationships and/or schooling and practical concerns.

Discussions aimed directly and solely at personal development, which might be described as "treatment", were present in only very few interactions and young people made very rare reference to these. What we may be seeing is, again, the difference between what social workers say they aim to do or achieve in developmental terms and what actually goes on in their interactions with young people. Such expectations, though, may relegate in the social workers' minds the importance to young people and their parents of more tangible issues concerning behaviours, relationships and practical needs by feeling that they should be doing something else instead. Our evidence here and elsewhere suggests that social workers do not necessarily have to focus on developmental issues for gains to be made in areas such as "self-esteem", "maturity" or increased "confidence". Some young people who benefited in these areas did not necessarily talk about them directly with their social workers. There is a difference between recognising developmental needs, which in our view is essential, and directly addressing them. In other words, when social workers deploy their skills and knowledge in the areas of active problem-solving and on issues of immediate concern to young people and their parents, then developmental needs are usually met as well.

Returning to the debate about the balance between care and control in supervision, some social workers, as already hinted at, used challenge and direction as an integral part of their counselling techniques. For example, one social worker remarked how she "challenged" offending while stressing the welfare orientation of supervision. The young person seemed to divorce any control element from her experience of supervision and viewed her social worker as someone "listening to her problems". Another social worker, who discussed with a young person his not going to school and his offending, was perceived by the young person as someone who 'made me appreciate the consequences of not going to school' and another one said that he was 'made to see sense'. These and other young people did not appear to perceive the social worker's intervention as intrusive or controlling. A range of similar comments made by both social workers and young people, confirmed Singer's (1989) observation that it was often difficult to say when a response was "care" or "control". The boundary line between the two seemed a very flexible one.

Other young people, though, objected to what they perceived to be intrusive methods. For example, one social worker who described the content of counselling as consisting of discussing 'work prospects, drugs and the financial situation' was perceived by the young person as 'always checking on you'. Some referred to the social worker as 'nagging' all the time or 'taking your time'. One even said: 'I hate listening to her'. How intervention was perceived largely depended on the quality of the relationship established between the young person and the social worker.

Besides helping to promote better relationships and reduce tensions, the other main rationale for attempting to work with the families of young people is that the family can become a source of continued support and a long-term social base for the young person, even if he/she no longer continues to live there. There are obvious dilemmas about how frequently to meet with the young person alone, jointly with other family members or with only the family members, e.g. parents. For example, a total family approach could deprive the young person of usually much needed individual help and could also restrict him or her in attempts to break away emotionally and eventually physically from the family. The management of family meetings is currently influenced by three theoretical perspectives and the techniques associated with them: systemic, psychodynamic and behavioural. In their accounts social workers referred in general to 'family work' or 'a family approach', but it was not possible to clarify whether they referred to the application of any one systematic approach or of an eclectic one.

Focus of supervision

In the social workers' view, the content of supervisory contacts with young people centred on practical concerns to do with money, jobs and self-care, discussions around anti-social behaviours, and on schooling and family relationships.

At least a fifth said they raised issues about offending/drugs and other anti-social behaviours. A typical comment was 'challenged his offending' or 'confronted him with his school behaviour'. Though a significant percentage of young people could not remember what they talked about with their social workers at the last meeting, overall they confirmed the social workers' view.

Most individual meetings with parents were dominated by discussion of the parents' handling of the young person and family tensions. According to social workers, in over a quarter of cases general, practical and emotional support was provided to parents in their own right. While parents confirmed this pattern, some did not recognise social work efforts directed at them for a change of attitude towards the young person. They thought that most effort was directed at changing the young person alone.

Separate meetings with young people were more common than joint ones involving other family members. Young people and parents only infrequently described purposeful joint family meetings, and less often than the social workers did. Our data referring to actual meetings backed the parents' and young people's views. The total picture that emerged was one of few planned joint meetings.

Frequency of supervision contacts

Approximately one-third of young people had at least a weekly meeting with their social workers, about 10 per cent once a fortnight and a similar percentage at least once every month. Overall, around half the young people on supervision saw their social worker at least once a month. For the rest it varied between less than a month, according to need or infrequently. Though there was no relationship between frequency of contact and outcomes, at the same time all the young people who said they benefited a lot from supervision had at least one contact every month. As resistance to supervision usually led to less frequent contacts, it could mean that social workers concentrated on those who were more accessible. In approximately six out of every 10 cases, social workers either never met or met very infrequently with parents, such as at reviews or when there was a crisis.

While in a number of cases contact seemed to have been well planned and with a particular purpose in mind, in others it was less so. For example, the comment would be made that the young person or parent could not be seen because they were 'not usually there when I drop in' or 'depends who is there when I visit' or 'very little one to one. I leave it to the group' or 'keep contact by phone'. Research in the 1970s and later has criticised what were described as either 'routinised' and 'formalised interviews' or unplanned home visits (Pearce, 1976).

Different perceptions of outcome

The study used a multiple approach to examine outcomes and the general benefits of supervision over the whole period as perceived by each of the participants (for details, see Triseliotis *et al*, 1995).

Social workers and young people identified approximately one in every six young people as having benefited a lot from supervision, with parents identifying about one in every five (Table 6.1). Looking at negative outcomes, social workers identified 19 (or 38%) young people in whose case they said supervision made no difference or not much difference. In contrast, a considerably higher proportion of young people (28, or 60%) and of parents (18, or 56%) said that supervision either did not help at all or made not much difference. It is a cause for concern that more than half of the service users perceived no gain at all from the intervention.

There was a tendency on the part of social workers to place more young people in the "some" benefit category compared with young people themselves and parents, who tended to polarise outcomes either as "good" or "bad". The situation was made more complex, as we shall be seeing later, because there was not always congruence among the three parties about who were the young people who benefited a lot or a little.

Table 6.1
Amount of benefit derived from being on supervision as perceived by each of the three parties

	Social workers		Young people		Parents	
	N	%	N	%	N	%
Benefited a lot	8	16	8	17	7	22
Some benefit	22	44	10	21	5	16
Not at all/ not much difference	19	38	28	60	18	56
Don't know	1	2	1	2	2	6
Total	**50**	**100**	**47**	**100**	**32**	**100**

Turning specifically to the young people's views, one in every five said they were "very satisfied" with how things turned out for them over the year overall. Three out of every five were "quite satisfied". At the other extreme, one in seven were not satisfied at all. Young people who made a resolve at the start of supervision to reduce or stop offending were more likely to achieve this in a year's time than the rest. Social workers, too, who used challenge and openness within a supportive and caring relationship, were also more likely to help the young person to reduce antisocial activities. From their comments, some of the young people implied that challenge sometimes put them in a better position to examine their behaviour or make decisions.

Looking towards the future, a third of young people said that the overall service they had had from the social services would help make their future better. However, nearly half indicated that it would make no difference and one in every 10 said that it would make their future worse. Those who said that the service they had had was likely to make their lives better were also more likely to say that supervision had helped them with their problems, compared with those who said that it would make no difference. There were some young people who were very appreciative of the help and support they had received to stop getting into trouble or to enable them to begin to manage more independently at 16, but not everybody viewed improvements as being the result of supervision. Those who eventually had to move away from home into care were glad to have the break from the difficulties at home. A significant number of the young people and parents who did not feel that supervision was of benefit said they were unlikely to turn to the social services for help in the future.

Giller and Morris (1978), who interviewed 21 children who were being supervised by the probation or social services department in one city and 22 sets of parents, found that around 80 per cent of the children said that supervision was 'helping' them. These more optimistic findings may be related to the fact that Giller and Morris only carried out one interview without a follow-up. In addition, they confined their sample to one agency and we know from our own study that there can be significant variations between agencies.

What was found to be helpful or unhelpful

Social workers reported that the benefits of supervision included:

- general support;
- a reduction of problem behaviours;
- developmental gains;
- practical/material help and keeping the young person out of care.

Young people valued supervision for:

- exercising a restraining influence on their antisocial behaviours;
- being involved in activities/groups/outreach and problem resolution in relation to school, money or housing.

Parents valued supervision when it:

- succeeded in keeping the young person away from trouble with the law and with drugs;
- gave the young person somebody to talk to;
- helped with school and with organised activities.

When it came to unhelpful aspects of supervision, social workers referred primarily to lack of response from the young person or the family. They spoke of the young person's lack of motivation for change, difficulty in engaging with the young person and the resistance of the family situation to change efforts. It was only after specific questioning that social workers made reference to resources as a relevant factor. Young people agreed with social workers on two of these reasons, i.e. the situation at home and their own behaviour, but added a third which was the behaviour and actions or inactions of social workers. They referred to social workers as not keeping promises or never doing anything of practical value. A few simply said they did not like their social worker.

On the positive side, young people provided a number of clues of what they liked about their social workers and made them easy to talk to. These included:

- being straight and taking trouble;
- understanding and listening;
- informality which included occasional outings together;
- continuity;
- keeping confidences.

The following are a few typical examples:

I could talk to her [social worker] if I was in trouble or if I thought I was going to go pinching.

She helped me understand things better and always someone at end of phone.

Helped with school, over job and money budgeting.

Organising activities.

Supervision it helped to avoid care.

Dissatisfied parents attributed the absence of benefits to two main reasons:

- the young person's continued unacceptable behaviour for which they did not necessarily blame the social worker, except that social workers could have been more firm;

159

- the inaction of the social worker/social services.

In the latter category they included the absence of diversion-type activities, of respite and the infrequency of contact between the young person and the social worker or the social worker and themselves. They were illustrated with comments such as: 'more activities', 'more frequent talk' or 'more contact'.

Our view, supported by some of our findings, is that it is not enough to provide an effective service in one area of work as a trade-off to compensate for deficiencies in another. For example, the lack of adequate supervision cannot be compensated for by attendance at a group and vice versa. Neither will activities by themselves deal with conditions such as unemployment, poor life chances, housing short-ages or the absence of a network to which the young person can attach himself. In other words, social workers tended to offer either personal help or group work/activities, whereas a combination of both appeared to lead to better outcomes. Our findings also suggest that a number of social workers had not appreciated the high value placed by parents and young people on diversion-type activities. Resources that a number of social workers said they would have liked to use included:

- different types of educational facilities;
- more group and outreach activities;
- suitable accommodation for respite purposes;
- access to specialist facilities.

The Audit Commission (1996) survey observed that activity-type schemes were unevenly available in different parts of the country, but that in some parts, precious facilities were underused.

Relationships and behaviours
A high percentage of young people and social workers said they got on well or very well with each other, but getting on well with the social worker did not always result in benefits from supervision or change in behaviours. However, all the young people who said they got on "very well" rather than "well" with their social workers also said that

supervision benefited them a lot. These same young people also said that they found their social workers easy to talk to. As with the young people, parents who were getting on "very well" with their social workers were also likely to say that the young person benefited a lot from supervision. The obvious question is whether those who can benefit from supervision are those also able to form relationships. Our data suggest that this was not a one-way process and that the personal qualities of the social worker were also important. Some young people, who on the Rutter Scale appeared to be displaying some highly disturbed behaviours, appeared to form "good" and occasionally "very good" relationships with their social workers.

The amount of benefit young people derived from supervision was unrelated to their initial levels of self-esteem as measured on the Coopersmith Scale (1990). In effect, young people with very low and high levels of self-esteem were said to have benefited or not about equally from supervision. There was also no connection between the extent of benefit from supervision measures and the levels of disturbance as measured on the Rutter Scale (1967). Irrespective of which of the three parties' views we took into account, there was no association between benefits from supervision and levels of disturbance. In effect, young people with low, medium or high scores of disturbance were as likely to benefit or not from supervision.

What happened to the 55 who were initially on supervision?

Of the 55 young people who were on supervision at the start of intervention (though we only reported on 50 here), 20 (36%) were continuing a year later, while another 12 or (22%) went into care/prison and 23 (42%) ceased to be on supervision, with some of these moving on to forms of independent living. The most common reason quoted by social workers for the young person going into care was offending behaviour and drugs, followed by the situation at home, usually a combination of these two factors. Difficulties with a number of those young people who were not accommodated were continuing, especially offending. In two cases, offending had led to court appearances and to non-custodial resolutions.

Concluding remarks

This paper has looked at the content and methods of supervision deployed by social workers when supervising young people in the community and also at the general outcomes. Though less than half the young people were said to have benefited from intervention, nevertheless social workers were able to help some young people who on objective tests came out as being very "disturbed". On the whole, social workers appeared uncomfortable with issues of control and uncertain of whether to make too many demands on the young people to examine their behaviours. Harris and Webb (1987) also noted that probation officers, compared with social workers, made more demands on their clients. Whether intervention was perceived by the young person as care or control, helpful or unhelpful, largely depended on the kind of relationship developed with the social worker (see also Sainsbury, 1975, in relation to work with families).

Individual and family interviews, along with resources in the form of groups and activities, were often used as either/or rather than to complement each other. Significant differences also found between agencies largely depended on whether comprehensive services, such as individual and family interviews and the deployment of community resources were consistently deployed, and the extent to which specific youth strategies, in collaboration also with other agencies, had been developed. Whether keeping something like eight out of 10 young people on supervision out of care over a year was a satisfactory achievement or not is a matter for further debate. Our data suggested that the difference found between going into care and staying in the community largely depended on the tolerance of the environment, including the family. That tolerance itself could be increased or under-mined depending on the range of support and diversion resources available. More supportive and co-ordinated individual and family counselling, along with a range of practical services, could help parents looking after teenagers to absorb some of the stress and helplessness that they experience, especially during periods of crisis. Graham and Bowling (1995, p. 4) also urge for more consistent efforts 'to harness sources of social control within the criminal justice system, families, schools and neighbours'.

Though our findings point only to modest achievements, they also suggest ways that could help increase parental and community tolerance and lead to more satisfactory supervisory outcomes. Besides more focused policies for this age group, clarity about the purpose of supervision and appropriate planning, a range of community-based resources are also required to cover:

- different type of educational facilities;
- more group and outreach activities;
- suitable accommodation;
- access to specialist facilities;
- above all, social work time in the form of individual and family work.

All the above have to be part of a package tailored to individual needs and circumstances and should not be used as alternatives.

Acknowledgement

This article is based on material used for Triseliotis *et al* (1995).

References

Asquith S. (1983) *Children and Justice*, Edinburgh: Edinburgh University Press

Audit Commission (1996) *Misspent Youth*, London: HMSO

Bottoms A. and McWilliams W. (1979) 'A non-treatment paradigm for probation practice', *British Journal of Social Work* 9:2, pp. 159–202

Coopersmith S (1990) *Self Esteem Inventories*, Palo Alto, C.A.: Consulting Psychologists Press

Department of Health (1996) *Children in Care in England and Wales March, 1994*, London: Department of Health

Giller H. and Morris A. (1978) 'Supervision orders: the routinization of treatment', *Howard Journal* 17:3, pp. 149–159

Graham J. and Bowling B. (1995) 'Young people and crime', *Research Findings*, 24:1–4, London: Home Office Research and Statistics Department

Hardiker P., Exton K. and Barker M. (1991) *Policies and Practices in Preventive Child Care*, Aldershot: Avebury

Harris R. (1980) 'A changing service: the case for separating "care" and "control" in probation practice', *British Journal of Social Work* 10:2, pp. 163–184

Harris R. (1991) 'The life and death of the Care Order (Criminal)', *British Journal of Social Work* 21:1, pp. 1–17

Harris R. and Webb D. (1987) *Welfare, Power and Juvenile Justice: the social control of delinquent youth*, London: Tavistock

Home Office (1988) *Punishment, Custody and the Community*, London: HMSO

Jones R. (1983) 'Justice, social work and statutory supervision', in Morris A. and Giller H. (eds) *Providing Criminal Justice for Children*, London: Edward Arnold

Marsh P. and Triseliotis J. (eds) (1993) *Prevention and Reunification in Child Care*, London: Batsford

Morris A. and Giller H. (ed.) (1983) *Providing Criminal Justice for Children*, London: Edward Arnold

Parsloe P. (1976) 'Social work and the justice model', *British Journal of Social Work* 6:1, pp. 71–90

Pearce I. (1976) 'Differing perceptions of interview behaviour and the nature of delinquency', *Social Work Today* 6, pp. 71–90

Pratt J. (1985) 'Juvenile justice, social work and social control. The need for positive thinking', *British Journal of Social Work* 15:1, pp. 1–24

Rutter M. (1967) 'A children's behaviour questionnaire for completion by teachers: preliminary findings', *Journal of Child Psychology and Psychiatry* 8:1, pp. 1–11

Sainsbury E. (1975) *Social Work with Families*, London: Routledge & Kegan Paul

Scull A. (1983) 'Community correction: panacea, progress or pretence?', in Garland D. and Young P. (eds) *The Power to Punish*, London: Heinemann

Singer L. (1989) *Adult Probation and Juvenile Supervision*, Aldershot: Avebury

Spicker P. (1990) 'Social work and self-determination', *British Journal of Social Work* 20:3, pp. 221–234

Triseliotis J., Borland M., Hill M. and Lambert L. (1995) *Teenagers and the Social Work Services*, London: HMSO

7 When is evaluation a scientific activity, when is it not?

Many of John's writings were about his own studies and his reviews of wider research included considerable detail on design issues, the pros and cons of different methods and common limitations in research. Below is a rare example of an article exclusively devoted to the nature of evaluation, i.e. empirical work undertaken to understand the nature and effects of placements and services. A strong case is made for using a mix of methods and data sources, both quantitative and qualitative, in order to understand process and context as well as outcomes. The conclusion is that social research can learn from the physical science paradigm, but needs also to take account of values and human complexity. The article was first printed in the Scandinavian Journal of Social Welfare *(7:2, pp 87–93, 1998).*

Introduction

I would like to digress for a while by making reference to Herodotus, the Greek historian. As most of you will know, Herodotus wrote a lot about the Greco-Persian wars of 500–400 BC. However, he integrated into this "magnificent tapestry" of the Persian wars some of the most marvellous stories ever told. Examples of his stories include: How do Babylonians marry off their young women? How do you catch a crocodile? One other story, a cruel one, is about language development and involves possibly the first description of a positivist piece of "research".

Jones (1997) reminds us that Herodotus, being both a genius and a curious person, picked up these stories during his travels around the Mediterranean. "History" comes from the Greek word "historic", meaning "research enquiry", and for Herodotus that meant enquiry into all human life, 'the sum of human experience as he knew it'. He was the kind of historian who was always looking for explanations about things. Contrast this with the equal brilliance displayed by his successor Thucydides, who had no time for stories and turned history into what Jones (1997) again describes as 'the narrow study of war and politics'. It is claimed that historians in the past 200 years have learned better, and come to realise that Herodotus's way was right all along. Even so, history also has a place for the equal genius of Thucydides in his ordering of thoughts and words.

Which brings me to my topic of 'When is evaluation a scientific activity and when is it not?'. There is no shortage of contesting paradigms for the coveted mantle of science. Evaluative paradigms and semi-paradigms are paraded, each one claiming to be superior or the real seeker of the truth. With regard to social work it may seem easier to spot the truth in the academic environments where most of us work, rather than in the messiness of everyday social services activities. As Ruddock (1981) pointed out in relation to education: 'in evaluation as in other forms of enquiry, there is a danger of imposing a conceptual order upon an empirical chaos' (p. 1).

The main thrust of my paper is to put forward a composite/ pluralist approach as being more appropriate for most of social work's outcome requirements. There is nothing new in this suggestion. The well-known social psychologist Donald Campbell advocated the synthesis of paradigms in his William James Lecture delivered at Harvard University in 1977. As expected, strong criticisms followed from both experimentalists and naturalists, the argument being that each is underpinned by irreconcilable epistemological principles which cannot be mixed.

Evaluative research in social work

In social work the term "evaluation" is mostly used to judge the impact of services on users and their success in achieving their stated objectives. Thus it is closely linked to outcomes and effectiveness and to a cause-and-effect sequence. The main argument is that social workers, managers, users and the wider public will want to know, each for a different reason, about the outcome of social work programmes and particularly those related to children. Outputs evaluation assumes a relationship between means and ends and I guess governments would not be funding research programmes if they did not believe such a relationship existed. Trinder (1996) has suggested, though, that the rush for evaluative input/output type studies in the 1990s is politically motivated as a way of avoiding difficult and politically embarrassing questions about understanding.

While there are many stakeholders in social work outcomes, Knapp (1984, p. 29) reminds us that social workers and others in the caring professions have to make decisions between different alternatives all the time, sometimes with little guidance as to the merits of alternative choices. One of many examples is decisions between different types of counselling or between different types of substitute care for children. There is considerable consensus that evidence-based social work can provide a firmer base for practitioners and policy-makers to make more informed choices or be able to justify their decisions. What is more controversial is the credibility of the evidence and which design is best suited to deliver it.

There are different forms of evaluation within the social work services, including that of service evaluation, which stops short of measuring user satisfaction and change. In my view it is more desirable, even though more complex, if service process and outcome variables are linked, including the structures and context within which service is provided. While it is important to understand the impact of a social work method on outcome, something that experimental and semi-experimental designs can do with considerable validity, by itself it is not enough. We need to know more than that, including the basis on which the method was used in the first place and the delivery process. Evaluation which is focused solely on the outcome of intervention methods becomes largely staff evaluation. It is in this context that qualitative studies help us to understand the input, the process and the "why". The familiar experimental design of "situation, input, process and outcome" does not usually address these complexities. For example, the well-known experimental study of probation outcomes (IMPACT) had very little to say about the treatment offered.

The pursuit of the relationship between inputs and outcomes, and the search for causation, are at the centre of most evaluative studies of this kind, even though causation itself is a very elusive concept. Furthermore, we are reminded that 'the significance of outcomes can only be evaluated by reference to some kind of comparative standard' (Parker *et al*, 1991, p. 50). When it comes to social work the problem is compounded because its goals, processes and methods are not only disputed but are too diverse to lend themselves to simple experimental testing. If there is no agreement about the nature of social work and how much of its activity is science and how much is art, how can it be specified and its outputs measured? For example, Jordan (1978) and England (1986), far from seeing social work as a scientific activity, put the emphasis on it being illuminated by art and literature. If this is so, perhaps it should also be evaluated on the same elusive criteria as literature!

What is scientific?

What is scientific has been a matter of debate and dispute among epistemologists and philosophers for as long as man's recorded history has existed, and I doubt that we are going to resolve it here. Traditionally the term scientific has been identified with the experimental design developed by the physical sciences and that has become the hallmark against which all other designs are usually judged. The paradigm's main claim is the search for truth based on observable and quantifiable data which are open to experimental verification.

The power exercised in our minds by the word "scientific" is undeniable. Even the British government joined the battle in the early 1980s when it insisted that the then "Social Science Research Council" be renamed by excising the word "science" from its title. The main argument put forward was that social research was not scientific. If there was any doubt, this debate illustrated, among other things, the power of the word "science". Any research coming from a council that has the word "science" in its title is bound to be seen as adding to its prestige. If the word "science" has so much power, it goes without saying that evaluative studies in social services/social work have equally to be seen to be scientific to be taken seriously.

A composite definition provided by the *Oxford Dictionary* defines "scientific" as: 'the use of careful, systematic and accurate study and observation, and testing the soundness of conclusions according to rules laid down in exact science'.

The dictionary is clear that science is concerned with 'the material and functioning of the physical world'. No reference is made to the human world. Who defines, therefore, what is scientific and what is truth depends as much on context as on method. As a result, a reasonable question to be asked is whether a single definition or a single paradigm can take account of both the physical and human worlds. Agreement could possibly be more easily reached on some of the concepts such as 'careful, systematic and accurate', but it becomes more problematic when notions of truth and testing are added. Nobody would dispute the scientific demands for "reason and logic", or indeed the need for rational enquiry, which come more easily from the physical than the social sciences. The onus, as a result, for proving its scientific credentials lies more often with the social than the physical sciences.

If science is simply the "search for truth" and possibly for certainty, we should ask whether there is more than one route to this end, all of which may be equally valid, especially when context and constraints are taken into account. A major bone of contention is that the scientific paradigm, especially when applied to human situations, assumes that there is one reality, whereas we are more complicated creatures than that. The reductionist search for truth, through the use of solely experimental designs, tends to look for exclusively "black and white" outcomes, resulting in denying all possibility of human complexity, contradiction and ambiguity. Along with its often single-facet approach to behaviour, the design can be of limited value to decision-makers who have to consider a series of factors operating in a situation. One of the strengths of qualitative methods is that they are better suited than experimental designs to take account of the "messiness" which is characteristic of most social work activities and provide multiple understandings and outcomes.

Leaving aside the fact that the scientific paradigm cannot always be transferred fully to the social sciences, the paradigm itself has its limitations even in the physical sciences, and has come under considerable criticism. Chalmers (1982, summarised by Robson, 1993 p. 1), in his treatise on the philosophy of science, presents the following as a widely held common sense view of science:

Scientific knowledge is proven knowledge. Scientific theories are derived in some rigorous way from the facts of experience acquired by observation and experiment. Science is based on what we can see and hear and touch, etc. Personal opinion or preference and speculative imaginings have no place in science. Science is objective. Scientific knowledge is reliable because it is objectively proven knowledge.

However, Chalmers goes on to "demolish" this view of science by demonstrating that none of the above statements are defensible, either as an account of science or as an account of how scientists (including "hard-line" scientists) actually go about "doing science". Among other things he shows that ultimately there is no fully proven scientific knowledge. The Director General of the Institute of Mechanical Engineers in a letter to *The Times* (28 August 1996), while criticising the development of an "unscientific culture" in Britain, went on to acknowledge that 'this is not to say that the scientific community is infallible. Inaccurate observation, biased interpretation and confused reporting, even within what we consider conventional science, has lowered credibility.' He went on to give two recent examples, that of reports on cold fusion and BSE. I could also add all the current wrangles among mathematicians of when exactly the new millenium should start.

I am told that even in some aspects of geology you cannot experiment and that physicists know they cannot measure anything absolutely accurately. The astronomer Herman Bondi is quoted as saying that in the natural sciences 'facts' are rarely as 'hard as is often assumed' (quoted by Raynor, 1984). Ian Stewart (1992), the scientist, argues that human beings cannot obtain an objective view of the universe because everything we experience is mediated by our brain. Because of this, he adds, we sometimes see patterns that do not exist.

Furthermore, intellectual constructs, like epicycles or laws of motion, may either be deep truths about nature or clever delusions.

Although there are limits to the scientific paradigm, it does not mean that we know, as far as the physical sciences are concerned, of any other better qualified way to tell us about things beyond those limits. Whatever we think about some of the advances of science, it is difficult not to recognise spectacular achievements in some domains. When it comes to the social sciences and especially social work, we can learn from the scientific paradigm, but we also have to take account of the complexity of the human personality that we usually have to deal with. Others have argued that the distinction should not be between scientific and non-scientific research, but between "good" and "bad" research, though "good" and "bad" have themselves no objectivity. Finch (1986), for example, rightly argues that the validity of qualitative methods depends just as much as that of statistical methods on the care and discipline with which they are used.

Design and field compromises

Because of the kind of constraints operating, outcomes research in social work has mostly involved a series of paradigm and other compromises. Constraints have all along been imposed by:

1. the design;
2. the funding body;
3. agencies and respondents.

1. The design

The merits and limitations of each of the two main paradigms have been rehearsed at length elsewhere and I intend only to make a brief reference to them here.

The positivist/experimental design

Experimentation, as represented by the scientific paradigm, involves a series of well-established stages. A fully experimental design has to respond to the requirements of every stage, including sample randomisation, the manipulation of one or more variables, pre-test and post-test measurements and the control of other variables.

No doubt, when transferred to social work and the wider social sciences, the emphasis of the experimental design on causality and the prediction of behaviour raises issues of determinism which are unacceptable to many. Unlike the physical sciences, not only is causality difficult to demonstrate, but outputs involving human beings rarely involve absolutes. To use Whitaker *et al*'s (1984) phrase, outcomes are a mixture of 'benefits and losses'. Furthermore, it is rare that a fully experimental design can be used in social work situations because of moral, methodological and pragmatic considerations. Besides ethical considerations, a major difficulty is that social events, unlike physical ones, are changeable, have many causes and "multiple" effects. These qualities cannot be easily controlled within an experimental design which mostly pursues limited objectives, rather than multiple ones, including understanding. Neither does the design recognise experiences and subjectivity, which are central to most human interactions, concentrating instead on facts. Yet social workers have to deal with both facts and feelings. As Fay (1975, p. 200) points out: 'social orders are changing as a result of their dependence on natural phenomena, their interactions with other social systems and the growth of knowledge and changes in ideas and values of their constituent members'.

It cannot be denied that the scientific paradigm has clarity on its side even if not full objectivity. Macdonald and Roberts (1995), though, are uncompromising, arguing that 'for the determination of social work effectiveness there is no substitute for controlled experimental research guided by the philosophy of science known as logical positivism' (p. 320).

The naturalistic/qualitative design

Positivism has been challenged, mainly by humanists, on the basis that social scientific explanations are inadequate without reference to the social and subjective world. The world, it is argued, is not waiting "passively" to be measured. If positivism arose out of the scientific experimental design, out of humanistic ideas sprang a number of post-positivist related paradigms such as the naturalistic, interpretive, phenomenological, ethnographic, and so on. As opposed to facts and statistical computations to establish causation, these paradigms go for understanding and explanation and sometimes interpretation of subjective data, aiming to discover the intentions which "actors have in whatever it is they are doing".

As with experimentation and tests, validity is also a problem with the naturalistic paradigm. The understanding of other people's intentions is far from clear or unproblematic and this is a major reason why social work cannot rely solely on a single paradigm where the possibility of misinterpretation of data looms large. Other questions and doubts raised in relation to studies which rely wholly on an analysis of qualitative material without other checks include the fact that people being interviewed know it and are already affecting or changing their behaviour. An interviewer's expectations and biases can also influence answers to questions by the way questions are being asked. Snapshot-type interviews can only capture the feelings of the moment, which can be transient and influenced by the respondent's prevailing mood. Similarly, retrospective studies can be biased by intervening events, hindsight and current stresses and circumstances.

In my view, a composite/pluralist approach offers more safeguards, not only by using qualitative and quantitative data acting as a check on each other, but also through such other methods as triangulation. Further safeguards would be replication, the availability of data to accredited researchers, and claims being checked by respondents and through inter-judge tests. A number of additional safeguards are now being put forward to increase validity and reliability in qualitative research (see Miles and Huberman, 1984; Lincoln and Guba, 1985; Strauss and Corbin, 1990).

A composite/pluralist design?

A composite/pluralist design basically aims to synthesise aspects from the two main paradigms to suit the problem under investigation. It is an attempt to find a credible alternative to the existing dichotomy between cognition and emotion, the subjective and objective, and between absolutism (Plato) and relativism (Sophists). While it could be said that social work has neglected the value of experimental and quasi-experimental designs, Henwood and Pidgeon (1992) equally argue that psychology has undervalued the role of qualitative research. If it is to adhere to the notion of "good" scientific research, a composite/pluralist design has to seriously take on board the principles of "careful", "systematic" and disciplined study. In doing so, it can borrow from the experimental design ideas such as: sample selection and randomisation (RCT – randomised controlled trial), objectivity and neutrality, the manipulation of variables, measurement, including pre-tests and post-tests, linking outputs with inputs and replication. Though the experimental design by itself is not always enough, a number of researchers have demonstrated its value (see e.g. Gibbons, 1981; Gibbons *et al*, 1995).

We have also seen that the naturalistic paradigm, while helping to provide meaning and explanation for human interactions, is exposed to too many dangers of subjectivity, value judgements and preferences. Nevertheless, the following are some of its strengths, which when carefully used should benefit a pluralist design: case study, focused interviews and conversations, observation, controlled analysis and interpretation of experiences and interactions and ideas surrounding the development of grounded theory.

Because of its flexibility, a pluralist design can be in a much better position to accommodate a user participation model too. Though time-consuming and more costly, it can also perform a kind of internal validating role (see also Trinder, 1996).

More precisely, a composite/pluralist design could take on board any one of the following strategies or a mixture, depending on the matter under study.

Randomisation to experimental and control groups
There is no conflict in my own mind about the value of randomisation and controls, or at least as near approximations as possible. Although randomisation is not impossible in social work, nevertheless there can

be both ethical and practical objections to it in many instances. In spite of this, a number of researchers have demonstrated that there can be ways round it. For example, some users receiving a different type of service or some but not others receiving a service, but without involving randomisation; or users are allocated to different types of workers, such as trained and untrained; or some are offered something extra that would not be available to anyone without the study (see e.g. Reid and Shyne, 1974; Goldberg, 1978).

The use of comparative samples
An obvious alternative way is the use of comparative samples. A comparative sample lays one set of policies and the actions that follow from them alongside another helping to evaluate or establish how similar or different their impact has been on users. The social policies of an agency or region, though guided by national legislation and sometimes standards, still leave plenty of opportunities for diversity – sometimes too much. Change sometimes begins through limited and local actions, often through state and national initiatives, and sometimes through international action. One other advantage of comparative samples is that they can help to provide internal validity, which is such a highly desirable commodity. The comparative approach is also in a unique position to exploit the impact of social policy decisions which some maverick authorities sometimes put into action. Possibly one of the better known examples of a policy initiative later being used for comparative purposes was the records of a Kansas mental hospital where it was the practice at one time to castrate patients in the hope of reducing violence. The records were later used to study longevity.

Issues of measurement
Perhaps my main scepticism about the experimental or quasi-experimental design when applied to social work relates to its almost blind faith in pre-tests and post-tests, believing that they provide absolute truths (Macdonald *et al*, 1992). There is an assumption that tests are always both reliable and valid and are science's answer to some of our uncertainties. Some may be both reliable and valid, but

others may be reliable because they keep reproducing the same results, but that does not make them also valid. Many of you will be familiar with the Hawthorn experiment. It is difficult also not to be reminded of some of the measures being used to test racial awareness and self-concept in black children. The largely single facet and narrow questions asked, such as about the colour of dolls, fail to address the complex issues of identities. Some of these tests were developed without being preceded by grounded theory on the experience itself.

In spite of what I have said, I believe that pre-tests and post-tests have a definite place in output studies. However, such tests can only provide an indication of outcome and have to be combined with qualitative methods. In our recent study of teenagers, we used pre-tests and post-tests of adjustment and self-esteem but combined them with triangulation involving qualitative interviews with young people, parents and social workers (Triseliotis *et al*, 1995). In a small-scale study aiming to evaluate adjustment and changes in foster children, McAuley (1996) also demonstrated the value of a composite design by combining statistical and qualitative methods, including pre-tests and post-tests, the use of controls from classroom populations and of prospectivity.

The value of qualitative data

Possibly the biggest contribution that the naturalistic paradigm could make to a pluralist model is that of focused interviews and observation, case studies and in the analysis of qualitative data. Qualitative approaches are indispensable in providing in-depth description and evaluation of a holistic or multidimensional concept of outcome. They can take account of the awareness among many researchers that people's behaviour is less determined by "objective facts" and logic, and more by their own perceptions and how they construct reality. Furthermore, qualitative data can help to make us more aware of the kinds of evaluative questions we should be asking of users of the services. All carefully thought out qualitative studies contribute towards grounded theory building (see Triseliotis, 1973; Sainsbury, 1974; Fisher *et al*, 1986). Above all, they can help to 'interpret, illuminate, illustrate and qualify empirically determined statistical relationships' (Walker, 1989, pp. 15–21) and to reduce and possibly eliminate the problems identified with ratings and answers to closed questions.

No doubt a major limitation of using only case studies or small samples is that we do not know how representative they are. As others have pointed out, it is also hard to know whether the connections that are seen by the respondents, or by the researcher, reflect the way the world actually works, or the way those involved wish to see or present it. This is where large survey numbers can provide representativeness and greater confidence about general application. One big asset, however, of using large survey methods for outcome studies is that large numbers of users can be reached and their views sought on the impact of the services on themselves, mostly through ratings about different levels of satisfaction. Sinclair (1996) makes the point that allowing for the problems identified with ratings, a statistical model using regression analysis and other techniques can be built into the model to trace the relationship between the variables or elements.

One obvious question that arises from what I have said is about the scientific credentials of a composite/pluralist design. Does it enhance the value of output studies in social work or is it an affront to the integrity of the two main paradigms? The design I am suggesting is the one that many researchers in the area of separated children in Britain have been using and trying to develop over the years. As others have pointed out, the design lacks a theoretical or philosophical underpinning, which is similar to the criticisms directed at the pragmatic approach (see Fuller, 1996). The naturalist Edward Wilson put forward the view that one of the great challenges, intellectually, is to find a way of combining the best in scientific knowledge and thinking and concept and creativity, with the best of the humanistic, and to develop a scientific culture (quoted by Rowe, 1996). Some of the philosophical arguments put forward by Sayer (1984) for his so-called "realist" approach would have a place in a composite design. These matters, though, are perhaps best left to epistemologists and philosophers.

2. The funding body

I said at the start of this paper that the second major constraint operating on evaluative output studies is the compromises imposed by the funding body. Nowadays the funding body is usually a government department and occasionally a foundation. Funding bodies are the customers who say what they want and we the researchers, in other words the contractors, do it and the customer pays. Those who pay the customer also "like to call the tune". The emphasis placed by the customer on usable facts, rather than on qualitative data, on cost cutting and time limits impose constraints on the design and the data collection methods to be used. It is not surprising that so much research in some countries is confined to student populations who are easily reached, even if unrepresentative!

Governments, as the customer, often set their own priorities, wanting research that is usable and quickly obtained at the lowest possible cost. Besides political agendas pursued by some governments through research, fund limitations put constraints on the size of samples, including obtaining comparative groups, when one of the strengths of the pluralist design is big samples and comparability, not to mention prospectivity and longitudinal studies. There is no disguising the fact that the current preference is for studies which put the emphasis on value for money rather than on explanation and understanding. Answers to wider questions which help to advance the general knowledge of the subject have to be seen as hopeful by-products. If they happen, well and good. Does, however, answering only part of the question amount to collusive falsification or not?

On the positive side, even commissioned research is subject to peer review, acting as a quality assurance measure and in some way contributing towards design improvements. We have also seen examples of a fair amount of social work research recently being incorporated into new child care legislation, mainly because a number of related, if not replicated, studies confirmed each other.

3. Constraints imposed by agencies and respondents

Apart from the constraints imposed by the design and the funding body, there are equally those imposed by respondents in the form of agencies making their samples available and of the time made available by respondents themselves. Besides lengthy negotiations about access to staff and users' records, we are all anxious to convince managers that demands on staff can be kept to a minimum. This compromises not only sampling, but all the other research stages, including triangulation.

When it comes to respondents, possibly the biggest constraint is access and sample loss, which do raise serious questions about the "scientific" basis of any study. One such example is the high percentage of losses, sometimes amounting to 66 per cent, suffered by some American studies evaluating outcomes in relation to intercountry and other forms of adoption.

Conclusion

I have tried to make the case for the use of a composite/pluralist design as being more suited to most social work outcome studies, in contrast to a solely experimental or naturalistic design. This should not be taken to mean that there are no occasions when either of these paradigms does not have a contribution to make. I have come to believe that outcome studies in social work can approach the ideal in testing hypotheses and reaching predictions by taking the best from each of the two main paradigms and moulding them into a third design. The search for design complementarity should be guided by the requirements of the subject under study rather than the other way round.

If the search for objectivity, truth and certainty is sometimes problematic in the physical sciences, it is infinitely more so in social work, where objectivity is mediated by experience. We cannot stand outside ourselves and our knowledge and neither can any other type of scientist. Much of our knowledge and understanding has come, not only from experiments and quasi-experiments, but also from experiences and the kind of worlds we have constructed, analysed and interpreted. A composite/pluralistic design underpinned by the relevant philosophical and theoretical arguments and principles should eventually come to be accepted and respected as fulfilling the scientific criteria of "careful, systematic and accurate" study. In a recent paper, Little (1998) argues that the truth or authority of findings in social work research are assessed somewhere between a theory of social work research (which should be related to a theory of social work practice) and epistemology. If it is to approximate the ideal of systematic, dispassionate and reasoned evaluation, a composite design will require continued refinement, improvements and development.

References

Bryman A. (1988) *Quantity and Quality in Social Research*, London: Unwin & Hyman

Campbell D.T. (1977) 'Descriptive epistemology: psychological, sociological and evolutionary', lecture given at Harvard University

Chalmers A.F. (1982) *What is this thing called science?* (2nd edn.), Milton Keynes: The Open University

England H. (1986) *Social Work as Art*, London: Allen & Unwin

Fay B. (1975) *Social Theory and Political Practice*, London: Allen & Unwin

Finch J. (1986) *Research and Policy*, London: Falmer

Fisher D., Marsh P. and Phillips D. (1986) *In and Out of Care*, London: Batsford

Fuller R. (1996) *Evaluating Social Work Effectiveness: A pragmatic approach*, Ilford: Barnardo's

Gibbons J. (1981) 'An evaluation of the effectiveness of social work intervention using task-centred methods after deliberate self-poisoning', in Goldberg E.M. and Connelly N. (ed.), *Evaluative Research in Social Care*, London: Heinemann

Gibbons J., Gallagher B., Bell C. and Gordon D. (1995) *Development After Physical Abuse in Childhood*, London: HMSO

Goldberg T. (1978) *Helping the Aged*, London: Allen & Unwin

Henwood K.L. and Pidgeon N.F. (1992) 'Qualitative research and psychological theorizing', *British Journal of Psychology* 83:1, pp. 97–111

Jones P. (1997) 'Introducing the hot new movie star – who was born 2,500 years ago', *The Mail*, 19 March, p. 9

Jordan B. (1978) 'A comment on "theory and practice in social work"', *British Journal of Social Work* 8:1, pp. 23–25

Knapp M. (1984) *The Economics of Social Care*, London: Macmillan

Lincoln Y. and Guba E. (1985) *Naturalistic Inquiry*, San Francisco C.A.: Sage

Little M. (1998) 'Whispers in the library: a response to Liz Trinder's article on the state of social work research', *Child & Family Social Work* 3:1, pp. 49–56

McAuley C. (1996) *Children in Long-term Foster Care*, Aldershot: Avebury

Macdonald G. and Roberts H. (1995) *What Works in the Early Years?*, Ilford: Barnardo's

Macdonald G., Sheldon B. and Gillespie J. (1992) 'Contemporary studies of the effectiveness of social work', *British Journal of Social Work* 22:6, pp. 614–643

Miles M.B. and Huberman A.M. (1984) *Qualitative Data Analysis*, London: Sage

Parker R., Ward H., Jackson S., Aldgate J. and Wedge P. (1991) *Assessing Outcomes in Child Care*, London: HMSO

Raynor P. (1984) 'Evaluation with one eye closed: the empiricist agenda in social work research', *British Journal of Social Work* 14:1, pp. 1–10

Reid W. and Shyne A. (1974) *Brief and Extended Casework*, London: Columbia University

Robson C. (1993) *Real World Research*, Oxford: Blackwell

Rowe D. (1996) 'The comforts of reason', in Kennard D. and Small N. (eds) *Living Together*, London: Quartet Books

Ruddock R. (1981) *Evaluation: A consideration of principles and methods*, Manchester Monograph 18, The University of Manchester

Sainsbury E. (1975) *Social Work with Families*, London: Routledge & Kegan Paul

Sayer A. (1984) *Method in Social Science: A realist approach*, London: Routledge & Kegan Paul

Sinclair I. (1996) 'Research proposal submitted to the Department of Health', London (privately circulated)

Stewart I. (1992) 'In the beginning was the number', *The Guardian*, 19 June

Strauss A.L. and Corbin J. (1990) *Basics of Qualitative Research*, Newbury Park, C.A.: Sage

Trinder L. (1996) 'Social work research: the state of the art (or science)', *Child & Family Social Work* 1:4, pp. 233–242

Triseliotis J. (1973) *In Search of Origins*, London: Routledge & Kegan Paul

Triseliotis J., Borland M., Hill M., Lambert L. (1995) *Teenagers and the Social Work Services*, London: HMSO

Walker D. (1989) 'We would like to know why: qualitative research and the policy-maker', *Research, Policy and Planning* 7:2, pp. 15–21

Whitaker D., Cook J., Dunn C. and Rocliffe S. (1985) *The Experience of Residential Care from the Perspective of Children, Parents and Caregivers*, report to the ESRC, University of York

8   Foster carers who cease to foster

Written in a context of growing use of foster care and increasing worries about the adequacy of the number of foster homes available, this article from Adoption & Fostering *(22:2, pp. 54–61, 1998) reported on evidence from foster carers and agencies in Scotland about why they stopped fostering. Nearly half had given up for positive or neutral reasons, such as adopting the foster child or moving home. However, many reported problems, stresses and dissatisfactions with the children or their families and/or a lack of support and understanding from the social work agency. Agency records about reasons for ceasing to foster underestimated carer dissatisfaction.*

Introduction

In recent years concern has often been expressed that there is a looming crisis in fostering as a result of difficulties in recruitment and retaining carers (see National Foster Care Association, 1997). Issues of supply and demand have often featured prominently in fostering literature over the last 50 or so years, but specific information has been lacking. In particular little is known about who ceases to foster and why. The only published research known to us on the matter is what came to be known as the "Portsmouth study", carried out some 20 years ago (Jones, 1975), and Gregg's (1993) study also based on samples drawn from a single agency in England. In addition, Pasztor and Wynne (1995) provide a summary of American studies on the subject. The dearth of studies in this area is illustrated by the fact that Berridge's (1997) excellent review of foster care research for the Department of Health makes reference to only one study which was part of more extensive research carried out within a single English authority (Cliffe and Berridge, 1991).

We report on this issue from a much larger study which was prompted mainly by concerns about the supply and demand of foster carers in Scotland. The study was set up in 1996 with the twin aims first, of establishing who the carers are and second, identifying the policies, structure and organisation of the fostering services in 32 local authorities and one voluntary agency. The two parts of the study were designed to complement each other. The key aims were:

1. To examine the characteristics, motives and social circumstances of those who foster and seek explanations concerning the retention and loss of foster carers; describe the experience of fostering, including contact issues between parents and children; and evaluate post-placement support and general experiences of the fostering service.

2. To identify the policies, organisation and structures of the new social work departments for fostering, including the agencies' fostering needs, recruitment approaches, the preparation, assessment and training of carers, continued placement support to children and carers, the assessment of children and the matching processes followed, financial arrangements and monitoring mechanisms.

Phase one of the study, which was carried out in 1996, identified the characteristics and lifestyles of active and former carers and, more important, how they perceived the operation of the fostering services in 16 Scottish local authorities and in one voluntary agency. This article reports findings from this phase, but with the main focus on the former carers and why they gave up fostering. Where appropriate, data are contrasted with similar information from active or continuing carers. Knowing the former carers' views of why they ceased to foster, though only one of a number of aspects that have to be taken into account, nevertheless provides valuable feedback for agencies in developing their fostering services. The perspective of the agencies was pursued during the second phase of the study which took place in the summer period of 1997.

Sampling methods

Identifying exact figures of who ceased to foster and why was far from straightforward. Not all of the sampled authorities had accurate lists of those who ceased or, if they had, the lists did not always give the reasons why people had stopped fostering. Furthermore, modern systems of information technology had hardly been used to keep up-to-date information on issues of supply and demand, foster carer availability, preferences, and so on. The implications for policy-making, planning and monitoring arising from the absence of such basic information are obvious.

After a rather complex and laborious process, including tapping the memories of staff, we were able to piece together what we think is a reliable picture of those who ceased to foster in 1994 and 1995 and why. We are confident that in relation to two-thirds of the agencies featuring in the study we were able to obtain fully accurate inform-ation. With the remaining one-third we may be over- or under-estimating losses by about one per cent.

Methods of data collection

Information on carers who ceased to foster was obtained in three ways:

1. *Postal questionnaires* Of 216 former carers identified by the 17 agencies, postal questionnaires were sent out to 201 of them. (No questionnaires were sent to 15 carers who had been de-registered following mainly allegations of abuse.) Of the question-naires sent out 97 (or 49 per cent) were returned. (One arrived too late to be included in the analysis.) The response rate was less satisfactory than the 74 per cent obtained from continuing carers.
2. *Agency records* Information was also obtained from staff and agency records on why the 216 carers gave up fostering. Eventually a picture was compiled on 149 (or 69 per cent) of the original 216 who withdrew or who were asked to withdraw. Data from this exercise were invaluable in helping to check with the replies received from carers through the postal survey.

3. *Personal interviews* Personal interviews were also held with 27 former foster carers who ceased to foster. These were randomly selected after excluding those who left fostering because of retirement. The interviews provided in-depth material which helped again to act as a check on the statistical data and on information obtained from staff and records. This form of triangulation has helped to provide a more accurate and consistent picture of why these carers gave up fostering.

The proportion who gave up fostering

During the two-year period preceding the start of the study, the 17 agencies had incurred a total loss of 216 carers. Between them the same agencies had 1,184 active foster carers, so the annual loss was around nine per cent. Translated into national figures for Scotland this would result in an annual loss of around 160 foster carers in relation to a total of about 1,900 fostering households. As was to be expected, there were variations between agencies. The lowest loss of four per cent was experienced by the only voluntary agency featuring in the sample which had 51 active carers on its books. The highest loss of 13 per cent was incurred by a middle-sized agency with almost 100 active foster carers.

Our figures are similar to those reported from a recent survey carried out by the National Foster Care Association (NFCA) of English local authorities. The agencies in that study who answered the question on losses reported an overall eight per cent loss, with a quarter of these experiencing more than 10 per cent (Waterhouse, 1997). No explanation was given about the nature of the losses. In contrast, the Portsmouth study, though poorly documented as far as actual numbers were concerned, identified an annual loss of around 27 per cent (Jones, 1975). Some American studies suggest up to 50 per cent losses within the first year of fostering (Pasztor and Wynne, 1995). With no previous Scottish studies to compare with, we cannot say whether these findings represent an improvement or not.

Background characteristics

The study contrasted a number of personal and background characteristics shared by former and continuing carers such as marital status, number of own children, religion, housing, ethnicity, health, educational qualifications, employment and social class. No significant differences were found between those who ceased to foster because of dissatisfaction with some key aspect of the operation of the fostering service and the active ones, except that those who ceased were more likely to:

- have poorer health at the time of giving up (female carers);
- have somewhat larger families and more own dependent children;
- be active worshippers (female);
- hold non-manual occupations (female);
- have larger houses.

Unlike Jones (1975), this study found no significant differences between age at recruitment and ceasing to foster.

Motivation to foster

When it came to their stated motivation to foster, no discernible differences could be identified between former and continuing carers. The same concerns and interests had attracted both the former as well as the continuing carers. Even certain differences found between female and male carers that were identified in the active group persisted within the group who ceased.

Overall, and except for those who enter fostering with a view to adoption or because it suits their family's circumstances at a particular point and time, looking for the carers' motives as a key reason for ceasing to foster does not appear to be a productive line of enquiry. It is possible that better methods of preparation and selection in the last decade or so have led to greater uniformity in the type of person who comes into fostering now.

The foster children

The study also contrasted the number and type of children fostered at any one time by continuing and former carers, the ages of the children, sibling groups, children with mental or physical disabilities fostered, type of fostering undertaken (including community care schemes for adolescents), difficulties presented by the children, breaks and holidays taken. No significant differences were again found except that former carers were more likely to:

- be fostering under five-year-olds;
- have had fewer breaks;
- say they were not undertaking the kind of fostering they preferred;
- have had more difficulties with parents over contact.

Why carers ceased to foster

We now turn to the more vital question of why these former carers gave up fostering. The table overleaf presents side by side the primary explanations offered by the surveyed former foster carers and those stated by fostering staff/social work records.

While the main reasons for which foster carers cease to foster are diverse, there are also a number of consistent patterns which can be grouped into two broad categories: (1) internal factors connected with the fostering services; and (2) external factors.

1. Internal factors connected with the operation of the fostering services included:

    - outright dissatisfaction with the operation of the fostering services;
    - the children's behaviours;
    - impact of fostering on own family/no privacy;
    - burn-out/stress/no respite;
    - allegations;
    - biological parents' behaviours.

The above areas of dissatisfaction amounted to 57 per cent of all the

Table 8.1
Why carers ceased to foster based on the views of former carers and fostering workers/records

Explanations	Former foster carers' primary reason		Fostering staff's primary reason	
	N	%*	N	%
Dissatisfaction with the service	25	26	3	2
Retirement or illness	18	19	32	22
Adopted the foster child	17	18	19	13
Children's behaviours	16	17	8	5
Needing to work, move, no space	14	15	30	20
Impact on own family, no privacy	12	12	13	9
Stress, no respite	10	10	6	4
Allegations	5	5	17	11
At own request or had enough	–	–	12	8
Biological parents' behaviours	4	4	–	–
End of unique placement	2	2	4	3
Other (bereavement, no placements)	5	5	5	3
Total	**128**		**149**	

*The percentages are based on multiple responses and do not add to 100.

responses. If we were to add those who said they had left because of ill-health resulting from the stress of fostering, then around three-fifths of carers left because of some aspect connected with the operation of the fostering services. These reasons did not always have to do with the behaviour or attitudes of social workers or the agency. A large part of it was related to the general implications arising from caring for some very problematic children. There was no evidence to suggest that those who ceased were fostering more problematic children compared to the rest. Hardly any black, Asian or mixed-race children featured in the study. The Portsmouth study too found that about half the responses of those who ceased were in some way connected with the operation of the fostering services (Jones, 1975), albeit withdrawals were much higher in that study.

On this basis the fostering services in Scotland can expect to have an annual loss of around six per cent (between 80 and 100 carers), who leave because of dissatisfaction with fostering including the children's problems and for having had no placement. In contrast Gregg (1993), based on his study of the carers of a single agency in England, claims that for foster carers ceasing to foster is 'a natural process'. Furthermore, though the social work support they received could have been improved, it was generally appreciated and found to be helpful. Inevitably studies based on single agencies simply show what is happening in that agency and findings cannot be generalised.

2. External factors included:

- the adoption of the foster child;
- illness/retirement;
- no space or needing to work;
- moving house.

Retirement and illness featured in almost a fifth of the responses offered (eight retired and four withdrew because of illness). With one exception, the 17 carers (or 18%) who withdrew after adopting the foster child were some of the most satisfied with the fostering services. Other key explanations offered by carers included moving house, the need to work or no space. A few had been fostering for the sole reason of fostering only one child known to them. Once this was completed they withdrew.

Levels of congruence found between former carers and fostering workers/records

Though there were a number of similarities in the explanations offered by former carers and social workers of why carers ceased to foster, there were also notable differences. Fostering workers significantly underestimated the proportion of carers who withdrew because of dissatisfaction with the fostering services, the foster children's behaviours, stress and parental interference. They "exaggerated" the numbers of those who left because of moving house and/or the need to work, illness or retirement and "own request" (see Table 8.1).

The most glaring difference between the two groups was the much higher proportion of carers to fostering workers, who said they had left fostering because of outright dissatisfaction with the operation of the fostering services (26% to 2%). It could be argued that those who returned the postal questionnaire or spoke to us were not a true representation of all those who ceased to foster and that the fostering workers' views were more representative. We tried to check this by comparing the levels of congruence (where we had the names) between the views expressed by social workers and those of former foster carers. Where foster carers gave as their main reason for withdrawing the 'lack of social work support', the 'attitudes and behaviour of social workers' or 'the activities of the social work department', fostering workers tended to say the carers had withdrawn 'at their own request', 'own decision' or that 'they had had enough, or 'because of work commitments'.

It seems that in part carers' real reasons for ceasing to foster were not conveyed to fostering staff or adequately recorded. In other instances social work records used generalised explanations like 'own request' and 'own decision' which obscured the problem.

We can also make some comparisons between the explanations offered by the former carers who gave up because of factors associated with fostering, and those offered by continuing ones when describing times they felt like giving up. There were many similarities between the two. Both spoke about children's problems, chronic lack of social work support and related issues concerning the operation of the fostering service, including stress and effect on own family. On the basis of these findings, the difference between the two groups was one of degree rather than of substance. Eventually the pressure or a crisis become too much for some individuals, tilting the balance towards withdrawal.

Working relationships with the fostering services

Next we contrasted the perceptions of former foster carers with those of active ones on the quality of relationships with the children's social workers, link workers and the agency as a whole. The ratings of satisfaction offered by the former carers were, as expected, below those of continuing ones. The same applied when it came to the levels of support and whether expectations had been met or not.

However, it was thought that to obtain a truer picture all those carers who gave up for external reasons should be left out of the analysis, which should concentrate instead on the 50 carers who left because of definite dissatisfaction with some key aspect of the operation of the fostering services. These form the basis for the next section.

The overall picture that emerges from Table 8.2 is that just over half the former carers rated their relationship with the social workers and the agency as "good", or "very good", but the rating for "very good" was notably lower. As we say in the main report, carers were very discriminating between "very good" and "good". Somewhat more favourable ratings were given to relationships with the link workers. However, compared to continuing carers, former carers rated all three types of relationships significantly lower. Perhaps it was to be expected

Table 8.2
Contrasting the rating of relationships between continuing and former carers who left because of dissatisfaction with some aspect of the fostering service

Relationship level	Relationship with social workers		Relationship with link worker		Relationship with agency	
	Cont.	Former	Cont.	Former	Cont.	Former
Level	%	%	%	%	%	%
Very good	46	31	68	40	37	18
Good	32	22	22	31	45	36
Neither good nor bad	13	14	8	20	13	26
Poor	6	18	1	7	4	12
Very poor	3	14	1	2	1	8
Total	**100**	**99**	**100**	**100**	**100**	**100**

that, as far as relationships were concerned, former carers would feel more disillusioned compared to continuing ones.

Much of the dissatisfaction of the former carers with the children's social workers centred around the latter's failure to visit often enough or provide sufficient background information on the child, being unresponsive to requests for help and support when the children were being difficult, being unappreciative of their efforts and not being available when needed. Typical comments included: 'no support from child's social worker'; 'could have done with more support'; 'lack of commitment from certain social workers'; or 'poor matching'.

Worse in the eyes of the carers were telephone calls or other messages never being returned or being told the social worker was always somewhere else and unable to come to the phone: 'calls to child's social workers not being returned'; 'no say in what happens'; or 'being left to cope on our own'.

There were a variety of other comments suggesting that as carers they had very little say in what happened to the children and there was little recognition of them as members of a working team or as partners.

Support

Another comparison made between the two groups of former and continuing carers was in the amount of support received.

Table 8.3
Levels of support as perceived by continuing and former carers

Level	Continuing %	Former %
Very good	37	12
Good	35	20
Neutral	18	40
Poor	7	16
Very poor	3	10
Total	**100**	**98**

The pattern found with relationships was repeated here but more strongly. Significantly fewer former than continuing carers described the level of support as "very good" or "good". Correspondingly, more former carers described support as neutral ("half and half") or as "very poor" to "poor". Former carers repeated some of the comments made earlier, especially infrequent visits, unavailability and unresponsiveness to requests for help. Nevertheless many were satisfied with the support contact but still gave up.

When asked to say whether their overall expectations of fostering had been met, only 29 per cent of those who gave up because of dissatisfaction with the fostering services said that they had. This contrasted with just over half of active carers who said their expectations were fulfilled. Their main explanation for the apparent disappointment was of fostering turning out to be much harder than they had expected and the lack of support from the fostering services.

Fostering experience

We also compared former and current carers' characteristics, and views on the service, in relation to their length of service. Carers who ceased to foster had an average of 7.5 years of fostering experience compared to 7.0 years of continuing ones. Even taking account of only those who ceased because of dissatisfaction with some aspect of the work of the fostering services, their fostering experience still amounted to an average of 7.3 years. It cannot be said, therefore, that those who withdraw do so only after a short period of caring. Just under half had fostered for less than five years, but over a quarter had fostered for more than 10 years (see Table 8.4). In fact only nine per cent had fostered for less than a year compared to 40 per cent found by Jones (1975). However, almost all those who gave up before the first year was over were the ones who were dissatisfied with the fostering service.

The large percentage of carers leaving after a year prompted Jones (1975) to write that 'there is little to be gained from higher recruitment of foster parents if large numbers of recruits cease to foster only after a

Table 8.4
The number of years former carers had fostered compared with continuing carers

No. of Years	Former carers		Continuing carers	
	N	%	N	%
0–5	45	48	418	52
6–10	25	26	179	22
11–20	23	24	170	21
21–30	2	2	34	4
30+	–	–	5	1
Total	**95***	**100**	**806**	**100**

*One missing

short period as an active foster parent' (p. 41). There is no answer, perhaps, to the question of how long carers should be expected to foster before they give up. Would the perception of themselves as doing a professional job or having a career make any difference, or does the demanding nature of the job impose its own time limits? As we say in the main publication, carers on the whole do not see themselves as making a career out of fostering.

Factors that triggered the final decision

Apart from those who retired or stopped fostering because of other external factors, the decision by the rest of the carers to cease fostering was not usually taken lightly. In the view of many, the situation had been building up over a period of time, but the final decision was usually triggered by some recent event such as action or inaction by the social work services, the behaviour of the placed child, deterioration of health, the need for a break or the end of a placement. Typical comments illustrating the precipitating factor included: 'disillusionment with the social work department'; 'trying to argue with social workers for better matching'; 'lack of support'; 'child's bad behaviour increased'; 'the end of placement seemed a good time' or 'we could not take any more; 'our health and our family's life were affected'.

While the majority said that once they decided to stop nothing would have made them change their minds, there were a few who indicated that changes in attitudes within the social work services might have stopped them from giving up. Typical comments included: 'with more support'; 'if the social work department's attitudes were different'; and 'changes in the social work department'.

Some of the above comments were repeated when asked what, if anything, might bring them back to fostering. A number mentioned changes in the operation of the fostering services, more space in their house, better health, better pay and better conditions of service or after their adopted child settled down. The total numbers of possible returnees, assuming their grievances were attended to, did not amount, however, to more than 10 per cent of all those who ceased to foster.

Summary

The annual loss of foster carers for all reasons found among 17 agencies in Scotland was around nine per cent. There were variations between agencies but these were not usually high, suggesting a uniform practice across the country. The annual losses sustained for reasons relating to the operation of the fostering services amounted to almost six per cent or between 80 to 100 carers lost annually across the whole of Scotland. In England, with over 20,000 carers, this percentage would amount to around 1,000 carers lost each year. The losses are much lower than those found in the Portsmouth study some 20 years ago (Jones, 1975). Former carers fostered for an average of 7.5 years, which may not seem low, though some agencies in the sample demonstrated that they could keep their carers longer.

There was no evidence that the majority of foster carers gave up easily. The reasons why they withdrew were diverse, but almost three-fifths were related to some aspect connected with the operation of the fostering services and the rest to external factors. Background characteristics and declared motivation were in most respects similar to those of active carers. The eventual decision to cease fostering by those who are dissatisfied is a culmination of four main interacting factors:

- a past history of unresponsiveness and unavailability of social work support;
- the child being more difficult than expected;
- unresponsiveness to requests for help and support during the most recent crisis;
- impact on own family.

The lower than expected losses should not lead to complacency. Many of the dissatisfactions expressed by those who ceased to foster were also shared by a significant proportion of continuing foster carers and require urgent attention. They include infrequent social work visits, unavailability of social workers, the stand-by service covered by staff who are not knowledgeable about fostering, absence of partnership, lack of information on the children's background, the children being more difficult than expected, stress arising from the fostering task and low pay. Meanwhile, fostering staff may have to establish more accurately and also properly record the main reasons for which carers give up.

References

Berridge D. (1997) *Foster Care: A research review*, London: The Stationery Office

Cliffe D. and Berridge D. (1991) *Closing Children's Homes*, London: National Children's Bureau

Gregg P. (1993) *Why do Foster Parents Cease to Foster? A study of the perceptions of foster parents*, M. Phil. thesis submitted to the University of Southampton

Jones E. (1975) 'A study of those who cease to foster', *British Journal of Social Work* 5:1, pp. 31–41

National Foster Care Association (1997) *Foster Care in Crisis*, London: NFCA

Pasztor E.M. and Wynne S.F. (1995) *Foster Parent Retention and Recruitment: The state of the art in practice and policy*, Washington DC: Child Welfare League of America

Waterhouse S. (1997) *The Organisation of Fostering Services*, London: NFCA

9   *Delivering Foster Care*: conclusions and overview

The previous chapter drew on one aspect of a national survey of fostering in Scotland and now we see an overview of the full findings of that survey, many of which were echoed in a comprehensive English study a few years later (Sinclair et al, 2004). The Scottish study found a number of positives about the service, notably the role of the placement link worker which was normally well valued. Recruitment and loss of foster carers were overall largely in balance, but shortages occurred in some areas and few had enough foster families to allow for much choice when placements were made, often in an emergency. This chapter, reprinted from the book Delivering Fostering Care *(Triseliotis et al, 2000), makes many suggestions to improve recruitment and enhance fostering as a more professional, partnership-based service.*[9]

Introduction

We have reported here the findings of a study which looked at the delivery of foster care from the perspective of foster carers and local authority fostering agencies. The study was prompted mainly by concerns to do with the perceived inadequate supply of foster carers and with issues of recruitment and retention. Though the study was set up in Scotland, similar concerns were voiced in England.

The main task faced by the study was to establish the extent of the shortages, where these occurred, and to which type of need they applied most. Furthermore, it was necessary to obtain the carers' perspectives on the delivery of the service and identify how policy and organisational matters influenced such delivery, including the recruitment and retention of carers. In the process of doing so, four main sets of data were brought together:

---

[9]   The survey on which this chapter is based took place at a time when Scottish government was moving from 12 regional authorities to 32 smaller authorities with responsibility for children's services, a change that is mentioned in the text.

- the views of current and former carers;
- the views of service and senior child care managers;
- agency documents;
- the results of the census survey.

In this final chapter we bring together the strengths and limitations of the fostering services and emerging themes from the study and their implications for policy-makers, management, practice and national government. The main strengths of the Scottish and English fostering services, as perceived by the authorities and identified by the foster

Table 9.1
The strength of the fostering service

Authorities (Scotland)	Authorities (England)	Carers (Scotland)*
• Committed placement staff	• Skilled & dedicated staff	• The placement worker system
• Committed carers	• Experienced carers plus good partnership	• Preparation and training
• The quality of support offered by placement staff	• Good recruitment, assessment, training & support services	• The fee-paying structure (where available)
• The specialist nature of the placement service	• Independent placement service	• Group meetings/ support
• The fee structure (where available)	• Good management & commitment by agency	• Good recruitment, assessment, training & support services
• The greater integration of the fostering and residential services	• Generous/flexible financial systems	
• Of children placed, six in 10 went to first choice placements	• Clear procedures and standards	

* We do not have the views of carers in England.

Table 9.2
The main difficulties of the fostering service

Scotland (agency view)	England (agency view)	Scotland (Carers' view)
• Not enough social worker time	• Financial deficiencies	• Poor availability of child's social worker
• Shortage of foster carers	• Shortages of foster carers	• Inadequate support
• Budgetary constraints	• Poor sensitivity to placement issues	• The children's problems
• Some carers' attitude to training	• Staffing deficiencies	• Not valuing or listening by agency
• Tensions between placement workers and children's social workers	• Poor communication between placement workers and fieldworkers	• Insufficient information on children
• Lack of policy direction	• Scattered/diverse/ inconsistent service	• No team work
• Low pay for carers		• Low pay and poor financial practices
		• Fears about allegations of abuse

*Waterhouse (1997).

carers in Scotland, are outlined in the next two tables. Looking at these strengths, there is considerable overlap between the managers' and carers' views, especially around the commitment of carers, the specialist nature of the service, the support offered to carers by placement workers and the fee structure (where available). Though there are no similar previous studies to compare the findings with, what has emerged suggests that the fostering services are fairly consistent in the delivery of services. These strengths could account for the low losses of carers found.

When it came to the service's difficulties, there was very little difference between the authorities' views in Scotland and England but there were significant differences between these and the carers' views.

In spite of the many strengths identified, major gaps and limitations also remain. These impact, among other things, on issues of recruitment, retention and direct service delivery. For example, significant associations were found, on the one hand, between levels of carer satisfaction with certain aspects closely connected with the operation of the fostering services, with the role and activities of the child's social worker and the agency as a whole and, on the other, with prematurely ceasing to foster, finding the children more difficult, and expectations of fostering not being met. All the key themes as well as those outlined below have also been given a big profile in the recently published UK National Standards for Foster Care (NFCA, 1999).

Structures and organisation

While some councils and managers were still searching for the "best possible" structure for the fostering service, in other areas change was prompted mainly by budgetary constraints. Yet reducing manpower without sufficient safeguards could accentuate further some of the service delivery problems found by the study or undermine some of the achievements of the service. The study found that separate foster care units had some advantages over area team attachments, but there are other factors that each agency has to consider before deciding the structure of its fostering service. These include the size of an agency; geographical factors; the expertise available; the management and degree of co-operation between staff; and how the activities of the placement staff can be ring-fenced and protected.

A highly regarded asset of the service was its placement worker system which operated consistently across Scotland and was available to most foster carers. The distinctiveness of the placement part of the service, whether operating from single units, district units or based in area teams, combined organisational coherence with considerable expertise. It is this distinctiveness that in our view has proved to be the backbone of the service, eliciting high praise from carers.

Possibly because of this distinctiveness and of accumulated expertise, this branch of the service has wrongly come to be known as "the fostering service" to the detriment of the other part of the work undertaken by children's social workers operating from within area teams. This kind of identification goes beyond semantics in that it has shaped the attitudes of some staff and carers as to whose responsibility it is to deliver the fostering services, and perhaps contributed to some of the tensions found within the service.

As the study has also found, these two branches of the fostering service, that is, the placement service and the child's social worker service, currently operate with very different degrees of effectiveness. Fostering knowledge and expertise were said to be most evident among placement staff and least among children's social workers and their immediate managers. The challenge is to bring the latter part of the service up to the same standard as that of the placement service or unify the two into a single fostering service.

More radically, in our view, the challenge is on policy-makers and managers to gradually move towards the integration and unification of all their child placement services under a single management and service delivery system, without the loss of their distinctiveness. A highly knowledgeable, specialised and efficient service, untrammelled by other responsibilities such as child protection and emergencies, is required to engage in recruitment and respond to the needs of all looked after children, including the provision of direct support services to children and their carers. Integration is necessary at all levels, including management, with clear guidelines setting out who does what. This form of integration should also enable authorities to offer flexible packages to looked after children, their families and foster carers. Unlike now, a move in this direction should also empower managers to hold frontline staff and carers more accountable for their activities.

In the meantime, much more could be achieved by greater emphasis being placed on better co-ordination and communication between social workers, placement workers, carers and their immediate managers. This requires senior management giving more guidance to lower management on how to prioritise their staff's time and how to manage staff with performance criteria in mind. Currently, both higher and lower management are also handicapped in being able to exercise a full monitoring role because of the absence of sophisticated management information technology systems.

Fostering policies and strategies

Since the late 1980s, foster care has become the principal "out-of-home" form of care for children looked after away from home, exceeding that of residential care. In spite of this, there are many signs that foster care does not yet have the high profile that was traditionally reserved for residential care within local authorities. Like their predecessors, a number of the new councils made general, rather than specific, policy statements with no long-term fostering strategic planning. Detail was mostly missing, including how objectives were meant to be achieved, the kind of resources to be made available, and the specific roles to be played by staff.

The official policy of wanting to keep as many children as possible in the community, including foster care, but without additional resourcing and detailed strategies and plans, places social work staff under considerable stress. The child's social workers, especially, do not have enough time to assess children, visit them and their carers more frequently, or to engage in much direct work with children. There was some dismay among many placement managers because too much emphasis was placed on child protection compared to the fostering service. The thrust of the policies that were emerging was mainly directed towards maintaining the status quo, and largely failed to take account of the many challenges currently facing the fostering service, including:

- the changing nature of fostering and the type of child now being fostered;
- the proportion of children requiring foster care who are not being placed;
- the gaps in existing services, especially the provision of support to children and carers;
- the rising aspirations of the great majority of foster carers;
- demographic changes and employment factors that influence recruitment;

- the emergence of a non-statutory fostering sector.

While budgetary constraints faced by all local authorities were partly responsible for this, evidence also suggested that the fostering service was still being perceived in some quarters as a semi-amateur kind of activity undertaken largely by volunteer carers who had a special commitment to children facing adversities in their lives. With a number of notable exceptions, there was a failure at the top level of management and within certain councils to recognise the evolution of fostering into a professional service demanding wide-ranging skills and knowledge from those who deliver it, including carers. As a result, the profile of foster care found was rather low, the service in some authorities "marginalised" and not always commanding adequate attention within a climate of continued prioritising of resource allocation.

During the changeover from the regional to unitary authorities, many carers expressed concerns about the ability of the new authorities to properly resource the fostering service, drawing attention to their small budgets and the inexperience of some councillors and senior managers in the new councils as regards social work and fostering issues. Some of these concerns were later echoed by a number of child care and placement managers. Particularly, corporate-type management structures, and those heading them, were felt to be too far removed from the aims and daily concerns of the service to understand its needs and resourcing.

Recruitment and retention

One positive finding from the study was that, during the year 1996/97, new carer recruitment exceeded losses by 46 per cent, which helped to bring up the number of all foster carers in Scotland to 2,203 or one carer for about every 938 households. Some evidence was also found suggesting that a few of the new smaller authorities were able to tap carer resources previously not reached by the larger regional author-ities. The proportion of active carers, however, varies widely between different parts of the country, suggesting scope for much further improvement. The big cities, the central belt and the West of Scotland have most need for carers, but their recruitment levels were below average and in some areas well below.

If the recent recruitment rate is maintained, it could also signify an end to the gradual erosion of foster carer resources that has been happening since the late 1960s. Nevertheless, the majority of carers still decide to foster when it suits their family and personal circumstances and, similarly, leave when these change. This knowledge presents a challenge to authorities to make fostering attractive enough to encourage carers to see fostering as a career and stay on for longer. As an example, some authorities were able to hold on to their carers for an average of up to 10 years, compared to the overall average of seven years. Reaching an average of 10 years reduces the need for new carers by about a third.

There can be no complacency, though, concerning both the low level of losses of carers and improvements in carer recruitment. More than half of those who leave the service do so mainly because of dissatisfaction with some aspect of its operation, including the children's behaviours. Furthermore, around half of active carers at any one time think of doing the same, with many of their complaints being similar to the ones held by those who give up.

One of the most potent recruitment methods found was by "word of mouth". This, however, works best if the message that is spread is a positive one. Only satisfied carers can recommend fostering to their relatives, friends, neighbours and to people at work. It is not accidental, perhaps, that the study found many carers clustered in the same streets, neighbourhoods or villages, yet elsewhere there were none. Taking the carers' comments on a number of related questions on the subject, recruitment messages would also have to address some key issues that carers consider hold back others from putting themselves forward to foster. They include:

- lack of awareness among the public about child care and fostering needs;
- fears of not measuring up to agency expectations and being rejected;

- lack of confidence about being able to do the job satisfactorily;
- the poor image of the children and the stereotype that children needing fostering are "bad";
- the "poor" image of social workers and the apparent credibility gap between them and the public, including their failure to deliver promised services.

To address these more specific factors, authorities have to project fostering as a longer-term undertaking responding to career aspirations and as suiting both sexes. Furthermore, they need to show that the variety of children needing foster care could fit with the domestic arrangements of almost any household, including those of single people. It is also important to project:

- child care needs and the benefits of fostering to the children;
- an "honest" and balanced view of what fostering is about;
- the personal and financial rewards, including career prospects;
- the availability of continued training and support.

As stated in Chapter 5,[10] recruitment campaigns were mostly episodic and unsystematic, with no clear targets and lacking in clarity as to who to address, what issues to address, and how. The expectation of quick results clouded the views of some managers on the value of campaigns. Long-term strategies on recruitment were exceptional rather than the norm and foster carer recruitment did not permeate the whole agency, and sometimes not even its child care part. The urgency, in many authorities, was felt more by the frontline staff than by policy-makers and planners.

Staff who currently carry the responsibility for recruitment require expert advice from those with marketing skills, especially on how to develop recruitment strategies, how to address specific issues, and how to mount recruitment campaigns. Furthermore, carers will have to be involved at every stage, from policy to planning, recruitment, selection and training and be given a much more central role than at

---

[10] This and subsequent chapters referred to are from Triseliotis *et al* (2000).

present. We had many comments suggesting that experienced carers are in a much better position (than placement staff) to address some of the fears and uncertainties of the public and some of the public's perceptions and stereotypes about the children and social workers. Besides carers, young people, too, who are in foster care or have experienced foster care, birth parents and the carers' own children should have a vital contribution to make in activities associated with recruitment, preparation and training.

The study found that successful recruitment processes are typically local (word of mouth and the local press), but some kind of national initiative and co-ordination with local authorities could make additional contributions by:

- making use of national media more effectively, notably TV;
- pooling resources and considering campaigns between authorities;
- sharing ideas and targeting strategies;
- obtaining advice on marketing;
- retaining the services of carers who move across administrative boundaries.

Recruitment campaigns and activities are expensive and labour intensive to mount. To avoid duplication, neighbouring authorities should be encouraged both in this and other similar activities (training, stand-by service) to pool resources and to co-ordinate their work. Such co-operation could also result in more placement sharing to respond to some highly specialised needs that a minority of children present and which cannot usually be provided by small authorities. Although the study has not found a blueprint for recruitment, the following qualities appear to aid recruitment and retention greatly:

- a good knowledge of the area and of the agency's fostering needs;
- having a well-organised and responsive fostering service;
- having satisfied carers who are involved as partners;
- undertaking ongoing local recruitment campaigns;
- consistently involving carers and young people in recruitment, preparation and training;

- a high profile of the fostering service maintained by senior management and councillors;
- well thought-out financial arrangements, including payments to carers;
- maintaining continuity in recruitment.

Preparation and continued training for carers

Training received considerable praise from carers, but there was also a strong call for far more continued and systematic training to help enhance the carers' knowledge and skills. With over half the children referred for fostering placement presenting behavioural and emotional problems, carers were expecting to be equipped with more specific skills connected with the management of such behaviours and needs. Much more input was also expected in relation to children having a disability or health problem, issues on contact, and the emotional impact of fostering on carers and their families. Carers who felt prepared were less likely to say that they found the children more difficult than they expected or that they felt like giving up.

Chapter 6 highlighted the blurring of the stages and timing of family assessment, preparation, training, participation in support groups and continued training, calling for greater differentiation. It was far from clear where one stopped and another began. No doubt there are overlaps, but distinctiveness is also necessary. In this way training also begins to assume its importance and sets the scene for continued training. Overall, a more coherent, systematic and continued form of training was being requested by carers with the possibility of it leading to higher qualifications for those who wanted them.

Without diluting the importance of separate training for carers, we would also like to stress the necessity of periodic joint forms of training for all those involved in the planning and delivery of services to children. Besides helping to improve working relationships and reduce existing stereotypes about each other, it could also help to promote greater identification with the task and the agency as a whole. Some authorities are already doing a fair amount in this direction, but far more is needed.

A number of implications for policy and practice also arise from the findings set out in Chapter 9 on children who foster. For example, preparation, training and post-placement services could do much more than at present to involve and take seriously the preparation and support of the whole fostering family. So often the outcome of the placement depends on the attitude of the fostering household's children. Both own and foster children can carry many fears and anxieties which appear to be underestimated by those around them. Even when children appear to know, they do not also necessarily understand about what is happening and its likely implications for themselves and others. Like the adults, the children too need to be listened to, sounded out and prepared on their readiness to foster, how to anticipate and deal with difficulties, and how to handle sensitive background information. They need to be prepared for children leaving, given a higher profile in the agreement, and offered more concentrated support during and after the placement is ended.

There are also a number of other ways which could help reduce the possibility of difficulties arising for both own and foster children. For instance, careful assessment and matching are especially needed when placing children who have been abused or having abused others, children who have been badly rejected, or those who appear very needy for attention. It is important to refrain from placing children of the same age as that of an own child; this has been found by this and other studies to carry significant risks. Similarly, avoid the placement of children who are older than the carers' own by less than five years. The investment in time for more detailed preparation, matching and support should be made up by placements lasting as planned and carers continuing to foster for periods longer than the average of seven years found at present.

Role ambiguities and uncertainties

Role ambiguities, uncertainty about expectations, and some tensions appeared to surround the relationship between carers and children's social workers and that of child care area teams and of the placement service. These roles and relationships have always been difficult because of their complexity. It has not become any easier with the different types of fostering that have been introduced over the years and the more central role now expected of and often played by the children's parents. These developments have mainly resulted in more expectations being placed on both carers and social work staff. The introduction of a link worker into this equation, popular as it has proved with carers, has introduced a further possibility for confusion of roles and expectations and sometimes has given rise to divided loyalties. Perhaps unfairly, children's workers, because of the more controlling nature of their role, have sometimes been singled out for criticism.

We found uncertainty among many carers as to who carries overall responsibility for the child care plan and who is the first port of call when it comes to the need for support in relation to the child. Similar uncertainties and differences of opinion were also found among many service managers. Who does what is currently not clear and existing guidelines hedge the issue. Staff manuals examined were found to be vague, especially on the specific role of social workers in relation to the child and the foster carers. Because of this, and the unavailability at times of children's workers, carers made too many demands on link workers' time.

It was equally vague who was meant to act as the carers' first line manager and what the content of this role was seen to be. For example, would some of the carers' expectations for support be further met by the provision of a more structured form of supervision focusing on accountability, development and support? Contrary to the amount of literature surrounding the concept of supervision in social work, there is little or no reference to it in relation to carers and fostering and no agency made reference to this in relation to their carers.

How the two kinds of worker, including their managers and administrative staff, could complement each other in their work with the children and foster carers merits much more thought. As already mentioned, these two parts of the service currently operate at different levels of effectiveness. Besides responsibilities that should be laid on managers to promote better co-ordination, specific fostering agreements could be used to promote greater clarity and accountability. Some of the uncertainties, ambiguities and tensions found could be addressed by:

- clearer delineation of roles and clearer signposting of the areas of complementarity of the two types of worker;
- social workers having more time to spend with the children and their carers;
- more explanation and open sharing of differences and of different approaches, especially to questions of discipline and control;
- carers being seen as members of the fostering team and involved in all decisions and planning concerning the children;
- social workers becoming more knowledgeable and skilled in fostering work and direct work with children;
- improved management;
- more joint training of staff and carers to help dispel some of the misunderstandings and stereotypes held about each other and which would contribute towards better team work.

The assessment and matching of children

The Census of supply and demand highlighted the scale of the assessment and matching task facing the fostering service. Over a 12-month period, the fostering placement services can expect around 8,000 referrals. In England, this would amount to almost 80,000 children referred annually. Over half of these are referred as emergencies requiring foster homes to be found urgently within a climate of scarcities. The Census survey further established that two-fifths of the children referred for placement were either not placed within the period of the Census and two weeks after, or placed in households which were not a first choice because of the non-availability of placements. We do not know how many more children were not referred because of the knowledge that the prospects of finding a placement were low, though anecdotal evidence indicates this happens.

Contrary to what the theoretical and research literature suggest should happen, most placements made were supply led rather than led by the children's needs (Triseliotis *et al*, 1995a; 1995b). When it came to balancing needs, preferences and placement availability, certain groups of children presented the placement services with big problems and many of these children remaining unplaced. Placements were badly needed for:

- children from minority ethnic groups;
- those requiring long-term placement;
- offenders;
- children with disabilities, especially learning difficulties;
- those displaying behavioural/emotional problems and school problems;
- older children.

It was even more difficult, apparently, to achieve matching in smaller authorities because there was only a very small pool of carers available and inter-authority placements proved more difficult to negotiate. Budget constraints made it difficult for authorities to access placements from the non-statutory sector.

Beyond these resource and supply considerations, concerns were also found about the process of assessment and matching. Clear guidelines appear to be needed on a range of issues relevant to matching, including the form of assessment that should precede placement requests and which children are meant to be matched and which not. The obscure divisions found between "planned" and "unplanned" or between "temporary", "permanent", "short-term", "long-term" and "emergency" placements, besides their inconsistency, disguised the need for the assessment and matching of a much larger group of children than currently undertaken.

Matching intentions featuring in some manuals were at odds with what was happening in practice. The absence also of updated information technology systems linking carers' characteristics, levels of skills and preferences with children's needs led to a significant number of placement decisions being made on very limited data. It was encouraging, as found in Chapter 7, that the majority of placed children went to first choice placements, but questions could still be asked about the very high proportion of children referred as emergencies (55%). As a result, some children went to carers without proper assessment or sufficient background information, something carers resented.

Availability and support

Carers came into fostering because they were mostly motivated by the wish to do something for children in need and expected the service to have a similar commitment. In the majority of cases, the service was perceived by them to be responsive and there was a lot of praise, particularly for individual members of staff. When, however, the service was seen to fall short of a similar commitment and standard as their own, carers found this hard to comprehend and it forced them to question their decision to foster. It is in this context that a minority make the decision to leave. As a number of carers put it to us: 'If they [agency/social workers] are not doing things for the children, they are not helping us.'

Preparation before placement, training and foster care manuals usually lead carers to expect support in the form of visits, availability, team work, problem-solving and responsiveness to crises over a 24-hour period. In most carers' views, all these aspects of service delivery constituted support, but it was not always forthcoming. Most complaints were about infrequent visits, cancelled visits, unavailability, unresponsiveness, not being listened to or understood, and lack of support to themselves and the children by children's social workers. The scarcity of specialist services for children, in the form of psychological and psychiatric help, was increasing the pressure on carers to find solutions to some children's complex problems. The limitations in knowledge and expertise of the stand-by service was also pointed out.

Because of the kind of children they are asked to care for, it was also the view of many carers that it was essential that the 24-hour stand-by general service should have at least one person present who is experienced in fostering work. Furthermore, because of dissatisfactions with part-time staff expressed by some carers, management needs to develop the kind of structures that ensure availability and continuity between full and part-time staff.

The authorities, too, were criticised for not listening more, for not being appreciative enough and for not making sufficient resources available for adequate support to be provided to the children and their carers. Even a majority of satisfied carers said that these were all areas about which authorities could do more. Many of them commented on the increased demands on their time arising from having to attend meetings and reviews, visit schools and doctors, keep records, work with parents and promote contact, while confronting constant fears about false allegations of abuse.

It was exceptional for a manager to contradict the carers' views as outlined above. They acknowledged that looked after children did not receive, on the whole, the same attention and priority as "child protection" cases. A recurrent theme was that, when under pressure, children's workers were glad to simply have a "safe" place for the child, like a foster home.

The peripheral role of carers within the agency

The majority of carers are asked to care for and help some very vulnerable and sometimes troublesome children and they require more than recognition for what they are doing. They expect improved conditions of work and good training and team work to be made more of a reality. Yet their present status within authorities was found to be ambiguous and somewhat peripheral. They are neither members of staff nor exactly outsiders and feel that they have a low status within the organisation.

The official message, as it appears in manuals, is one of partnership, but this does not often match up with the reality of policy and practice. Partnership implies a redistribution of power with which authorities have yet to come to terms. Examples of partnership quoted by carers were few and this was confirmed by the authorities. Without diminishing the work of individual authorities and individual managers who have gone to great lengths to promote team work, carers largely perceived themselves as outsiders and of low status. Their current limited role in the planning and running of the fostering service largely reflected the ambivalent attitudes towards them held by authorities, reinforcing perceptions of themselves as being "second class" and of low status. Other experiences discussed earlier and under financial arrangements reinforced these feelings.

Carers appeared to be caught in a kind of double bind, that is, at times being seen as "paid professionals", who should be getting on with the job without needing support, and at other times being viewed as "amateurs" or "volunteers", who could not be trusted with information or with whom team work was not realistic. Overall, and not infrequently, a significant number of them came to feel isolated and alone.

Not surprisingly, perhaps, the carers' rapport with authorities as corporate bodies was found to be low. Their first identification was with the children, then their link workers, followed by the social worker and lastly the agency. They identified positively with individual members of staff rather than staff as representatives of the organisation. Increasing satisfaction and promoting greater identification between authorities and carers should also have a positive impact on recruitment and retention.

The carers and the children's parents

Some carers' commitment to the view that it is in most children's interests to have contact with their families was found to be rather weak. This could also explain the low proportion of contact visits that took place in the foster home. Carers and parents were sometimes physically set apart by the way contact is managed. This is not consistent with the thrust of the current legislation to promote continued parental responsibility and contact (unless contrary to the child's best interests). Neither is this consistent with research findings which demonstrate that continuing contact with parents, 'managed carefully by social workers where necessary', benefits the children and speeds up reunification (for a summary of the research evidence see Triseliotis, 1989; Berridge, 1997).

Most foster carers saw themselves as being "child-centred", i.e. that interest in children and/or a desire to help children were the key motivating factors that brought them into fostering. This means focusing on the individual child's well-being, often trying to restore their confidence and to help them overcome painful and damaging experiences. Birth parents were sometimes blamed for their children's hardship, which may make it difficult to include them in the restorative process. In our view, more consistent training and the carers' fuller participation in team work and ownership of the plan could promote greater commitment also to contact and restoration plans. The promotion of contact is as much a matter of planning as of attitudes. It has to feature more prominently in the care plans and agreements and be regularly monitored and reviewed.

Some manuals and managers made reference to carers working with the children's families, but with few exceptions the "how" of doing this had not been specified in writing. In interviews, some carers were uncertain of what this exactly meant and how it could be put into practice. An interesting example initiated by one agency in this direction, and referred to in Chapter 10, is worth exploring by other authorities. If wider expectations were to be placed on carers "to work with parents", then this needs to be supported by continued training, specified in-care plans and in-placement agreements, and reflected in levels of remuneration. It has also to be recognised, as a number of carers told us, that caring for the children left them with little time or energy to work with parents.

Assuring and controlling quality
In their pursuit of good quality practice, many authorities were trying to strike a balance between quality assurance measures to "guarantee" overall performance and avoid "disasters" through quality control. Ensuring that requirements and intentions are systematically observed, such as through panels, reviews and inspections, is a skilled and labour intensive process. It requires proper resourcing, good organisation and efficient management. Unsurprisingly, perhaps, the systematic observation of existing arrangements, while mostly intended, was still some way from being achieved at the time of the study. This task was further hampered by the absence of suitable management information and monitoring systems.

So far the participation of key stakeholders such as children, young people, their families and carers in the planning, review and evaluation of the fostering service has been patchy.

Financial arrangements

A number of major financial matters emerged that local authorities, individually or collectively, have to consider as a matter of urgency because they generate much dissatisfaction and have an adverse impact on both recruitment and retention of carers as well as morale. Much greater confidence has to be restored amongst carers concerning the efficient management of their pay, whether in the form of allowances, fees or individual grants. The lack of attention apparently paid to their grievances by most of the former authorities, along with the perception of their being peripheral to the service, as described earlier, again conveyed to some carers feelings of being "second class" and perhaps not worthy of attention.

Many carers were also puzzled and perplexed by the multiplicity of payment systems operating within and between authorities and so were a number of managers. Some carers were themselves uncertain of which type of payment scheme they were on. It was for this reason that many of them and a number of managers were in favour of a national scheme that offered realistic pensionable payments, which was also seen to be consistent and fair.

Achieving a better payment system was hampered by serious budgetary constraints facing many authorities and negative attitudes held by some towards rewarding carers for their services, along with a failure to appreciate the position of the fostering service in present-day society. This harbours dangers for the service. In spite of the fact that carers demonstrated high levels of commitment to their local authorities and to the care of local children, their loyalty could not be taken for granted. At the time of the study, the non-statutory sector was paying carers around three times more than the weekly fee paid by local authorities and making available more benefits and improved support packages.

Key policy recommendations

Specific policy issues requiring attention include the need to:

- raise the image and profile of the fostering service within councils. A number of authorities have already made strenuous efforts to involve their councillors and top managers, including other services in the provision of child care and fostering services. This needs to become a standard practice;

- develop up-to-date long-term fostering policies and planning strategies based on efficient management information systems;
- make available sufficient resources to enable staff to engage in long-term recruitment, undertake more direct work with children, and provide more support services to foster carers;
- adopt a more marketing-oriented approach to recruitment, including the adoption of longer-term strategies that recognise changing social, demographic and employment factors;
- integrate the organisation, management and delivery of all placement services without jeopardising the distinctiveness of each, in order to create a highly specialised, knowledgeable and responsive service for all looked after children;
- promote much greater team work and partnership between authorities and carers;
- establish more adequate systems for obtaining feedback from all stakeholders in the service;
- set in place consistent policies on the fostering of children by relatives;
- develop adequate systems of management information to aid fostering policy-making, long-term fostering strategies, planning, recruitment and the matching of children to carers;
- respond to the financial aspirations of carers and set in place mechanisms for the efficient payment of allowances and grants to them. As a temporary step, the attachment of pension rights to fees and enhanced allowances could go some way in meeting the carers' aspirations.

Considering the small size of many authorities and limitations of their resources, it will be to their advantage to encourage much more sharing in such areas as recruitment, training, expertise, stand-by support, placement sharing, and the monitoring and evaluation of the service.

Some specific recommendations for managers

Senior management have the opportunity to address a number of issues arising from the study, including:

- aiming for a single management structure for all services for looked after children, including the integration of all these services, while generally safeguarding their distinctiveness;
- clear statements about the respective roles of social worker and placement worker, especially in relation to decision-making, direct work with children, support to carers and the supervision of carers;
- guidelines on the content of children's assessment and on the matching process. (Not surprisingly, perhaps, many staff are frustrated about the many different types of reports they have to produce on the same child. A more uniform approach is required, perhaps such as the ones suggested in the Looking After Children Schedules.);
- improved co-ordination and communication between the various parts of the fostering service and especially between child care area teams and the placement service;
- the significant upgrading of the quality of the service currently provided to children in foster care and to foster carers by children's social workers to equal that offered by the placement part of the service;
- a 24-hour support service with staff who include one or more people who are knowledgeable about family placement issues;
- aiming for greater continuity in children's social workers and using part-time staff in ways that ensure availability and continuity;
- guidance to managers lower down the line on setting priorities, monitoring and managing in ways that ensure and control the quality of the service provided;
- the creation of lines of communication between carers' representatives and top management;
- ensuring that all those working in foster care have the necessary training to undertake such work. It is unacceptable that many carers appear to have more understanding of fostering and of children's needs than many children's social workers;

- increased forms of joint training involving staff from area teams, residential staff and carers;
- aiming for more coherent forms of training and continued training for all carers, while also distinguishing more clearly between preparation, assessment, training, support groups and continued training.

The plethora of fostering terms currently used to describe what are essentially similar arrangements or types of need are confusing and can mask the extent of need. Agreement is required for a more consistent classification of carers and of fostering terms to facilitate the development of a common fostering language. Such a step should aid recruitment campaigns, provide clarity when assessing and matching children, avoid possible misunderstandings when arranging cross agency placements and agreements, and present policy-makers and the public with a clearer view of what fostering is about.

Some key practice and training considerations

The majority of social workers working with children in foster care were providing an adequate and sometimes more than adequate service, but gaps remained. As a result, a significant number of carers had no confidence in the knowledge and expertise of their social workers to engage in problem-solving, when necessary. Some key requirements include:

- acquiring far more knowledge and expertise, than at present, on child development, placement issues and fostering, and direct work with children;
- getting to know better the children in foster care;
- demonstrating greater responsiveness, appreciation of carers and greater reliability;
- improving the quality of the assessment reports which are provided to placement staff for matching purposes;
- working in partnership with carers, providing them with information on the children and sharing with them in problem-solving where necessary;

- paying more attention to the foster carers' own children;
- helping carers and their children manage feelings over the ending of placements.

Some considerations for national governments

The study points to a number of initiatives at national level, including:

- outlining its own long-term strategy and resourcing of the fostering service;
- encouraging and organising recruitment publicity through the national media;
- providing advice on marketing skills to authorities that could help the recruitment of carers;
- encouraging greater co-operation and sharing between authorities;
- giving consideration to a national system for paying carers;
- the adoption of national foster care standards.

Overview

In final conclusion, the overall findings from the study suggest a service with many strengths. Much of the fostering work was permeated by a strong sense of commitment, along with a readiness to take risks and face challenges. Nevertheless, a number of key areas require much greater attention including:

- developing long-term strategies on fostering;
- adopting a marketing approach to recruitment;
- moving towards the integration of services for all looked after children, and separating them from child protection work and emergencies;
- improving methods of assessing and matching children to carers;
- significantly improving the support services available to children and carers, especially those provided by social workers;
- giving fuller expression to the concept of partnership with stakeholders;
- responding to the aspirations of carers for team work, continued training and improved conditions of service.

The above recommendations have to be seen as a total package, rather than one to select from. Failing that, the local authority fostering service is likely to become more fragmented. Furthermore, an increasing proportion of the more difficult children and those with disabilities are likely to go to the non-statutory sector at much higher costs to local authorities. Worse, it could eventually lead to the disappearance of a local authority fostering service.

References

Berridge D. (1997) *Foster Care: A research review*, London: The Stationery Office

NFCA (1999) *UK National Standards for Foster Care*, London: National Foster Care Association

Triseliotis J. (1989) 'Foster care outcomes: a review of key research findings', *Adoption & Fostering* 13:3, pp. 5–17

Triseliotis J., Sellick C. and Short R. (1995a) *Foster Care: Theory and practice*, London: Batsford

Triseliotis J., Borland M., Hill M. and Lambert L. (1995b) *Teenagers and the Social Work Services*, London: HMSO

Waterhouse S. (1997) *The Organisation of Fostering Services*, London: National Foster Care Association

10 Intercountry adoption: Global trade or global gift?

While John emphasised the importance of empirical evidence as a basis for policy and practice, he was equally passionate about the need to act ethically and against injustice. This is exemplified in the following critical analysis of intercountry adoption, which almost invariably has involved children born in impoverished circumstances in Asia, Latin America, Africa or Eastern Europe being adopted into "western" countries. John argued that international adoptions were only justifiable when tight regulations preclude abductions, trafficking and bribes. His attack on the market basis of much intercountry adoption concluded with a plea for genuine and reciprocal altruism as an alternative underpinning principle. This chapter is reproduced from Adoption & Fostering *(24:2, pp. 45–54, 2000).*

Introduction

This paper sets out to question the legitimacy of intercountry adoption because of the way a significant part of it is currently practised. My views on the subject are less about intercountry adoption as such, or about individuals who adopt from abroad, and more about political and social attitudes in both the sending and receiving countries which tolerate trading in children. In the course of the discussion three key issues will be raised:

- how the lack of legitimacy manifests itself;
- how intercountry adoption came to be in this position;
- suggested measures for achieving greater legitimacy.

How the absence of legitimacy manifests itself

Irrespective of what we believe as individuals, the practice of inter-country adoption cannot be considered in a legal or moral vacuum. The absence of legitimacy is manifested in five different ways:

1. a disregard for children's rights as set out in the UN Convention on the Rights of the Child (UNCRC);
2. the absence of legality;
3. lack of choice for birth parents;
4. disregard of empirically-based knowledge of what is known to be best for children;
5. the absence of an ethical base.

A disregard for children's rights as set out in the UN Convention

The UNCRC is meant to grant dignity and respect to children as human beings. These rights are also meant to be international and have been accepted globally. When it comes to adoption, Article 21 of the Convention is unambiguous:

> *The primary aim of adoption is to provide the child who cannot be cared for by his or her own parents, with a permanent family. If that child cannot be placed in a foster or adoptive family and cannot in any suitable manner be cared for in the country of origin, intercountry adoption may be considered as an alternative means of child care.*

State parties are expected to enact laws to reflect these rights, but international instruments such as these lack ways of enforcement. Furthermore, when laws are enacted it does not follow that they will always be enforced or respected. There is no shortage of examples of children's rights being frequently violated and intercountry adoption has contributed to this violation (see Asquith and Hill, 1994). Adoption is meant to be a service for children first, but part of it is practised on the premise that every adult, especially those who are wealthy, has the right to get a child from anywhere and almost by any means in order to be a parent. Just when it was thought that after three or so thousand years adoption was at last becoming a more child-centred activity, much of intercountry adoption has been shifting the emphasis back to the interests of the adults. In some respects intercountry adoption, and the trafficking in children that is a characteristic part of it, has set back the clock for the rights of children and has been a bad precedent for countries still struggling to develop child-centred legislation.

Studies in the USA have found that, on the whole, those who adopt from abroad consider themselves as having a right to do so and are annoyed at the need for investigations and the preparation of background reports. In their view, it is enough that their prosperity and social position guarantee the child a better life (Bartholet, 1993; Gailey, 1999). The USA is not alone in this. Broadly similar sentiments have been expressed in Britain (see an extensive article by Matthew Engel, *Weekend Guardian*, 29 May 1999, pp. 10–17).

Because children around the world are suffering, it suits the needs of some people in the industrialised countries to "rescue" a tiny number of them. We should have no illusions, though, that the proportion of children around the world exposed to deprivations, poverty and suffering is so huge that intercountry adoption is not even a drop in an ocean of need. I recognise that this does not make those adopted any less needy or vulnerable. However, the proposition that intercountry adoption offers children from the Third World a better future may be true at the individual, but not at the wider level.

The absence of legality

A number of sending and receiving countries have entered bilateral and other similar agreements, by which adoptions in one country are recognised in the other. Such agreements are usually reached after each country is satisfied that the practices of the other are acceptable, but until recently, there has been no yardstick of what is acceptable. Otherwise, much of intercountry adoption has relied on piecemeal legislation that has failed to safeguard the children's rights in such areas as the suitability of the adopters, matching or trafficking.

What gradually helped to enhance the legitimacy of domestic adoption in most industrialised countries was mainly legality, which was increasingly based on what was empirically known to be best for children. Alongside this were the widespread welfare programmes that brought significant improvements in the social and welfare conditions of all citizens, including children, resulting also in the overall extension of choice for parents.

Even after these improvements, domestic adoption in industrialised countries still raises serious questions about the respective powers and roles of parents and the state, the relative rights of children and parents, and the procedures and criteria which should govern those situations when plans for children are disputed, such as freeing for adoption (see Lambert *et al*, 1990). Intercountry adoption gives rise to all the same questions plus the trafficking that goes on.

Efforts to put some order to what are widely agreed to be unacceptable practices are not infrequently thwarted by powerful interests. Politicians in some countries, with the aid of some of the media, have come to recognise that there are votes to be gained when they urge no or minimum regulation in adoption in general. The same media are incensed at the idea of trade in children, but equally so, if obstacles are seen to be put in the way of adults when pursuing either domestic or intercountry adoption (again, see *Weekend Guardian*, 29 May 1999, pp. 10–17).

It is only recently that the international community, through the Hague Convention, has tried to develop standards and regulations, in line with the 1989 UNCRC. Maybe it is too early to expect results, but the agreement reached between countries in the early 1990s does not appear to have diminished the major abuses. Even in Britain, with its strong immigration controls, a judge was recently forced to confirm an intercountry adoption despite its illegality, because it was a *fait accompli* [(in *re* C (*a minor*) (*adoption: legality*), reported in *The Times*, 2 June 1998, p. 24]. (I will be returning later to the work of the Hague Convention.)

Lack of choice for birth parents

Domestic adoption in the industrialised world is now practised on the premise of choice for birth parents and freedom from compulsion, unless the courts have declared a child free for adoption against the wishes of parents. If economic and other external forms of compulsion are not allowed to undermine the basic rights of parents and children in the industrialised world, the same expectations should also be applied to the countries from which the children are brought to the West.

When it comes to the rearing of children, many parents in some Third World and Eastern European countries, faced with abject poverty and/or ill-health and with no basic state welfare provision as a fallback, find themselves with very limited or no choices. In relation to adoption they often act under compulsion and are sometimes exploited by corrupt agents, professionals and administrators. Unsurprisingly, perhaps, the parents' actions can lead to a conflict of interest developing between themselves and their children, with the children requiring protection.

Disregard of empirically-based knowledge of what is known to be best for children

A number of agencies and individuals in both sending and receiving countries have tried and managed to achieve high standards in the practice of intercountry adoption. No doubt many of them have the best interests of the children in mind and have made their own contribution to the development of new knowledge and skills in this area. Nevertheless, and because of the clandestine way in which a significant part of intercountry adoption is now being practised, empirically-based knowledge of what has been found to be good for children, their birth and adoptive parents is often disregarded or not systematically applied in such areas as:

- the preparation of would-be adopters for the additional tasks required of them for parenting children often of a different ethnic, racial, cultural and religious background;
- the matching of adopters to children;
- the collection of genealogical and other background information;
- the deployment of post-adoption counselling and other services (see Triseliotis *et al*, 1997).

The failure to deploy systematically available knowledge and skills in all the above areas can undermine the children's potential for development, including their genealogical and ethnic identity. With the exception of only a few countries, a large part of intercountry adoption is in the hands of private or third parties and organisations not always involving the participation of trained child welfare staff. Even where accredited agencies take part in the arrangements, not infrequently these operate outside the mainstream child welfare services, including what remains of domestic adoption. Under this system children adopted from abroad do not always benefit from the knowledge and skills developed over the years.

It could also be claimed that because of the separation, in many countries on the continent of Europe, of intercountry adoption from domestic adoption and from the wider child care field, it has led to the neglect of domestic children with special needs requiring new families (see Anderson, 1999, in respect of Sweden).

I am not suggesting by this that domestic and intercountry adoption are or should be in competition. Far from it. Different couples or individuals are usually interested in different children and the needs of children can be met by differently composed households. Legitimate ways of practising adoption, whether domestic or intercountry, are likely to benefit both groups of children.

The absence of an ethical base

The issues raised so far add to the overall absence of an ethical base in the practice of a significant part of intercountry adoption. Trading in children, kidnapping, fattening of children to be more saleable to fetch higher prices, lying to birth parents about the fate of their children or the production of spurious background reports on adopters, all add up to a catalogue of ignoble and unprincipled practices (see later for references). Furthermore, and possibly because intercountry adoption has become so widespread and is largely isolated from other child welfare services, its practices seem no longer to be questioned. We know that, on the whole, intercountry adoption works well, but the ends do not necessarily justify the means.

How did intercountry adoption come to this?

Intercountry adoption in the post-World War II period has experienced a number of phases in its development. Depending on the country, some or all of the following phases may be happening simultaneously:

1. compassion and humanitarianism;
2. the wish to create or expand one's family;
3. trading in children;
4. beginning international regulation.

Compassion and humanitarianism

The compassionate/humanitarian, altruistic response, or "the kindness of strangers", has always been present in the practice of all forms of adoption and substitute parenting (see Boswell, 1988). Within the ancient world, the stories of Moses and Oedipus fulfil the requirements of both intercountry and interstate adoption as a compassionate response to the fate of unwanted and exposed children. More recently, the humanitarian response has been continued in the aftermath of wars and natural disasters. Examples of this are to be found in some of the initial responses of American servicemen adopting children from Germany at the end of the last World War, the adoption of children orphaned during the Greek Civil War of the late 1940s and early 1950s, and the adoption of children "orphaned" or "deserted" as a consequence of the Korean and later Vietnam wars.

Most of the children who were adopted then also had the characteristics of children with special needs, that is being older and sometimes displaying many physical, cognitive and emotional deficits.

The wish to create or expand one's family

After about the middle of the 1970s and because of the dramatic decline in the number of domestic infants made available for adoption in most industrialised countries, those wishing to create a family or expand it now turned their attention to intercountry adoption. As a result, acts of humanitarianism went side by side with this new type of adoption until the latter came to predominate. Studies after the 1980s show a decisive shift in both the type of person adopting and the type of child being adopted intercountry. For example, the children were becoming much younger, mostly under two years old, and the adopters largely middle class, wishing to create or enlarge their family (Triseliotis *et al*, 1997, Chapter 9).

Trading in children

The third phase, which is currently a characteristic of a significant part of intercountry adoption and overlaps with 1 and 2 above, is that of global trade. No doubt children were sold before, but this practice took off in a big way after the early 1980s. Nobody knows exactly how many of the 35,000 or so children coming each year to industrialised countries to be adopted are bought. Article 35 of the UNCRC expects state parties to take 'all appropriate national bilateral and multi-lateral measures to prevent the abduction of, the sale of, or traffic in children for any purpose or in any form'.

There is no shortage of evidence on the trade in children (see Ngabonziza, 1991; Triseliotis, 1993). The UK Bill on intercountry adoption, which has now become the Adoption (Intercountry Aspects) Act 1999, recognised what has been said above by stating that one of its purposes was 'to regulate adoption to prevent trafficking in children' (p. 1).

The trafficking in children has also often been highlighted by the British press, as in this example:

> South of the border (USA), down Mexico way, duty-free shoppers are picking up bargains they can't find elsewhere in the world – babies. The land of tequila and sombreros is now the centre of a cruel and inhumane trade in children. Sometimes kidnapped, other times bartered or traded like wheat, the babies come from all over southern America into processing houses where they are fattened like cattle to appeal to the rich gringo women who desire them. (*The Scotsman*, 25 August 1998, p. 11)

There are many other stories of sales, kidnapping, stealing, exploiting, cruelty and the fattening and selling of children before they are adopted in the industrialised world. Nor can it be claimed that this is a problem exclusive to Third World countries, because there are also documented stories describing the sale of children within a number of Western countries, e.g. the USA and Italy. *The Times* newspaper revealed that in Ukraine corrupt doctors and officials were involved in the illegal sale of babies to Western Europe and North America by deceiving the children's 'impoverished mothers' that their new-born babies had died or would have a better life being brought up by the state. Apparently some children were sold for as much as 40,000 US dollars (*The Times*, 9 February 1996, p. 4).

Children from Russia now top the US intercountry adoption statistics. Though there has been some disillusionment recently with children from Eastern Europe because of the intractable emotional problems some are said to present, nevertheless they continue to attract higher prices because of their white colour (Gailey, 1999). Again *The Times* newspaper recently wrote that the sale of children from Russia, mainly for the US market, was 'by no means rare' (28 May 1999, p. 23). The legislation on intercountry adoption in Russia states that international adoption is only possible in 'exceptional, urgent situations in the interests of the child's health', but is so vague that it has left the way open to 'profiteering by unregulated agencies' (Bowring, 1999, p. 132).

The question could be asked whether the industrialised countries have created the climate which made possible this trade in children. Apart from the demand for babies to adopt, by the early 1980s new ideas and values associated with the operation of a free, and largely unrestrained market, became the cornerstone of most industrial governments' economic policy. The idea of trade and profit was suddenly becoming the hallmark of good policy and practice in other areas besides trade (see Elliot and Atkinson, 1998). The market, it was claimed, recognised no moral imperatives even in such matters as education, health, children or human relationships.

Davis (1995) referring to the United States describes vividly how adoption there had been developing fast into a service business, limited to childless couples 'willing to pay hefty fees'. According to the same source, not only had fees been rising but a number of 'for-profit agencies' had emerged as it had become apparent that many people were prepared to pay a high price to adopt either an incountry or intercountry child. The idea of setting up independent for-profit adoption agencies was also canvassed in Britain in the early 1990s but found no support.

Parents too, whether in the Third World or elsewhere where adoption is not properly regulated, have learned to shop around for the best deal. Market forces have been turning middle agents, birth parents and adopters into the main stakeholders. In this process, the children's interests may or may not be protected. Speaking of Germany, Textor (1991) wrote that:

> ... large amounts of money are sometimes paid to children's homes, birth parents or middlemen in exchange for the children. In some cases children are even stolen or registered immediately after birth as the biological children of a German couple. (p. 112)

In the sphere of human relationships intercountry adoption has revealed and exposed the weaknesses of corporate industrialised governments and of the helplessness, and sometimes corruption, of some Third World countries unable to develop non-profit democratic regulation as a way of stopping the trade in children. It may sound an exaggeration to say that intercountry adoption reflects, in a small way, the globalisation of the market and its excesses. In systems terms, thinking that dominates a supra system, such as global economics, eventually influences smaller systems and institutions as well, including that of adoption. Aspects of intercountry adoption have become a microcosm of what goes on in other walks of life when the supremacy of the market remains unchallenged. It includes the loose controls, the predominance of the profit motive, the absence of choice for the weakest and its endemic inequalities. In the way intercountry adoption is practised now, it is mostly open to those who are better off, though I have been told that in Norway a state subsidy can be made available to the less prosperous.

Beginning international regulation

The final phase in the post-World War II period for intercountry adoption comes in the form of beginning regulation from the early 1990s onwards, reflected mainly in the work of the Hague Convention on Intercountry Adoption (ICA). The work of the Convention will be discussed later but suffice it to say here that as we enter the new millenium, we find examples of adoptions being arranged and concluded based on international, mainly bilateral agreements, adoptions arranged by accredited or private agencies, and of a significant number based on trade.

Achieving legitimacy in intercountry adoption

In my view, intercountry adoption could achieve greater legitimacy by promoting:

- a rights approach to children;
- full international regulation;
- practising adoption as a gift.

A rights approach to children

The UNCRC offers a useful framework within which intercountry adoption could be regulated and practised. It is no more than a framework aiming to guarantee only basic rights to children, but it is good enough. The Hague Convention tried to base its own articles on intercountry adoption on the UNCRC, but in the process of doing so, many compromises had to be made. It reiterated, though, a child's right to be reared first by his or her own parents and in his or her own country, and for other solutions to be sought only when that is not possible. However, it is up to countries who ratify the Convention to give expression to these articles through their domestic child care legislation, and more important to observe it.

Full international regulation

Experience so far has shown that full international regulation is the only way to bring greater legitimacy to the practice of international adoption. Leaving it to individual countries, whether sending or receiving, to put their house in order will not happen. The Hague Convention on ICA which was set up in 1990 achieved a fair amount, mainly by initially bringing together over 60 countries who eventually signed their agreement to the Convention's articles (29 May, 1993). By the autumn of 1999, 27 countries had ratified and nine had acceded to the Convention. (Accession is essentially ratification by non-member states.) Of all Hague Conventions, the 1993 one on ICA has attained more signatories to ratification than any other Convention. Now that the new Adoption Bill has become law, the British government will also ratify it.

It is recognised that there are many difficulties in trying to apply universal principles to diverse realities, so as to bridge the laws of countries with competing images of childhood, varied systems and diversity in cultural traditions and values, rights and obligations. However, the evidence so far suggests that the main obstacle has not been this, but scepticism about children's rights and the adult-centred approach adopted by some participating countries at the Hague Convention. Because of these attitudes, the presently agreed articles of the Convention are and can be easily bypassed. As an example, the following two measures could, if agreed and applied, reduce significantly trafficking.

The first suggestion is the prohibition of all privately or independently arranged non-related adoptions, except those undertaken by recognised, approved and inspected agencies. The International Social Service (1996) has identified seven types of privately arranged adoptions, most of them unwelcome. Carstens and Julia (1995) also write that:

> Trafficking and the sale of infants is more likely to occur when independent adoption agents are involved because there is opportunity for improper financial gain at each stage of the adoption process.

The attempt, though, by the Hague Convention to ban all privately arranged adoptions was bitterly resisted by many countries, especially the USA where few of the 50 states regulate the profit status of individuals or organisations involved in adoptions.

Concerns have been expressed about a number of European countries, too, for allowing international adoptions to be arranged by non-accredited or approved agencies. Writing about France, Green-field (1995) comments that most families there adopting from abroad seem to take the independent rather than the agency route. The newspaper *Le Monde* reported that 3,666 children were adopted in France from abroad in 1996, adding that there was 'little regulation of these adoptions with intermediaries making increasing amounts of money and few checks made on the children's background' (16 February 1998, p. 7).

The second measure is to stop the many privately commissioned reports on adopters that are taken to the sending countries as proof of suitability. After obtaining the report, adoptive parents send their application or travel abroad without the involvement of an accredited agency. Even when a report is prepared by an accredited agency, it does not guarantee that no purchase will take place (Selman, 1993). It is claimed that in the USA, assuming you have the money, you can bypass even the minimum requirements for a suitability study. Apparently, when would-be adopters offer to double the fees, some agencies are happy to prepare the report over the telephone without face-to-face interviews or a home visit (Gailey, 1999). An article in *The Guardian* quotes a family from Montana whose assessment was based solely on a social worker coming round one morning 'for coffee and carrot cake'. Unsurprisingly, perhaps, the author of the article is critical about the detailed social and medical reports required in Britain (Matthew Engel, *The Guardian*, 16 February 1998, p. 7).

The questions of who finds the child, who does the matching and who makes the final arrangements are currently a murky area. It is not so much the individuals involved who are at fault, but the absence of suitable structures to provide confidence that the best interests of those involved, including the children, will be safeguarded. Though Britain banned third party domestic adoptions over 20 years ago, it is only recently that it has proceeded to extend the law to intercountry adoption. The 1999 Act also put beyond all legal doubt that the preparation of privately commissioned reports for purposes of adoption is a criminal offence. Norway no longer permits private adoptions. New laws have also been put in place in sending countries such as Romania, India and Sri Lanka to curb the worst excesses of intercountry adoption. The right climate seems to be developing to lend much greater support to the work of the Hague Convention, mainly to tighten controls and put teeth into its articles. To call for stricter international regulation may sound totalitarian. Donzelot (1980), writing on the policing of families, outlined what he called the positive aspects of 'social control' which need not be oppressive. Even the privatisation of social welfare, far from being a free for all, is going side by side with increased powers of inspection.

As late as the summer of 1998, that is before the collapse of the markets in Asia and later in Russia, for a government to try to regulate the implementation of global trade decisions was seen as being out of touch with the real world or just "plain daft". Within 18 months or so, things have been changing. Nobody now, apparently, believes any longer that markets work best if businesses are simply left to their own devices (Kaletsky, *The Times*, 22 April 1999, p. 24). Soros (1998), who made his millions through the operation of a free market, has also been calling for 'tough global controls'. President Clinton, too, speaking on television on 20 April 1999, said that international financial markets need to be regulated by international agencies. If the financial markets need regulation, why not also intercountry adoption?

Proper regulation is not only in the best interests of children and adopters, but also in the interest of those countries which currently play or are trying to play by the rules. Once the public knows that there is a legitimate and more dignified way of adopting, they are more likely to accept restrictions. For intercountry adoption to shed its badly tarnished image of a global market in babies, and to gain legitimacy, it urgently needs to demonstrate that in any arrangement:

- the child is in genuine need of a new family;
- adoption by a family abroad is in the children's best interests;

- the process follows closely standards of good practice set by accredited agencies;
- the laws of the sending and receiving countries strictly adhere to the Hague Convention on ICA;
- adoption is freely entered upon by all parties;
- the process involves no profit, including disguised inflated fees and expenses;
- the arrangements are covered by a comprehensive range of after-care services in the receiving country.

Prospective adopters, too, require protection from the possible excesses of those undertaking suitability studies and need to be given access to independent tribunals to safeguard their rights.

Adoption as a gift and an act of altruism

Finally, and what may sound utopian, is the proposition that both domestic and intercountry adoption should eventually be practised within the context of the gift relationship and with openness and contact being part of this arrangement. In the words of Titmuss (1970), a gift relationship implies freedom of choice and an act of altruism without obvious immediate returns. Besides blood donation in the UK, possibly the nearest other example of total altruism and freedom of choice is the donation of organs, such as kidneys.

Apparently the Romans, who were great on families and looked upon childlessness as a great calamity, would 'lend one another their daughter, sister and even sometimes their wives' as a way of ensuring that children were produced. It is claimed, in fact, that by about 200 AD the practice of adoption had been abandoned in favour of this form of "surrogacy" (Dupont, 1989). We cannot, however, declare this to be the ultimate gift because historians have not told us what the women felt or thought about it.

The scientists who originally invented the internet did not intend it to be used as a trade tool but to exchange information. Though this "icon of modern technology" was originally invented for military purposes, it was later mainly used by academics and even amateurs as a cheap and sometimes free method of distributing information, exchanging ideas and discoveries and communicating with colleagues. It was proving to be a "gift" to humanity that was helping to strengthen international social relationships (Levi, 1997). However, "lurking" behind this new technology is the free market which has taken it over. It has even been used to advertise children for sale (Gailey, 1999).

I will leave it to social anthropologists to debate the various shades of the notion of gift and especially the difference between the gift as part of a "circular" form of exchange and a gift given solely for its intrinsic value or for the relationships it creates. A gift, whether as part of an exchange system or as an act of total altruism, has its place in the way adoption could develop, thus greatly enhancing its legitimacy. A gift relationship, in many cultures, implies an obligation to give and to exchange and circulate the gift idea, but not necessarily to the same person. Furthermore, the compulsion to return the gift is only a moral one.

As an idea, giving on a non-commercial basis to the stranger or the unknown may sound like a panacea in an imperfect world. However, in any such arrangement we would still need to make certain that the interests of the children come first. In the same way that it is not right to sell children, neither is it right for them to be used as a means to promote global humanism. Obviously we would still need to know how the parents of the children and the adopters conceptualise inter-country adoption; in other words, whether donors and receivers use a "moral vocabulary" to explain their actions, visualising it as the fore-runner of an emerging global gift relationship, a commitment to global evolutionary humanism, or a more pragmatic one, such as economic considerations or simply the wish to parent a child.

The question could equally be asked of why we should expect the poorer people in the poorer countries to be motivated by lofty ideals or have regard for the needs of affluent total strangers, often of a different race, culture, religion and ethnicity? No doubt there are many other practical and moral questions to be considered. For example, does "donation" reduce the element of compulsion? Like the gift relationship, should some form of repayment or exchange be expected and in what form? Should any returns have to be on an individual basis or to the group or country as a whole? Ideally, reciprocity should not be directed to the individual who offers the gift but to that country's children as a whole. Funds could be earmarked for use solely for identifiable children's programmes in the sending countries via regulated, accredited and monitored non-governmental international agencies. Such bodies might also come to exercise positive influence on governmental child welfare policies through their:

- control of resources which they can dispense accordingly;
- direct contact with policy-making politicians;
- rigorous monitoring and evaluation of the projects;
- publication of annual reports.

There is, of course, no reason why individual families should not exchange gifts and continue to do so, provided that the initial match-ing and other arrangements have been done independently and without the possibility of trade and pay entering into the arrangements.

Conclusion

This article has questioned the legitimacy of some of the worst practices surrounding intercountry adoption and particularly the evils of its commercialisation. The initial humanitarian response to inter-national calamities and the evils of war has gradually been supplanted in ways not altogether welcome. In some respects, the way intercountry adoption is often being practised now has set back the clock for children's rights and the idea of adoption being a child-centred activity.

Globalisation may have weakened the arguments against inter-country adoption, but it has strengthened the anti-trafficking agree-ments and the need for strong regulation. While accepting that most forms of regulation, especially international ones, are of an evolutionary character, nevertheless the Hague Convention on ICA seems to have had little impact, so far, in stemming the trafficking in children. This is because its articles are insufficient or weak or both. The Convention requires much more support to enable it to exercise pressure on recalcitrant governments to put their house in order.

Finally, the idea was put forward in this paper for all forms of adoption to be based on the gift relationship and to be practised more openly than now. This is not a novel idea, but neither has it been systematically promoted. A fitting conclusion, perhaps, to adoption being practised within such a relationship is Hyde's (1999) wider comment:

> ... a bond precedes or is created by donation and it is absent, suspended or severed in commodity exchange ... We do not deal in commodities when we wish to initiate or preserve ties of affection ... Because of the bonding power of gifts and the detached nature of commodity exchange, gifts have become associated with community and with being obliged to others, while commodities are associated with alienation and freedom. (pp. 62 & 66–67)

Note

A previous version of this article was published in the proceedings of the conference titled *Mine-Yours – Ours and Theirs: Adoption, changing kinship and family pattern*, edited by Rygvold A., Dalen M. and Saetersdal B. (Department of Special Needs Education, University of Oslo, 1999).

References

Adoption (Intercountry Aspects) Act (1999) London: House of Commons

Anderson G. (1999) 'Children in permanent foster care in Sweden', *Child & Family Social Work* 4:3, pp. 175–86

Asquith S. and Hill M. (eds) (1994) *Justice for Children*, Dordrecht: Martinus Nijhof

Bartholet E. (1993) 'Adoption among nations', in *Family Bonds: Adoption and the politics of parenting*, Boston: Houghton Mifflin

Boswell J. (1988) *The Kindness of Strangers*, London: Penguin

Bowring B. (1999) 'Children of Russia: victims of crisis, beneficiaries or international law', *Child & Family Law Quarterly* 11:2, pp. 125–35

Carstens C. and Julia M. (1995) 'Legal, policy and practice issues in intercountry adoption in the United States', *Adoption & Fostering* 19:4, pp. 26–33

Davis D.F. (1995) 'Capitalising on adoption', *Adoption & Fostering* 19:2, pp. 25–30

Donzelot J. (1980) *Policing the Family*, London: Hutchinson

Dupont F. (1989) *Daily Life in Ancient Rome*, Oxford: Blackwell

Elliot R. and Atkinson D. (1998) *The Age of Insecurity*, London: Verso

Gailey C. Paper presented at the *International Conference on Intercountry Adoption*, Oslo, 6–9 May 1999

Greenfield J. (1995) 'Intercountry adoption: a comparison between France and England', *Adoption & Fostering* 19:2, pp. 31–36

Hyde L. (1999) *The Gift*, London: Vintage

International Social Service (1996) *Intercountry Adoption: Developing good practice*, Geneva: ISS

Lambert L., Buist M., Triseliotis J. and Hill M. (1990) *Freeing Children for Adoption*, London: BAAF

Levi P. (1997) *Collective Intelligence*, New York: Plenum

Ngabonziza D. (1991) 'Moral and political issues facing relinquishing countries', *Adoption & Fostering* 15:4, pp. 75–80

Selman P. (1993) 'Services for intercountry adoption in the UK: some lessons from Europe', *Adoption & Fostering* 17:3, pp. 14–19

Soros G. (1998) *Capitalism in Crisis*, London: Little Brown

Textor R.M. (1991) 'International adoption in West Germany', in Altstein H. and Simon R. (eds), *Intercountry Adoption*, London: Praeger

Titmuss R. (1970) *The Gift Relationship*, London: Penguin

Triseliotis J. (1993) 'Intercountry adoption: in whose best interests?', in Humphrey M. and Humphrey H. (eds), *Intercountry Adoption*, London: Tavistock/Routledge

Triseliotis J., Shireman J. and Hundleby M. (1997) *Adoption: Theory, policy and practice*, London: Cassell

11 Long-term foster care or adoption? The evidence examined

A recurrent theme of John's work concerned the respective merits of adoption and fostering, as seen in Chapter 2. This overview of research findings about outcomes noted that it is hard to achieve stability in foster care, while adoption more often provides security and positive outcomes in adulthood. The typically balanced conclusion states that the weight of evidence shows substantial advantages for adoption, but that long-term fostering 'still is the plan of choice' where young people do not want to be adopted and/or there is a high degree of birth family contact. It is reprinted from Child & Family Social Work *(7:1, pp. 23–33, 2002).*

Introduction

This paper examines, in the light of the research literature, the relative merits and limitations of long-term fostering and adoption. A key question often asked when considering the future of children who cannot return to their birth families is whether it matters to them, in the long run, to whichever of these two forms of substitute parenting they happen to go. The intention of long-term fostering is invariably that the child will live in the household on a "permanent" basis until they reach adulthood, and possibly beyond, forming a psychosocial base in their life. Because of this expectation long-term fostering is often referred to as "permanent". Yet the term "permanent" cannot objectively be applied because parental responsibility often continues to be held either by the local authority or by the birth parent. Furthermore, the child can be removed at the instigation of any one of four parties. Studies also confirm that within social services there is widespread confusion as to what exactly is meant by the terms "long-term fostering" or "permanence" (Triseliotis *et al*, 2000; Lowe and Murch, 2001). In contrast to long-term fostering, an adoption order confirms permanence through its legality, with all parental responsibilities being transferred to the adoptive family. The child can only be removed, like any other child, if the adopter(s) is found to be neglectful or abusive.

The research evidence

A cautionary note is necessary before these two forms of substitute parenting are contrasted. To start with, and unlike adoption, there is a dearth of studies in long-term fostering that go beyond the snapshot type approach. Because of the much greater stability associated with adoption, populations of adopted children and adopted adults have become the target of researchers from different disciplines. In addition, the studies to be contrasted here are not always comparable, for reasons which include:

- small samples or flawed samples, e.g. anecdotal;
- the lack of controls;
- the absence of before and after baselines for the children featuring in the study;
- failure to combine qualitative with more objective measures;
- the points in children's lives at which progress was assessed;
- the dearth of longitudinal studies;
- the exclusion of some categories of children, e.g. those with disabilities;
- the failure of some studies to distinguish between "permanent" fostering and adoption;
- with one exception, not separating breakdowns before and after the adoption order was granted;
- failure to separate adoptions by foster carers from other adoptions;
- reliance on the memories and/or sole judgement of social workers in establishing breakdown rates or whether placement objectives have been met.

Contrasts with past studies are also made more difficult because not only has the social context between then and now changed, but so have policies and practices in relation to children and families. As one example, most of the children in foster care now would, in the past, have gone to residential establishments because of their special needs such as emotional and behavioural problems and/or physical or mental disabilities. Those who went into foster care in the past do not even come into the care system now but are looked after at home with supportive services made available to their families. Because many children adopted now have special needs, i.e. display behavioural and emotional problems, are older at placement and/or have physical or mental disabilities, considerable overlaps in characteristics and circumstances can be expected between them and those going into long-term foster care (see Holloway, 1997a,b; Quinton *et al*, 1998; Rushton *et al*, pers. comm.).

As a result of what has been said, what is looked for is not the truth but the weight of evidence and probabilities. With these qualifications in mind, the following six key variables are contrasted:

- stability of long-term fostering and adoption;
- adjustment;
- sense of security and belonging;
- personal and social functioning;
- the subjects' retrospective perceptions;
- the substitute parents' perspective.

The stability of long-term fostering and adoption

When a placement is made in either long-term fostering or adoption the expectation is that it will last until the child reaches adulthood and beyond. However, some placements may be terminated prematurely and are referred to as "breakdowns" or "disruptions". What is a placement "breakdown" or "disruption" begs many questions, but for the purposes of this paper the studies' own definitions have been accepted. Breakdowns in long-term fostering can happen from the point the first placement is made to the time a child reaches adulthood. No study known to me has charted the children's pathways to adulthood with the stability of the fostering placement in mind. What most of them have done is to take a series of placements already in existence and chronicle their in-care history up to then. Some have also followed them up for one, three or five years noting breakdown rates on the way. What happens to long-term fostering after the five-year follow-up period is over remains largely unknown, though Sinclair *et al* (2000) comment that the number of changes of placements they found meant that very long-stay placements are almost bound to be extremely uncommon.

Overall breakdown rates

The overall breakdown rates noted by a number of key studies in long-term fostering, for all age groups and between two and five years after the placement was made, is around 43 per cent (Parker, 1966; George, 1970; Berridge and Cleaver, 1987; Rowe *et al*, 1989; Strathclyde Regional Council, 1991; Thoburn, 1991; Holloway, 1997a,b; Rushton, *et al*, pers. comm.). The average ranges from 60 per cent, found by one study at a time when mostly non-problematic children were meant to go into fostering (George, 1970), to 27 per cent found by a more recent survey when far more difficult children were being placed (Thoburn, 1991). This trend is also supported by Rowe *et al* (1989) and Rushton *et al* (pers. comm.), suggesting an improved delivery of foster care services.

Turning to adoption, the overall breakdown rate found for children placed with special needs is around 19 per cent, with the follow-up periods ranging from two to eight years after placement (Kadushin, 1970; Boyne *et al*, 1984; Tremitiere, 1984; Nelson, 1985; Festinger, 1986; Barth and Berry, 1988; Rowe *et al*, 1989; Borland *et al*, 1991; Strathclyde Regional Council, 1991; Thoburn, 1991; Lowe *et al*, 1999; Rushton *et al*, pers. comm.). The White Paper (Cabinet Office, 2000, p. 15) puts at 18 per cent all adoptive placements which broke down during 1999–2000 before an adoption order was made. Around four per cent of children return to care annually after the adoption order is granted (Statistics Section of the Department of Health, pers. comm.). Overall breakdown rates, however, disguise differences due to the age of the child at placement, which is known to be a crucial factor in placement stability. The next stage therefore analyses breakdown rates by age groups.

Pre-school children

Contrasting breakdown rates between children placed in long-term fostering and adoption at the pre-school stage is made additionally problematic because some studies have taken the ages of four, five or even seven as their cut-off point, while others have excluded those aged under four. With this in mind, an analysis will first be made of breakdown rates reported for children placed when aged nought to one, followed by breakdown rates for those placed mainly at the pre-school stage.

Three studies give an average breakdown rate of 30 per cent after three to five years for children placed in long-term fostering when aged nought to one (Parker, 1966; George, 1970; Berridge and Cleaver, 1987). More recent surveys, though, found hardly any breakdowns for either adoption or long-term fostering 30 months to six years after the placements had been made (Thoburn, 1991; Rushton et al, pers. comm.). Because the vast majority of children placed in adoption before the 1970s were very young, no breakdowns were expected and hardly any attention was paid to this aspect by researchers. However, a summary of nine US studies, looking at adoption before 1970, found the overall breakdown rate to be just under two per cent (Kadushin, 1970). Two recent British studies reported that, of children placed when under a year old, none had broken down within a five- to six-year period (Holloway, 1997a,b; Castle et al, 2000).

Turning to the whole pre- or just post-school age group, adoption studies from about 1980 onwards show a consistent average break-down rate of around five per cent between two and five years following placement (Table 11.1) (Kadushin, 1970; Boyne et al, 1984; Tremitiere, 1984; Kaye and Tipton, 1985; Barth and Berry, 1988; Rowe et al, 1989; Borland et al, 1991; Thoburn, 1991; Lowe et al, 1999). Long-term fostering breakdowns for the same age group and for approximately the same follow-up period average 22 per cent. For example, three studies put breakdown rates at an average of 39 per cent (Parker, 1966; George, 1970; Berridge and Cleaver, 1987), but two later surveys show a dramatic fall to less than four per cent, broadly the same as adoption (Rowe et al, 1989; Thoburn, 1991). In fact, the Rushton et al (pers.

Table 11.1

Contrasting breakdown rates between fostering and adoption for children placed at around the pre-school stage*

Long-term foster care

Study	Breakdowns (%)
Parker (1966) (after 5 years)	38
George (1970) (after 5 years)	47
Berridge and Cleaver (1987) (after 3 years)	32
Rowe *et al* (1989) (after 13–23 months)	4
Thoburn (1991) (after 30 months)	3
Rushton *et al* (pers.comm.) (after 6 years)	0

Adoption

Summary of US studies (after 3–5 years)	6
Rowe *et al* (1989) (after 13–23 months)	2
Thoburn (1991) (after 30 months)	3
Borland *et al* (1991) (after 3 years)	6
Lowe *et al* (1999) (period not specified)	4
Rushton *et al* (pers. comm.) (after 6 years)	0

*Studies with fewer than 30 in their sample and those whose sample basis was unclear or anecdotal were left out in this and other calculations.

comm.) study, covering both adoption and long-term fostering, found no breakdowns among children placed when under six years old, six years after the placements were made.

Overall, if we include past studies, then breakdowns among the adoption group were significantly lower compared with the fostering group. However, if we include only studies carried out in the last 10 or so years, then hardly any differences would be found. This could be attributed to improved policies and practices.

Children placed between the ages of five and 12

Again, because of the different cut-off points selected by different studies the upper age limits can differ. With this in mind, Table 11.2 shows that up to the mid-1980s three studies reported the overall rate of long-term fostering breakdowns for this age group to be over 50 per cent (Parker, 1966; George, 1970; Berridge and Cleaver, 1987). Three subsequent surveys suggested a significant drop (Rowe *et al*, 1989; Thoburn, 1991; Rushton *et al*, pers. comm.), but a fourth recorded again high rates of 52 per cent (Holloway, 1997a,b). Since about 1980,

Table 11.2
Contrasting breakdown rates between children placed in long-term fostering or adoption during latency

Long-term foster care

Study	Age at placement	Breakdowns (%)
Parker (1966) (after 5 years)	5–12 years	57
George (1970) (after 5 years)	5–12 years	68
Berridge and Cleaver (1987) (after 3 years)	5–12 years	46
Rowe *et al* (1989) (after 11–23 months)	5–10 years	23
Thoburn (1991) (minimum 30 months)	5–8 years	19
Holloway (1997a,b) (after 5 years)	5–10 years	52
Rushton *et al* (pers.comm.) (after 6 years)	6–11 years	34

Adoption

Study	Age at placement	Breakdowns (%)
Summary of US studies	5–11 years	15
Rushton *et al* (1988) (after 8 years)	5–9 years	19
Rowe *et al* (1989) (after 13–23 months)	5–10 years	11
Borland *et al* (1991) (after 3 years)	6–10 years	11
Thoburn (1991) (after 30 months)	5–8 years	12
Holloway (1997a,b) (after 5 years)	5–10 years	7
Rushton *et al* (pers. comm.) (after 6 years)	6–11 years	27

adoption breakdowns for a broadly similar age group have averaged 15 per cent (summary of US studies; Rushton *et al*, 1988; Rowe *et al*, 1989; Borland *et al*, 1991; Thoburn 1991; Lowe *et al*, 1999; Rushton *et al*, pers. comm.). The main surprise here is the high breakdown rates (27%) found by Rushton *et al*, in an as yet unpublished study which followed up the children six years into their placement.

If studies carried out before about 1990 are included, then long-term fostering experiences would show significantly higher breakdown rates compared with adoption. However, if studies carried out after about 1990 were contrasted, then they would show that fostering breakdowns are still higher, but the gap between these two forms of substitute parenting is narrowing (though Sinclair *et al* (2000, p. 40) point out that the chance of long-term placements lasting is 'very low'). Some recent studies reflect the increasing number of very problematic children being placed in both adoption and long-term fostering (Holloway, 1997a,b; Quinton *et al*, 1998; Rushton *et al*, pers. comm.).

Placement of adolescents

Far more adolescents are likely to be placed in long-term fostering than in adoption, but exact figures are not available. Of the 2,700 children who left care through adoption in 1999/2000, 179 (or 6.6%) were aged 10 and upwards (Department of Health, 2001). Whether placed in long-term fostering or adoption the breakdown rates for adolescents can be very high. Between a third and more than half are likely to disrupt within a three- to five-year period (fostering studies: Parker, 1966; Berridge and Cleaver, 1987; Rowe *et al*, 1989; Thoburn, 1991; Holloway, 1997a,b; Rushton *et al*, pers. comm.; adoption studies: summary of US studies; Rowe *et al*, 1989; Thoburn, 1991; Borland *et al*, 1991; Strathclyde Regional Council, 1991; Holloway, 1997a,b; Lowe *et al*, 1999; Rushton *et al*, pers. comm.).

Though the overall breakdown rate suggests somewhat lower breakdowns in favour of adoption, this disguises the fact that a proportion of older children are adopted by their foster carers after the placement stabilises. Possibly because of the high breakdown rates expected, agencies appear cautious nowadays about placing adolescents for adoption. For example, the number of adolescents placed in 2000 was half the number placed in 1996 (Department of Health Annual Statistics). While it cannot always be presumed that a placement that breaks down does not involve some benefits to a child, the real challenge is in being able to recognise the 50 per cent or so who can profit from either adoption or long-term fostering without exposing children to unnecessary failures. The overall picture that emerges about breakdowns is a mixed one. While some recent studies suggest a narrowing of the gap between adoption and long-term fostering breakdowns, a sombre message comes from Sinclair and colleagues (2000): 'These figures suggest that the chance of very long-term placements is low. Only six per cent of the sample had been in the same placement for six years or more' (p. 40). Later on they add that 'very long-term placements are clearly exceptional' (p. 41) and, on p. 272, that 'it [foster care] rarely offers permanence. Its placements are too liable to break down.'

Adjustment

Identifying and measuring children's behavioural and emotional difficulties is often complex and imprecise, and made more so by the absence, in most studies, of the children's "before and after" placement baselines. A further dilemma is whether to look for intermediary outcomes, i.e. during childhood, or for more final ones after the child reaches adulthood.

Adjustment in childhood

Fostering

Two early snapshot type studies which took place at a time when it was thought that only non-problematic children went into foster care reported that around a third of them were "disturbed", some seriously, compared with seven per cent in the general population (Thorpe, 1974; Rowe *et al*, 1984). More recent studies suggest that around half the children in fostering display high levels of emotional and behavioural problems (Holloway, 1997a,b; Minnis, 1999; Schofield *et al*, 2000; Sinclair *et al*, 2000; Triseliotis *et al*, 2000). Some of the studies report that the difficulties were irrespective of the child's age. Brand and Brinich (1999, p. 1227) noted from their analysis of extensive statistical data in the USA that young children in foster care had 'significantly higher scores on the behaviour problem scale than children in any other placement type'. The same authors also added that, compared with others, adoptive parents were seeking help at a lower threshold.

Adoption
Most studies report that adopted children placed as infants, or when very young, hardly differ in adjustment from the general population (Seglow *et al*, 1972; Maughan and Pickles 1990 – NCD study; Lambert and Streather, 1980; Plomin and De Fries, 1985; St. Claire and Osborne, 1987; Bohman and Sigvardson, 1990; Brodzinsky, 1993). A somewhat discordant note is struck by a New Zealand study which found that adopted children were more likely to have higher rates of "externalising" but not of "internalising" behaviours (Fergusson *et al*, 1995). In the case of adoption of older children and those with special needs, as with fostering, between a third and a half were found to be displaying problems of some intensity, with little improvement being noted after a year (Holloway, 1997a,b; Howe, 1998; Quinton *et al*, 1998; Rushton *et al*, pers. comm.). On the other hand, within a two-year period, the under two-year-olds adopted from Romanian institutions made excellent progress, in spite of the gross deprivations to which they had been exposed (Rutter *et al*, 1998).

Like breakdown rates, "adjustment" in childhood as an outcome variable is becoming less important now for contrasting long-term fostering and adoption because recent studies, mentioned above, have found very high adjustment problems in both groups. Rushton *et al* (pers. comm.) also showed that while the long-term foster children in their study had some differences in their pre-placement backgrounds, their problem profile was very similar to the adopted group.

Adjustment in adult life

Possibly the most accomplished longitudinal study contrasting infants, some of whom went to adoption and others to long-term fostering, and with community controls, is the one by Bohman and Sigvardson (1990) from Sweden. This study found that at age 18 "maladjustment" in the fostering group was two to three times more frequent than among controls and in relation to the adoption group (albeit the foster carers were described as having 'stable families' but did not have the higher financial, educational and occupational status of the adopters). However, the authors concluded (p. 104):

> *The results of our longitudinal studies indicate that the long-term prognosis for adopted children is in no way worse than for children in the general population, provided that the adoptive family is psychologically well prepared for the task of rearing a non-biological child.*

The findings of the NCD British longitudinal study confirmed similar findings in relation to those adopted (Maughan and Pickles, 1990).

Other studies suggest that when it comes to the placement of children with "special needs", adoption can have the capacity to help reverse the negative impact of early traumas, but that there is also a limit to such recovery (for a summary of studies see Clarke and Clarke, 2001). Equally, we know that many children whose placements last can benefit considerably from long-term fostering (see Triseliotis, 1980; Triseliotis and Hill, 1990).

Sense of security and belonging

Attention was drawn in the early 1980s to findings suggesting that long-term fostering, unlike adoption, appeared then to leave the children feeling unusually insecure and lacking a full sense of belonging to their substitute family (Triseliotis, 1983). Other studies were to confirm this finding (Tizard, 1977; Rowe *et al*, 1984; Hill *et al*, 1989; Bohman and Sigvardson, 1990; Triseliotis and Hill, 1990). These studies identified two key areas around which the insecurities were concentrated:

1. Anxiety and uncertainty on the part of the child and their carers arising from the impermanence of their situation

Because of the lack of legal security, which meant that the placement could be terminated at any time, many children and foster carers were left in a continual state of anxiety of what might happen next. A typical comment by one child was:

As a foster child you still worry. (Hill *et al*, 1989)

The foster child's insecurity was further stressed by more recent studies reporting that a small group of carers gave indications that if the child's behaviour was to get much worse, or their own children were seen to suffer as a result, then the foster child might have to go (Schofield *et al*, 2000; Sinclair *et al*, 2000; Triseliotis *et al*, 2000). This appears to contrast with the reported perseverance demonstrated by most adoptive parents. Rowe *et al* (1984) also highlighted the element of insecurity operating in long-term fostering by saying that the children did not necessarily feel secure, and the number of changes that occurred while the study was in progress, plus the fact that nearly half the placements had been in some jeopardy at some stage, showed that their fears were not without justification (pp. 224–225). Bohman and Sigvardson (1990) attributed the poorer performance of fostered young people to the same insecurities, adding that there was no guarantee that the child might not some day be returned to the biological mother or father. The foster carers also expressed concerns about their insecure position and the researchers went on to add: 'It is inconceivable that this insecurity has not influenced the relationship between foster parents and the children' (p. 105).

2. Ambiguity of position

The ambiguous position of children in long-term fostering appears to make many of them feel that they "belong" to nobody. They do not live with their biological parents, and often are not in touch with them, yet their carers are not their "parents", and neither can they call them "mum" or "dad" by right. This ambiguity appears to lead to a sense of unusualness and difference, experienced especially in school and at play. Other happenings in their lives reinforce the sense of "difference", such as a separate surname from that of the substitute family, the anxiety of being moved and sometimes the comings and goings of short-stay children in the household (see Triseliotis, 1983; Hill *et al*, 1989; Bohman and Sigvardson, 1990; Triseliotis and Hill, 1990). The following are typical comments made by foster children moving to adoption (Hill *et al*, 1989):

A foster home is in-between.

Fostering is about moving on and on . . .

Most children in the same study who moved from long-term fostering to adoption stressed the advantages of the latter in terms of:

Legality:

It is something permanent and by law.

They are legally my mum and dad. I can call them mum and dad.

Security, continuity and permanence:

I belong.

You cannot be taken away.

Being a proper part of the family.

We can conclude that even when long-term fostering lasts, the children still feel less secure and have a weaker sense of belonging compared with those who are adopted. This is possibly the main defining difference between these two forms of substitute parenting. Though around 375,000 adopted adults (possibly half of the total) have so far searched for more information about their origins and/or sought reunions with birth relatives, the evidence suggests that this is not because they wish to replace their adoptive parents. For most of them the adoptive parents retained a firm place in their relationships and affections (Triseliotis, 1973; Howe and Feast, 2000).

Personal and social functioning

Personal and social functioning covers such areas as mental health, educational attainments, employment and economic security, housing circumstances, criminal behaviour, alcohol and drug abuse and family life. Very few studies known to me have contrasted these in relation to adults who had formerly been fostered long term or adopted. One series of studies, though, concluded that compared with those adopted, those formerly fostered long term were "somewhat" less able to form relationships or carry out the parenting role; fewer had continued their education beyond the statutory school-leaving age; far more were likely to be unemployed and draw social security benefits and/or be homeless. At the time of the study, around one in 10 in both groups had seen a psychiatrist in their adult life, and criminal convictions after the age of 16 did not differ significantly between them (Triseliotis, 1980; Triseliotis and Russell, 1984; Triseliotis and Hill, 1990). These findings were largely confirmed by Bohman and Sigvardson's Swedish longitudinal study (Bohman and Sigvardson, 1990).

Dumaret's earlier French study, which also contrasted long-term fostering with adoption, reported that on all measurements the adopted group came out on "top" (Dumaret, 1985). However, a later study concluded that those fostered did not differ in terms of social functioning and integration from the rest of the population (Dumaret and Coppel-Batsch, 1998). A much less "rosy" picture is painted by a retrospective US cohort study which found high levels of unemployment, homelessness, drug abuse, arrests, violence towards partners or violence meted out to them by partners among adults who were formerly in long-term fostering (Benedict et al, 1996).

The subjects' retrospective perceptions

There is only one series of studies known to me which has contrasted the perceptions of adults who had grown up in long-term fostering with those who had been adopted (Triseliotis, 1980; Triseliotis and Russell, 1984; Triseliotis and Hill, 1990). Table 11.3 contrasts findings

Table 11.3
Self-rating of current life situations based on Triseliotis (1980) and Triseliotis and Russell (1984)

Type	Formerly fostered group: quality of experience			Adopted group: quality of experience		
	Very good to good (%)	Mixed (%)	Poor to very poor (%)	Very good to good (%)	Mixed (%)	Poor to very poor (%)
Coping in life	57	20	22	90	5	5
Sense of well-being	35	47	18	90	5	5
Fostering experience	67	7	25	82	9	9
Closeness to carers now	60	12	27	80	18	2

from these studies on perceptions of coping and well-being and on the foster care or adoption experience. In all the contrasted areas the adoption group emerge as doing significantly better. For example, 57 per cent of those formerly fostered rated their "coping with current life" as "very good" to "good", compared with 90 per cent of those adopted. Only 35 per cent of those formerly fostered rated their feelings of well-being as "very good to good", compared with 90 per cent of those adopted. The fostering experience was rated "very good to good" by 67 per cent of those formerly fostered, compared with 82 per cent of those adopted. Whereas 27 per cent of those formerly fostered said their current closeness to their former carers was "poor or very poor", only two per cent of those adopted said so. In Owen's (1999) study around 85 per cent of the children, who had been adopted when aged 6–11 and many of them now grown up, said they were getting on well with their parents and that they had been shown physical affection. This contrasted with only around 70 per cent from a community sample saying the same.

Where children in long-term foster care became integrated into their foster family and continued to live there beyond the age of 16 or

18 as members of the family, then levels of satisfaction could be high. However, a significant number had left their carers once they reached the age of 16 and one-third had lost all contact with them. They largely drifted between different birth relatives or joined the group of young homeless. A quarter of them had joined the armed forces compared with none from the adoption group (Triseliotis, 1980; Triseliotis and Russell, 1984).

The substitute parents' perspective

Retrospective studies on either the fostering or adoption experience as seen through the eyes of the carers after the children have grown up are again rare. However, one study asked foster carers to rate their experience of long-term fostering when the children were aged around 21 (Triseliotis, 1980). Over half (55%) expressed satisfaction with how the placement had worked out. In most of these cases the foster child had become part of the family and found a family for life. The remaining 45 per cent were split equally between those who indicated a less long-term commitment to the child and more to their role as foster carers and those who felt that the placement had not worked out as expected. Levels of satisfaction among those who had adopted infants and young children average around 80 per cent (Kornitzer, 1968; Raynor, 1980; Howe, 1996). Adopted people featuring in "search and reunion" studies have expressed similar levels of satisfaction with their adoption (Howe and Feast, 2000).

Few studies have yet elicited the retrospective views of those who adopted children with "special needs". However, high levels of satisfaction were expressed by single parents adopting older children; children with disabilities also did particularly well (Owen, 1999). Just over three-fifths (63%) of those who had adopted, or fostered long term, children of minority ethnic origin, some of them transracially, were also positive about the experience, with only 12 per cent generally being negative (Thoburn et al, 2000). Howe (1996) reported that 93 per cent of adopters said that although the children's growing-up period proved most challenging and demanding, nevertheless they had 'positive parent–child relationships'.

What future for long-term fostering?

The weight of the evidence examined suggests that adoption confers significant advantages to children who cannot return to their birth families, especially in terms of emotional security and sense of belonging. Yet it would be wrong to see this as an either/or situation because long-term fostering can still be the plan of choice especially for:

- children who are clear that they don't want adoption;
- those closely attached to their carers for whom a move would not be in their interests;
- children where there is a high level of continuous birth family involvement;
- situations where children, especially older ones, and their carers want time to get to know each other before perhaps making a final commitment.

Other things being equal, the ideal for children in long-term fostering who cannot return to their birth families is to be adopted by their foster carers, assuming this is also the expressed wish of the older children and their carers. Such adoptions can spare children the trauma arising from moving. Where old enough, the children must be consulted and listened to, and their views seriously considered and respected. This is also the best predictor of placement stability (Triseliotis *et al*, 1995; Sellick and Thoburn, 1996). Some older children will be clear that they do not want adoption or that they do not want to leave their foster homes. Others may prefer the benefits that go with adoption as outlined earlier. For young children who cannot express a clear view, others have to make the decision on their behalf after considering the facts and the empirical evidence available.

Some 13 per cent of carers adopt or want to adopt their foster children each year (BAAF, 2000; Sinclair *et al*, 2000). It is not clear to what extent social workers encourage foster carers to adopt, especially as in some cases this could result in the local authority losing some of them from continuing to foster. A decisive factor which has been found to enable long-term foster carers to adopt is the provision of adoption allowances. Hill *et al* (1989) reported that four out of every five adoption allowances went to carers adopting their foster children. However, an off-putting aspect about adoption allowances is that they are means-tested instead of attached to the child. The Adoption Bill that went to Parliament before its dissolution in 2001 did not go far enough in rectifying this.

Possibly the biggest planning dilemma arises when carers fostering a young child who cannot return to their family express a commitment to care long term, but not to adopt. Given some of the unpredictabilities of long-term fostering outlined earlier, the question is whether it is preferable to move a young child to an adoptive placement, thus breaking their existing attachments, or leave them where they are with a somewhat unpredictable future. Examples of such unpredictabilities include foster carers who in all honesty say they will look after a two- or three-year-old for the remainder of their childhood, only to give up after six, eight or even 10 years. At such a late stage it is almost impossible to find an adoptive home for the child, especially for a boy. The scenario that usually follows is a succession of temporary fostering placements with the child eventually growing up without a family to call their own and no social base in life. Yet uprooting can prove very traumatic to the child.

Judicial decisions

For parents long-term fostering keeps the door open for the child's possible rehabilitation with them and largely safeguards continued face-to-face contact. As a result they often ask the courts that instead of adoption the child should go into or stay in long-term fostering. The reality is that once a child has been in care for around two years the chances of rehabilitation to their parents are distant (see PIU, 2000, p. 84). Over the years a number of judges have come to recognise the advantages of adoption over long-term fostering, the most noted one being in *re H (1981) 3 FLR*. Ormond LJ said [of adopters]:

> . . . *adoption gives us total security and makes the child part of our family, and places us in parental control of the child; long-*

term fostering leaves us exposed to changes of view of the local authority, it leaves us exposed to applications and so on, by the natural parent. This is a perfectly sensible approach, it is far from being an emotive one.

One reason given by some judges for not granting an adoption order and opting instead for long-term fostering is where there are still hopes of rehabilitation or there is frequent contact between a child and members of their birth family. Other things being equal, of course, in cases where a parent or relative cannot make a home for a child but has a meaningful emotional link with them, emotional and genealogical continuity could be preserved by providing for post-adoption contact.

Summary and conclusions

Allowing for all the methodological difficulties in contrasting data from different studies, two broad conclusions can be drawn from this paper. First, because of the type of child currently being adopted or fostered, differences in breakdown rates and in adjustment between these two forms of substitute parenting are diminishing and in some age groups evening out. Yet at least one recent study reported that foster care rarely offers permanence. Its placements are too liable to break down (Sinclair *et al*, 2000). Second, compared with long-term fostering, adoption still provides higher levels of emotional security, a stronger sense of belonging and a more enduring psychosocial base in life for those who cannot live with their birth families.

The main limitation of long-term fostering is its unpredictability and the uncertain and ambiguous position in which the children find themselves. Taken together these conditions appear to generate long-standing feelings of insecurity and anxiety in children. One other possible explanation for this is the different expectations placed on adopters and foster carers and the different commitment that is brought to the task by each of these two groups of substitute "parents". For example, studies suggest that when difficulties arise adopters, on the whole, persevere against the odds (Howe, 1996, 1997; Quinton *et al*, 1998) while long-term foster carers may be readier to give up. The nature of their task, including their contracts, allows for opting out (Schofield *et al*, 2000; Sinclair *et al*, 2000; Triseliotis *et al*, 2000). It is too early yet to predict the impact of the special guardianship order proposed in the Adoption (England and Wales) Bill 2001, which is meant to provide for greater security to children and their carers. Whether the order will be used eventually to fulfil this expectation or some of those currently adopted will instead be kept on a special guardianship order is too early to say. The acceptance of the order may also come to depend on the circumstances under which it can be reversed.

Finally, when deciding between these two forms of substitute parenting, account has to be taken of each child's individual needs and circumstances and those of their carers, including the range of available resources in terms of placements. In the same way that the same shoe cannot fit every foot, adoption is not the answer for every child who cannot return to their family. Long-term fostering still has a firm place in planning, as shown earlier. Furthermore, a significant number of those whose placements last find a family for life, albeit lacking some of the more intense qualities found with adoption. All decisions in child placement involve an element of risk. It is possible only to reduce it, rather than eliminate it, by balancing the child's age, levels of adjustment, current attachments, the child's wishes (where old enough) and the strength of their carers' commitment.

References

Barth R.P. and Berry M. (1988) *Adoption and Disruption Rates: Rates, risks and responses*, New York: Aldine de Gruyter

Benedict M.I., Zuravin S. and Stallings R.Y. (1996) 'Adult functioning of children who lived in kin versus non-relative family foster homes', *Child Welfare* 75:5, pp. 529–549

Berridge D. and Cleaver H. (1987) *Foster Home Breakdown*, Oxford: Blackwell

Bohman M. and Sigvardson S. (1990) 'Outcome in adoption: lessons from longitudinal studies', in Brodzinsky D.M. and Schechter M.D. (eds) *The Psychology of Adoption*, New York: Oxford University Press

Borland M., O'Hara G. and Triseliotis J. (1991) 'Permanency planning for children in Lothian Region', in Social Work Services Group (ed.) *The Outcome of Permanent Family Placements in Two Scottish Local Authorities*, Edinburgh: Scottish Office

Boyne J., Denby L., Kettering J.R. and Wheeler W. (1984) *The Shadow of Success*, unpublished research report, Westfield: Spaulding for Children

Brand E.A. and Brinich M.P. (1999) 'Behaviour problems and mental health contacts in adopted, foster and non-adopted children', *Journal of Child Psychology and Psychiatry* 40:8, pp. 1221–229

BAAF (2000) Paper presented to the National Adoption Standards Working Group, London: BAAF

Brodzinsky D.M. (1993) 'Long-term outcomes in adoption', *The Future of Children* 3:1, pp. 153–166

Cabinet Office (2000) *Adoption: A new approach*, White Paper, London: Department of Health

Castle J., Beckett C. and Groothues C. (2000) 'Infant adoption in England', *Adoption & Fostering* 24:3, pp. 26–35

Clarke A. and Clarke A. (2001) 'Early adversity and adoptive solutions', *Adoption & Fostering* 25:1, pp. 24–32

Department of Health (2001) *Annual Statistics of Looked After Children*, London: Department of Health

Dumaret A. (1985) 'Scholastic performance and behaviours of sibs raised in contrasting environments', *Journal of Child Psychology and Psychiatry and Allied Disciplines* 26:4, pp. 553–580

Dumaret A. and Coppel-Batsch M. (1998) 'Effects in adulthood of separations and long-term foster care: a French study', *Adoption & Fostering* 22:1, pp. 31–39

Fergusson D.M., Lynskey M. and Horwood L.J. (1995) 'The adolescent outcomes of adoption: a 16-year longitudinal study', *Journal of Child Psychology and Psychiatry* 36:4, pp. 597–616

Festinger T. (1986) *Necessary Risk: A study of adoptions and disrupted adoptive placements*, New York: Child Welfare League of America

George V. (1970) *Foster Care*, London: Routledge & Kegan Paul

Hill M., Lambert L. and Triseliotis J. (1989) *Achieving Adoption with Love and Money*, London: National Children's Bureau

Holloway J.S. (1997a) 'Outcome in placements for adoption or long-term fostering', *Archives of Disease in Childhood* 76:3, pp. 227–230

Holloway J.S. (1997b) 'Foster and adoptive parents' assessment of permanent family placements', *Archives of Disease in Childhood* 76:3, pp. 231–235

Howe D. (1996) 'Adopters' relationships with their adopted children from adolescence to early adulthood', *Adoption & Fostering* 20:3, pp. 35–43

Howe D. (1997) 'Parent-reported problems in 211 adopted children: some risk and protective factors', *Journal of Child Psychology and Psychiatry* 38:4, pp. 401–411

Howe D. (1998) 'Adoption outcome research and practical judgement', *Adoption & Fostering* 22:2, pp. 6–15

Howe D. and Feast J. (2000) *Adoption, Search and Reunion*, London: The Children's Society

Kadushin A. (1970) *Adopting Older Children*, New York: Columbia University Press

Kaye E. and Tipton M. (1985) *Evaluation of State Activities with Regard to Adoption Disruption*, Washington, DC: Office of Human Development Services

Kornitzer M. (1968) *Adoption and Family Life*, London: Putman

Lambert L. and Streather J. (1980) *Children in Changing Families*, London: Macmillan

Lowe N. and Murch M. (2001) *The Plan for the Child: Adoption or long-term fostering*, London: Report to the Department of Health

Lowe N., Murch M., Borkowski M., Weaver A., Beckford V. and Thomas C. (1999) *Supporting Adoption: Reframing the approach*, London: BAAF

Maughan B. and Pickles A. (1990) 'Adopted and illegitimate children growing up', in Robins L.N. and Rutter M. (eds) *Straight and Devious Pathways from Childhood to Adulthood*, Cambridge: Cambridge University Press

Minnis H. (1999) *Results of the Foster Carers Training Project*, pamphlet, Glasgow

Nelson K. (1985) *On the Frontiers of Adoption: A study of special needs adoptive families*, Washington, DC: Child Welfare League of America

Owen M. (1999) *Novices, Old Hands and Professionals: Adoption by single people*, London: BAAF

Parker R. (1966) *Decision in Foster Care*, London: Allen & Unwin

PIU (2000) *Prime Minister's Review of Adoption*, London: The Cabinet Office

Plomin R. and De Fries J.C. (1985) *Origins of Individual Differences: The Colorado Adoption Project*, New York: Academic Press

Quinton D., Rushton A., Dance C. and Mayes D. (1998) *Joining New Families: A study of adoption and fostering in middle childhood*, London: Wiley

Raynor L. (1980) *The Adopted Child Comes of Age*, London: Allen & Unwin

Rowe J., Cain H., Hundleby M. and Keane A. (1984) *Long-term Foster Care*, London: Batsford

Rowe J., Hundleby M. and Garnett L. (1989) *Child Care Now*, London: BAAF

Rushton A., Treseder J. and Quinton D. (1988) *New Parents of Older Children*, London: BAAF

Rutter M. and the English and Romanian Adoptees Study Team (1998) 'Developmental catch-up and deficit following adoption after severe global early privation', *Journal of Child Psychology and Psychiatry* 39:4, pp. 465–476

Schofield G., Beek M., Sargent K. with Thoburn J. (2000) *Growing Up in Foster Care*, London: BAAF

Seglow J., Pringle M. and Wedge P. (1972) *Growing Up Adopted*, Windsor: NFER

Sellick C. and Thoburn J. (1996) *What Works in Family Placement*, London: Barnardo's

Sinclair I., Wilson K. and Gibbs I. (2000) *Supporting Foster Placements*, London: Interim report to the Department of Health

St Claire L. and Osborn A.F. (1987) 'The ability and behaviour of children who have been "in-care" or separated from their parents', *Early Child Development and Care* 28, pp. 187–354

Strathclyde Regional Council (1991) 'Fostering and adoption disruption', in Social Work Services Group (ed.) *The Outcome of Permanent Family Placements in Two Scottish Local Authorities*, Edinburgh: Scottish Office

Thoburn J. (1991) 'Family placement', in Fratter J (ed.) *Family Placement*, London: BAAF

Thoburn J., Norford L. and Rashid S. (2000) *Permanent Family Placement for Children of Minority Ethnic Origin*, London: Jessica Kingsley

Thorpe R. (1974) 'The social and psychological situation of the long-term foster child with regard to his natural family', Unpublished PhD thesis, University of Nottingham

Tizard B. (1977) *Adoption: A second chance*, London: Open Books

Tremitiere B. (1984) *Disruption: A break in commitment*, York: Tressler-Lutheran

Triseliotis J. (1973) *In Search of Origins*, London: Routledge & Kegan Paul

Triseliotis J. (1980) *Growing Up Fostered*, London: Report to the Social Science Research Council

Triseliotis J. (1983) 'Identity and security in long-term fostering and adoption', *Adoption & Fostering* 7:1, pp. 22–31

Triseliotis J., Borland M. and Hill M. (2000) *Delivering Fostering Services*, London: BAAF

Triseliotis J., Borland M., Hill M. and Lambert L. (1995) *Teenagers and the Social Work Services*, London: HMSO

Triseliotis J. and Hill M. (1990) 'Contrasting adoption, foster care and residential care', in Brodzinsky D.M. and Schechter M.D. (eds) *The Psychology of Adoption*, New York: Oxford University Press

Triseliotis J. and Russell J. (1984) *Hard to Place: The outcome of adoption and residential care*, London: Gower

12   *The Adoption Triangle Revisited:* summary and conclusions

The summary chapter included here comes from a late study published by BAAF (2005) where, together with Julia Feast and Fiona Kyle, John returned to the subject matter and issues he covered more than 30 years before (Chapter 1). The changes that had come about partly as a result of In Search of Origins *meant that large numbers of adoptive families in England and Wales now had experience of searching and reunions, in accord with new legal entitlements, even though this had not been expected at the time of the adoptions. The research found much congruence in the feelings of loss and mutual interest among the birth parents, adopted people and adoptive parents. Re-establishing contact usually had complicated effects, but in most cases all three parties recognised more gains than disappointments.*

Introduction

Based on information obtained from the perspective of all three members of the so-called adoption triangle, this study reported predominantly on two specific stages of adoption. First, the experiences of giving up a child for adoption some 40 to 50 years ago, rearing an adopted child and growing up as an adopted person. Second, the more recent experiences of all three groups surrounding the search and reunion process and its outcome for each after an average of eight years. The birth mother's feelings and thoughts were charted from the time of the pregnancy to the post-reunion period, and those of the adopted child from being raised as an adopted person to the aftermath of the contact and reunion experience. Finally, the adoptive parents shared their views, feelings and thoughts about raising the adopted child and the impact on themselves and the adopted person of the search, contact and reunion. Besides eliciting and recording each group's separate experiences, it was also possible to contrast them in matched dyads and triads. A key focal point was a study of the outcomes of what Hill (1991, p. 21) described as:

> ... the shift in adoption paradigm from previous ideas based on secrecy and unitary identity to one embodying greater honesty and recognition of the continuing duality of adoptive parenthood and identity. That double nature occurs whenever genetic and social parenthood are partially or wholly separated, whether through adoption, assisted reproduction techniques, divorce or widowhood.

Previous studies have looked at some of these issues from the perspective of a particular group but rarely from that of all three. Furthermore, no study known to us has included sizeable samples of people in the same adoption triad. In addition, this study has included both mothers who were sought by their sons and daughters and those who sought their child. Like the preceding study (Howe and Feast, 2000), this one too covered searching and non-searching adopted people, but the sample of those not searching was small. As a result, levels of significance referring to them were only quoted when these were robust and where there was descriptive material to support them. To summarise, the main sample consisted of:

- 93 birth mothers, of whom 61 were sought and 32 were searchers;
- 126 adopted people, of whom 104 were searchers and 22 non-searchers;
- 93 adoptive parents, 77 of whose children were searchers and 16 sought.

Included within the sample were:

- 78 birth mother dyads (adopted person, birth mother);
- 86 adoptive parent dyads (adopted person, adoptive parent(s);
- 38 triads (adopted person, adoptive parent(s) and birth mother).

The study elicited both retrospective and more recent experiences and took a longitudinal perspective that allowed for contrasts to be made before, between and after experiences. Retrospective and self-reporting accounts are inevitably, perhaps, influenced and coloured by time and the changing social context, but by asking a number of related questions it was possible to look at the data from different angles. As far as the more recent events were concerned, that is since the search began and the subsequent reunions, the fact that the sample had included many who were related, i.e. birth mother, adopted people and adoptive parent(s), offered additional safeguards through cross-checking. As has been shown in earlier chapters, considerable congruence was found, especially within the dyads of birth mothers and adopted adults and of adoptive parents and adopted adults. Overall, significant agreements were found between the groups on a range of variables, but also some important differences such as between birth mothers and adopted people, adopted people and adoptive parents, searchers and non-searchers or males and females. Fewer contrasts were possible within the triads because many of their experiences as triads were not exactly comparable. In addition, the views of a small and rather unrepresentative sample of birth fathers have been included.

Birth mothers and adoption

Policy and practice in the UK, and in many other western countries, have come a long way since the opening of the birth records to adopted people after the mid-1970s. Leaving aside the compelling moral arguments for doing so, what mostly persuaded legislators then to open the sealed records was research-based evidence demonstrating the value and benefits of such a step to adopted people. Since the original study, *In Search of Origins* (Triseliotis, 1973), which contributed to the opening of the records, there have been over a hundred other studies in the UK and elsewhere reaching broadly similar conclusions and confirming the positive impact of the opening of the records on adopted people's lives. The new studies also provided further insights on the search and reunion process and outcome. What has held back equivalent provision for access to birth relatives, mainly parents, has been the absence of similar studies, identifying what benefits such a step might bring to them without causing undue distress or harm to either the adopted person or their family. In spite of this limitation, changes have been made in the recent past, culminating in the provisions of the Adoption and Children Act 2002, which were discussed in Chapter 1.[11] Provisional findings from this study contributed to the debate at the time.

Research available on birth mothers until recently was mostly of a qualitative type which, even though valuable, lacked proper sampling approaches (see Chapter 2).[12] Their main weakness was a reliance on samples of birth mothers who had mainly approached an agency, were self-selected or who had been recruited through the media. Although the reported experiences of these mothers were real to them, this study has shown that they were not representative of the experiences, attitudes and outlook of all mothers, i.e. those who had not approached agencies and had not sought the adopted person. The differences found between searching and sought birth mothers were equivalent to those identified by the first part of the study in respect of searching and non-searching adopted people (Howe and Feast, 2000). It must be remembered that we still do not know the perspectives of those birth parents who refused contact altogether when approached directly by or on behalf of the adopted person.

In this study the views, thoughts and feelings of birth mothers were sought in respect of four different stages of their lives that were linked to the adoption decision and its aftermath. It covered the pregnancy, the child's birth and the parting, from parting to the stage of being sought or starting to search, and finally from contact up to an average of eight years later.

From the pregnancy to the parting with the child

The amount of shame, stigma and secrecy that surrounded non-marital births for some decades up to about the late 1960s is now history, but most of those mothers who suffered from the exclusion,

---

[11]   Referring to Triseliotis, Feast and Kyle (2005).
[12]   As Above.

condemnation and pressures are still around, trying to come to terms with the adoption decision and the way it has impacted on them and their child. It would be too easy to condemn the birth mothers' parents for the way they reacted, including the withholding, by the majority, of emotional and practical support and the eventual pressure on their daughters to part with their children. They, too, were largely both the products and perhaps the victims of the same prevailing ethos and harsh moral code of the period. Similarly, the social and institutional structures of the period had almost no place for women giving birth to a child outside of marriage. Adoption was seen as freeing the child born outside wedlock from the stigma, and as Howe *et al* (1992) point out, it was the women who bore its negative effects. The high proportion of women who said that their self-esteem had been affected (40%) confirms Goffman's (1969) studies suggesting that 'a spoiled identity' usually develops from the receipt of consistently negative messages from those around us.

Mander (1995) interviewed birth mothers, mainly from a medical perspective, and reported that the attitudes of various professionals with whom the mothers had contact did not differ much from the censorious views of many parents. She added that the feelings and thoughts that dominated the lives of many mothers in her study were shame, isolation, lack of control and guilt (see also Winkler and van Keppel, 1984; Bouchier *et al*, 1991; Howe *et al*, 1992; Modell, 1994). What was found from the present study was that resistance to pressures to have the child adopted required strong personal resources and sufficient external emotional and practical support, which were mostly unavailable to many birth mothers who found themselves largely isolated. Not being able to make decisions based on choice increased their sense of frustration and powerlessness, even though they hardly expressed any anger about what happened to them. Birth mothers who said that the adoption decision was largely theirs were less likely to report either poor mental health or be searchers. The same mothers also said that they felt more 'vindicated' in their decision after seeing how well their child had been brought up and how well he or she had done as a result. It could be argued that, under the prevailing conditions of the period, far from these mothers being "selfish" for parting with their child, they were probably well adjusted because they could anticipate the difficulties ahead. A father or mother who surrenders his or her child today would possibly feel, or be made to feel, more guilt because of the different social conditions.

Apart from the actual parting with the child, what pained most of these mothers was the pretence on the part of their families that nothing had happened, rather than recognising a major loss equivalent to bereavement, and therefore having to keep their sorrow private without being able to grieve more openly for the loss of their child. Witney (2004) quotes Sprang and McNeil (1995) as saying that 'normal grief is sanctioned by society but stigmatised grief is disenfranchised, isolates the bereaved and denies them expression. Their sorrow remains hidden and unrecognised' (p. 56). Friends and siblings, especially friends, proved at the time to be the most support-ive, possibly because they were of a new generation and more ready to look at things differently. Even during these early stages, significant differences were found between sought and searcher birth mothers, with the latter having had more censorious parents who were more prepared to withhold their support from their daughter and also pressurise her towards adoption. Because of the mainly censorious attitudes towards the pregnancy, there were hardly any accounts of mothers enjoying it.

Although only around one out of five of the relationships with the child's father were described as 'casual', after the pregnancy or the child's birth, three-quarters of the relationships came to an end. Mothers and fathers decided in about equal proportions to terminate the relationship and in the rest it was a mutual decision. Based on the mothers' accounts, some birth fathers panicked and disappeared from their lives. The low level of support provided by birth fathers largely mirrored that of the mothers' parents, and it was well below that provided by siblings and especially friends. However, as we found from the few fathers we recruited, many were themselves young and inexperienced, and felt as confused as the mothers. In contrast to the negative perception of the child born outside marriage in western-type societies in the recent past, Washington (1982) wrote that African cultural mores valued any infant as being of fundamental importance for the community. 'In this context', he wrote:

> ... *procreative activities which insured the survival of the group were held in high regard and those couples who conceived offspring as a result of the valued sexual liaisons were able to claim increased status and prestige in the community.* (p. 298)

Unsurprisingly, perhaps, many mothers referred with some envy to current conditions that offer far more choices to single parents but little anger was expressed about what happened to them then. We can only speculate that any anger may have been turned inwards in the form of guilt about parting with their child in a society that valued the bearing and rearing of children, albeit within marriage. It is also possible that, because the study took place some eight years after contact had been established, any harboured anger had given way to the satisfaction derived from the mostly positive outcomes of the contact and reunion experience. Since the 1950s and 1960s, when most of these mothers had parted with their children, there has been a revolution in public attitudes and a decisive shift away from strict codes of sexual behaviour towards freer expressiveness and to different types of relationships and partnerships. The emphasis has shifted from fidelity to the quality of relationships and self-fulfilment. The shame and guilt usually experienced by those who failed in the past to observe the sexual moral code have little or no place in a post-modernist western society. More than a third of children are now born within partnerships, not marriage, and single mothers head a high proportion of households with children. Introducing a series of articles on the family in the 21st century, Roseneil and Budgeon (2004) observed:

> *At the start of the 21st century, 'the family' is a sociological concept under severe strain. Processes of individualisation are rendering the romantic dyad and the modern family formation it has supported increasingly unstable, and the normative grip of the gender and sexual order that has underpinned the modern family is ever weakening. As a result more and more people are spending longer periods of their lives outside the conventional family unit.*

Later, in the same journal, the authors make the point that 'the hetero-sexual couple, and particularly the married, co-resident heterosexual couple with children, no longer occupy the centre-ground of western societies and cannot be taken for granted as the basic unit society' (Roseneil and Budgeon, 2004, p. 140). The apparent current emphasis on individual expression and choice were not available to many mothers expecting a non-marital child at the time. It is also a far cry from the predominant theoretical explanation of 30 to 40 years ago, which came from psychoanalysis, that mothers giving birth to a non-marital child suffered mostly from psychopathology, with the pregnancy being the acting out of conflict and unmet need within the mother (e.g. Young, 1954).

The years before contact

If the pregnancy and parting were difficult and upsetting stages, the majority of mothers experienced the period between the parting and the search as equally distressing and sad, with the loss weighing heavy on their minds. Although distressed, the majority still enjoyed good emotional health. For 40 per cent of them, the dominant effect of the parting during this stage was the sense of loss, with its accompanying sadness and depression. Professional writings discussed by Brodzinksy (1990, p. 309) are in agreement with the idea that, when given the opportunity to grieve openly and fully in a supportive environment, human beings will experience a reasonably satisfactory resolution to their feelings about loss. Parkes (1975), too, noted that a satisfactory resolution assumed the availability of opportunities to mourn and grieve with the support of others. The importance of support was further highlighted by Brown and Harris (1978), whose study showed that women who had a confidante as a form of support were less likely to develop depression. Grief theory also suggests a range of different stages which those who experience loss, such as death, normally go through: from initial denial or isolation, to confusion or anger, bargaining, depression and acceptance (Kubler-Ross, 1970). Others have noted that the realisation of the magnitude of the loss can lead to the onset of "despair" and depression (Bowlby, 1980; Parkes, 1975). Although some mothers in this study likened the loss of their child to bereavement, one difference was that they could not share their grief because those around them mostly failed to acknowledge the loss. Equally, the view of professionals then was that the parting with the child was an altruistic activity on the part of the mother, who could see that it was for the good of her child. Such attitudes could again have inhibited mourning for the child. For example, Mander (1995, p. 191) noted from her study that the way the various professionals communicated with the mother limited her scope for expressing her grief.

For many of the rest in this study, as several described it, it was a 'limbo' period because the child was neither dead nor had they contact with him or her. Above all, what many of them found was that they could not forget or "block off" what had happened and a persistent, and for some unrelenting, thought was wondering whether their child was well, had a happy life and would like to meet them one day. Reporting on the same theme, Fravel *et al* (2000) explained the "not forgetting" by saying that although the child is physically absent from the birth mother's life, he or she remains psychologically present in her mind. Others have pointed out that the possibility of the reappearance of the "relinquished one" serves to impede, by delaying or prolonging the mother's grief (Mander, 1995). This study found that it was different for those mothers who said that it had been their own decision to part with their child. They mostly reported being able to get on with their lives, believing that they had done the right thing and adding that they had few regrets and were not consumed by guilt.

Besides feelings of loss and grief, 79 per cent of mothers in this study reported guilt as one of a number of lasting impacts arising from the parting decision; almost a fifth (17%) reported it as the main impact. The guilt arose mainly from the realisation that, irrespective of the circumstances, they had rejected their child. Although no mother reported low self-esteem as a main impact arising from the adoption decision, 40 per cent quoted it as one of a number. Lewis (1971) has suggested that parents who cannot keep their infants have a sense of worthlessness and much guilt. The anxiety arising also from the pressure and felt need to keep both the birth and the adoption secret impacted equally heavily on many mothers, with almost a fifth (19%) reporting it as a main impact and 64 per cent as one of a number. The fact that many still felt they could not talk about it increased both their sense of isolation and the anxiety of being found out. In fact, half of them had not told their other children or husbands/partners about the adoption until shortly before or after contact was established. As some explained, they were caught between the desire to have news of their child, and perhaps meet one day, and apprehension that the secret would come out and, perhaps, shock their new family. Telling and explaining to their other children appeared to cause a greater sense of guilt than telling husbands and partners. Except for a small number, for the majority it was a relief to find that, when told, their new family's response was on the whole understanding and far from condemnatory. Difficulties did arise, however, especially for sought mothers, but in the end they had no regrets, they said, because of the relief at having shed the secret and shared the feelings associated with it.

During the same period, i.e. between the parting with the child and contact, almost all mothers (98%) said that one of their thoughts was about whether their child was well and happy. Their main wish was to know what had happened to their son or daughter. Over half (52%) singled this out as their main preoccupation. The main coping mechanism most mothers developed was holding on to the belief that the child went to a "good" home as promised by the adoption agency. Having news of the child could have gone further, some said, to alleviate doubts about the parting, and the anxiety and guilt they felt. Compared to sought mothers, searcher ones were more likely to report being more anxious and worried about their child. Significantly, more of them also reported poorer physical and mental health, lower self-esteem, taking more alcohol and attributing all this to the adoption. However, there was no significant association between being pressurised to consent to the adoption and being a searching mother.

Other studies have also suggested a relationship between parting with a child for adoption and impairment in psychological functioning, but there is no agreement about its extent (see Rynearson, 1982; Winkler and van Keppel, 1984; Bouchier et al, 1991; Logan, 1996). Only a tiny number of birth mothers in this study reported having been diagnosed with a mental health problem before the adoption (three out of 93). However, almost a quarter reported having been diagnosed with such problems, mostly for depression, between the parting with the child and contact, and almost all were from the searcher group of mothers. It cannot, of course, be inferred with certainty that the poorer mental health reported could be attributed to the loss of the child, because other factors may have intervened. Poor mental health, however, was less likely to be reported by mothers who said that adoption had been their personal choice. Previous studies that found significantly higher levels of mental health problems among birth mothers had relied heavily on mothers who took the initiative to enquire or search, were self-selected or were recruited through the media (see Winkler and van Keppel, 1984; Bouchier *et al*, 1991; Modell, 1994; Logan, 1996). By including both searching and non-searching mothers in this study, it was possible to obtain a more balanced view about the mental health of both. With the exception of searcher mothers, half of whom had been diagnosed at some point with poor mental health, birth mothers, on the whole, were not found to be significantly different from the average in the population before contact took place. Although parting was experienced as a sad and guilt-ridden experience by many mothers, and significantly more so by those who later set out to seek their child, the great majority were able to get on with their lives and with their new families, although many said that what had happened had changed them for life and left its scars. Overall, searcher mothers had been affected more severely by the loss of the child and possibly felt the need to repair the loss more than non-searchers. Lazarus and Folkman (quoted by Brodzinsky, 1990 p. 306) have suggested that adaptational outcomes in response to a stressful situation are the result of an interaction between the individual's perception of the event, their repertoire of coping behaviours, personality characteristics, and the social realities which surround the situation. The combination of family, institutional and social disapproval experienced by these mothers from pregnancy to confinement and beyond, and the lack of choice for most, could also have led to learned or imposed helplessness described by some writers such as Seligman (1975).

Being sought or seeking

The great majority of birth mothers were both excited and elated at the news that their son or daughter was trying to establish contact with them. The study, however, from the outset had not included mothers who might have rejected any form of contact. Of those who initially responded and featured in the study, there was no evidence that most of them were inconvenienced, except for a handful of sought mothers who were annoyed or angry that control had been taken out of their hands and their privacy "invaded". These were mostly mothers who had made a conscious decision from the start that adoption was the right thing to do. However, following an average of eight years after contact was established, hardly any birth mother regretted the event. Although a minority of sought mothers had previously initiated unsuccessful searches themselves, the majority had held back, feeling they had no right to do so, afraid that their sons or daughters might reject them or that they might upset the adoptive family. Searcher mothers entertained similar concerns but eventually their strong desire to establish contact overcame their other considerations.

The dominant expectation had to do with the wish to find out whether their sons and daughters were well and had a good adoption. Searcher mothers were more likely to express heightened fears of their child not having been happy, whereas sought ones were more concerned with whether they would get on with their son or daughter and be liked by them. This was followed by a kind of expiating wish, that is, to explain why the adoption had occurred and tell them how much they loved them and that they were not forgotten or rejected. Knowing that their child was well and had a good adoption, along with being able to explain to them why the parting had happened appeared to do away with some of the guilt arising from it. Although forming a relationship was part of their expectations, it did not hold centre stage before contact took place, but searcher mothers stressed it more than sought ones. For both groups of sought and searcher mothers, the excitement and pleasure of seeing their sons and daughters was also tempered by considerable anxiety, worry, and sometimes fear, that they might hear that he or she did not have a good adoption, that they might be blamed for the parting or that their son or daughter might not like them. A minority were worried about how a husband or their other children might react, because some of them did not know about the adoption. These fears largely did not materialise.

Contact and its outcome

Although not consciously planned by many, it was not unusual for the two phases of searching and contact to become part of the same process. For that reason, searching and contact became at times inextricably mixed. In the end, some form of contact was nearly always established and in the majority of cases sustained. Contact and reunion stood the test of time over an average of eight years, even though almost a third of mothers did not currently have face-to-face contact. Searcher mothers were more likely to lose contact at the initiative of the adopted person, who tended to find faults of incompatibility or make reference to the birth mother's emotional state or her making too many demands. Losing contact was disappointing and painful, but many of these mothers took the view that they had already gained a lot and been relieved of much of the guilt by having the opportunity to explain. However, even most of those who lost contact still felt the value of the experience and had no regrets. For the majority, contact continued to take place at least once every three to four months, but again more frequently for sought than searcher mothers. While sought mothers were likely to cite distance as the main obstacle, searchers were more likely to report that the adopted person was not always too keen to see them.

Looking at the overall picture, almost all birth mothers said that they were pleased that their sons and daughters had established contact or that they had searched for them, and 94 per cent added that the experience was positive. Only eight per cent reported that their expectations of contact had not been met, mostly among searchers, but no birth mother said she wished that she had not met her son or daughter. Those who had reported experiencing intense feelings of loss between the adoption and contact appeared to benefit most from contact and reunion. Other key benefits identified for themselves included:

No more:

- guilt (79%);
- sadness or grief (79%);
- confused feelings about their son or daughter (69%).

Improved:

- emotional outlook (60%);
- self-esteem (45%);

And:

- an enhanced life (64%);
- changed for the better (70%).

One of the less expected benefits, seldom openly declared as a main expectation prior to contact, was the establishment of new and durable relationships between birth mothers and their sons or daughters, frequently also involving other members of the family such as half-siblings and grandparents. On the whole, birth mothers looked at what they got out of contact without dwelling too much on experiences of rejection or of reduced contact. As will be seen later, they retained this outlook on other matters relating to the contact and reunion, tending, at times, to exaggerate the positives. A handful of mothers also expressed guilt arising from the contact and reunion experience, saying that they could not respond to their adopted son or daughter with the same love they felt for their other children. There were also a few who admitted to feeling 'envious' and 'jealous' of the adoptive parents for having watched their child grow up, something that they had missed and which was irreplaceable. However, when one looks at their responses, almost all birth mothers were contented and happy with what they got out of contact. Even when disappointed by not having face-to-face contact or only infrequent contact, they felt that having had news of their sons and daughters was a kind of bonus. Where a relationship was established, it was 'the icing on the cake' as one of them put it. Because of such acceptance, it might be suggested that these mothers did not, perhaps, feel that they deserved better and that contact was an expiation experience, especially as so little anger was shown against the conditions of the period that led to the adoption of the child. Their ready acceptance could be interpreted as a kind of apology to their sons and daughters.

On the more objective General Health Questionnaire (GHQ) score, which measured current emotional health, birth mothers came out well. The finding of no unusually high levels of emotional problems among all birth mothers, and of no significant differences between searchers and sought some eight years after contact, could suggest the positive impact of contact on all birth mothers but more so on searchers. This is in contrast to the mental health problems reported by almost a quarter of birth mothers, mostly searchers, which developed between the parting and contact. We could not, of course, be certain that other factors did not intervene in the lives of these mothers, who currently appeared to function no differently from the rest of the population.

Finally, a progression was identified for birth mothers from high levels of distress, grief and isolation from the pregnancy to the parting, to worry, fear and guilt during the period between the parting and contact, to little evidence being found for the continued presence or continued intensity of these feelings and thoughts after contact was established. It is a matter of conjecture whether, if they had been involved from the start in open forms of adoption, much of the pain and distress would have been avoided. For that we have to wait for the eventual publication of longitudinal studies in the USA (see Grotevant and McRoy, 1998 for an early account). However, for a minority of mothers, ranging from 10 to 20 per cent of cases, some of these feelings and thoughts persisted, mainly among the searchers group. Some of these mothers reported that, irrespective of the happy outcome, they still felt guilt for having given their child away. As one of them said:

The feeling of guilt never left me and probably never will, but I separate it from all the love I have had since we found each other.

Overall, for almost nine out of 10 birth mothers (89%), contact and reunion were said to have been a happy and satisfying experience. The rest either felt disappointed, wanted more contact, or said that they found it hard to cope with the intensity of their feelings aroused by contact. Half of these were unhappy with contact, dissatisfied with the relationship with their sons or daughters, wanted more contact, found it hard to cope with the intensity of the feelings it aroused, and were not satisfied with the overall outcome. We have no explanation for why this small group came to feel like this, neither were they pre-dominantly from the group of searchers. The small numbers did not allow for tests of significance to be conducted. Others have also reported that birth mothers who had contact with the adoptive family and the child, either ongoing, partly or fully disclosed, showed better resolution of their feelings than did mothers who never had such contact or had less open contact (Dominick, 1988; van Keppel, 1991; Cushman *et al*, 1997; Grotevant, 2000; Neil, 2000). In the birth mothers' view, contact was more likely to continue if it felt comfort-able; if there was compatibility or they had a lot in common; if there was depth in the emotional connection; if the son or daughter showed that they were glad to meet the parent; if the birth parent was sensitive to their son or daughter's feelings; or if the birth parent was not making too many demands.

Birth fathers

The accounts of the small number of birth fathers who featured in the study suggested hardly any differences from those of birth mothers. Although the possibly biased nature of such a small sample is recog-nised, nevertheless they confirmed that their experiences, feelings and thoughts over the years, their reaction when told that their sons and daughters were seeking them, and the subsequent contact and relationships had many similarities with those reported by birth mothers. Compared to the latter, however, birth fathers hardly reported poor mental health during the period from the parting to contact, but this could be because 14 of the 15 fathers had been sought by their sons and daughters. Recent accounts of birth fathers make no reference to their emotional or mental health (Clapton, 2003; Witney, 2004). In the case of birth mothers, it was those searching for their sons and daughters who mostly reported much of the poor mental health during that period. Like the birth mothers, the great majority of these birth fathers reported that contact, and the subsequent relationships that developed with their sons and daughters, helped them to cope better and come to terms with their feelings about the adoption. Most of them were very positive or positive and satisfied about the outcome. Furthermore, and again like birth mothers, they said that contact enhanced their outlook and changed them for the better; almost half said their self-esteem had improved and with one exception, the rest reported they were very glad they had been sought out. There was no evidence that the emotional health of these fathers had been damaged as a result of their loss and, on the more objective GHQ test, they came across as an emotionally well-balanced group. But again they may not have been representative of all birth fathers.

Overall, the birth fathers' descriptions of the type of relationship they had developed with the adopted person did not differ significantly from those developed by birth mothers. In the majority of cases, their sons and daughters agreed with these perceptions but in a minority of cases there were differences, such as whether the relationship was like that with a parent or friend. Occasionally, birth fathers tended to see more in the relationship than the adopted person did.

Growing up adopted

It was pointed out at the start that it was not the intention to repeat the first part of the study, which was published in 2000, but mainly to reflect on the adopted person's past and current experiences and circumstances in the light of those of their birth mothers and adoptive parents, and to address areas that had not been explored in the same detail before. However, a number of overlaps were inevitable. In their book, Brodzinsky *et al* (1992) acknowledge that being adopted is something that colours a person's relationship with his or her adoptive parents, his or her emergent sense of self, and the intimate relationships he or she forges for the rest of their life. 'If you are adopted', they add, 'you will think about that fact of your life now and again – maybe when a question arises about your genetic background, maybe when you encounter a particularly rough spot in your life, maybe every single day' (p. 1). To aid adoptive parenting, they set out in their book a model of 'normal adjustment to being adopted as it occurs throughout the life span'. The first part of this study (Howe and Feast, 2000) showed that the majority of adopted people who had searched or been sought, had adjusted well to their adoptive status and the search and reunion experience had benefited them significantly in a number of ways, but mostly in terms of genealogy and identity.

In this study, around 80 per cent of adopted people said that they felt happy about being adopted, felt loved by their parents and had developed a sense of belonging. A broadly similar proportion reported having developed very close or close relationships with their adoptive parents during childhood. There were no differences in reported closeness between mother and father. Although this was a retrospective reporting, closeness fell sharply during adolescence and it partly recovered by adulthood, but it never reached the closeness achieved during early childhood. Some eight years after contact, closeness stood at around 70 per cent. Those who were either feeling not close or distant were around one in seven, while the rest fell in between. The fall during adolescence, and the fact that it never regained the childhood levels later, may not be surprising. Adulthood implies a move to greater independence and a loosening of attachments from familiar figures and the seeking of relationships and intimacy outside the parental home. However, as this study has found, almost everyone kept the links with their adoptive family. The closer adopted people felt to their parents, the more openly was their adoption discussed within the family, the happier they felt about being adopted, the more they felt they belonged, the higher their self-esteem as found on a standardised scale and the better their emotional health as scored on the GHQ. Although closeness was not significantly affected by the presence of biological children within the adoptive family, significantly more of those brought up in such families said that they came to feel 'different'. Overall, the findings suggested that self-esteem and emotional health were related to the quality of the adoptive relationship.

Two feelings and thoughts that had dominated much of the lives of half the adopted people were those of rejection and loss experienced in relation to the parting from their birth family. Some experienced these feelings very strongly. Most of those who felt rejected were broadly the same as those who felt the sense of loss. For the adopted person, as Brodzinsky *et al* (1992) put it, 'the experience of loss is usually felt in the context of the search for self' (p. 12). In their view, for early placed children, the sense of loss is not consciously experienced until the age of five or so. In this study, the presence of strong feelings of rejection and loss increased also the motivation to search. Searchers were more likely than non-searchers to report such feelings. These feelings appeared to act as a strong motivating force for the search and wanting especially to find out 'why put up for adoption', and indirectly whether wanted or not. Why only half of them, though, came to feel the sense of rejection and loss is possibly explained by the findings suggesting that the closer their reported relationship to the adoptive parents, the less likely they were to have experienced these feelings and thoughts. As many of them explained, 'it was the love of my parents that did it' (meaning adoptive parents), suggesting again that close relationships and feeling loved by a parent acted as a protective shield against the development of such feelings. However, where they persisted, it was contact this time that was reported as having helped to extinguish or lessen their impact. As an example, 55 per cent of those who had felt rejected reported that any feelings of rejection disappeared after contact and 68 per cent said the same about feelings of loss. Those who reported the disappearance or lessening of feelings of rejection and loss were also more likely to report closer relationships to their adoptive parents. These findings raise again the question of whether more open forms of adoption from the start could have prevented such feelings from developing in the first place. For example, one writer maintains that, when a disruption such as this occurs in the biological link, the emotions associated with the break remain buried pending a reunion with the birth mother (Robinson, 2004). In this writer's view, both birth mothers and adopted people need to address their feelings of loss and grief through counselling. However, as this study found, such feelings are not inevitable nor are they experienced with the same intensity. As shown earlier, other factors appear to mediate, leading to the absence, decrease or increase of such feelings.

The search and contact

The wish to search and make contact with birth relatives appears to be heightened from adolescence onwards and the majority of those searching in Britain are women with an average age of around 30. There is no shortage of studies and writings explaining why adopted people search and what they expect from it. There is agreement that much of the search is for genealogical connectedness having mainly to do with establishing roots and identity. It could also be part of the move to independence and the search for new intimacies without necessarily discarding old ones. Some writers refer also to the search as the wish 'to undo the trauma of separation' (Andersen, 1988, p. 19) and/or for an explanation of why the 'rejection' or 'loss' (Triseliotis, 1973; Weiss, 1988). Not surprisingly, perhaps, adopted people in our study who took the initiative to search were more likely than non-searchers to have felt rejection and loss in relation to their birth family. Other expectations had to do with physical appearance and the recognition of oneself in others, or to find out about the circumstances and well-being of members of the birth family.

In this study, and as with birth mothers, a face-to-face meeting with a birth relative was usually viewed as desirable, but the possibility of a relationship did not initially appear as central to the search. It mostly evolved over a period of time and after the parties came to know each other. Along with excitement about the prospect of meeting a birth parent or relative, there was also uncertainty, nervousness and the fear of hurting or of being hurt. Uncertainty was mainly to do with what they might find, nervousness was to do with how to handle a face-to-face meeting in particular, and the fear was to do with hurting their adoptive parents, their birth relative or themselves. After an average of eight years following contact, eight out of 10 were still in some form of direct or indirect contact, with around 70 per cent having face-to-face contact. The frequency of contact varied a lot, but most typical was a few times a year. Two-thirds of those in contact also described close to very close relationships with their birth mother, thus only slightly lower compared to current relationships with their adoptive parents. For around 25 to 30 per cent, direct contact had ceased at the initiative of the adopted person or the parent/relative. Who rejected whom was not always easy to establish, but the most common explanations were incompatible interests, the birth mother's alleged problems and rejection by a birth parent. Many of the relationships described appeared strong and rewarding, but they mainly acted as an extension, rather than a substitute, for other relationships such as with the adoptive parents. Around a third had established contact with a birth father, three-quarters with at least one sibling and almost half with a grandparent. Although these relationships were fluid and their strength variable, finding a half-brother, half-sister or grandparent gave great pleasure to many adopted people.

Around half of adopted people featuring in the study identified many benefits from the search and contact and almost a similar proportion identified some; only five per cent said they derived no benefit at all from contact. The benefits were similar to those identified by previous studies, such as that of Howe and Feast (2000). These mainly included receiving background information, finding answers to many questions such as knowing 'why they were given up', 'physical recognition', 'knowing their birth relatives were mostly well', 'developing new relationships' and much practical information such as about medical history. Much of this, they reported, improved their sense of identity and of who they were; they came to feel more secure and more complete; they achieved higher levels of self-esteem and of emotional functioning; and their feelings of loss and rejection decreased or disappeared. There was also considerable relief in finding that the birth parent was well. A psychoanalytic explanation could be that the relief was from finding that their anger over the adoption had not damaged the birth parent.

All these benefits were more likely to be reported by those who had declared close relationships with their adoptive parents and an equally close one with the birth mother. It looked as if the good start given to

them within the adoptive family was an important factor that contributed to these outcomes, but we cannot be certain. There were
indications that non-searchers were more likely to report benefits
than those who searched, but many of those who searched also
reported many benefits. Contact having been terminated by the
adopted person or the birth mother did not mean that there were no
rewards or gains. Around eight out of 10 were glad they had searched
or had been contacted and a similar proportion felt that their original
expectations had been well or very well met. Overall, and though it is
recognised that other factors may have intervened, there were indications that a close relationship with the adoptive parents, including
feeling loved and developing a sense of belonging, acted as protective
factors and also impacted positively on other areas of the adopted
adults' life, including on the contact and reunion experience. Although
not exactly comparable, a study of children in adoptive families that
included birth children found that greater mutuality (closeness)
between mother and child was associated with lower levels of child
behaviour problems. The authors concluded that mother–child
mutuality is child specific within families and that there was no
evidence of passive gene-environment correlation, suggesting that the
link between lower levels of mutuality and higher levels of child
behaviour problems is not only reflecting overlapping genetic
influences on parent and child behaviour (Deater-Deckard and Petrill,
2004).

A consistent proportion of between 10 to 20 per cent of adopted
people, found more among searchers than non-searchers, reported
that feelings of rejection and loss persisted and that being adopted had
affected their marriage, well-being, education, career and relationships.
Broadly, the same group reported lower self-esteem and poorer
emotional health and they were also less likely to be satisfied with the
outcome of contact, saying that their expectations of contact had not
been met. For this group, it was hard to separate that which related to
the adoption from other factors in their lives. There were indications
that non-searchers were less likely to report such feelings. However,
there was no significant overlap between this small group of adopted

people and a similar proportion of birth mothers, who felt equally dissatisfied over a number of issues concerning the outcome. A lower proportion of seven per cent of adopted people had both low self-esteem and poor emotional health as scored on more standardised tests. The same group was also more likely to give negative answers to outcome questions about being adopted or about the contact and reunion experience. For example, adopted people who entertained strong feelings of rejection and loss were more likely to rate the contact and reunion experience as less positive.

Although numbers of those from a black or minority ethnic background were small, their comments suggested that the main experience that stood out for many of them was the racism they had experienced, mostly at school, their awareness that they were different, not fitting in with those around them or of not being fully accepted by members of their wider adoptive family. This was also confirmed by the first study, which covered a larger sample (Howe and Feast, 2000). Ethnicity and "race" issues appeared to matter to this group and the few who moved within a more ethnically diverse environment were more positive. Although there are no easy answers, inevitably the tension between the need to provide for the cultural and racial identity of children and also provide a secure social base in their lives can only be met if a sufficient number of matching and suitable placements can be found. Failing that, an ethnically diverse environment, good preparation and ongoing support could go some way to make up for other shortcomings (see also McRoy *et al*, 1984).

Like earlier studies, the majority of adopted people responding to this and the first part of the study (Howe and Feast, 2000) reported on how identity-enhancing they found the reunion, including the information gained through it and the relationships established. There was also evidence that the contact and reunion were experienced as even more positive by those who were already feeling well settled. The accounts from adopted people suggested that aspects of the new information gained, including answers to the central questions 'Why?' and 'Who am I?', appeared to be integrated with other aspects of the adopted person's identity to contribute towards a more whole self. In other words, the biological heritage and psychosocial rearing were blended in a kind of duality that left the majority of adopted people satisfied. Although the circumstances are not exactly similar, Tizard and Phoenix (1993) reported from their study that children of dual heritage and ethnicity raised by their families appeared to successfully integrate in themselves both aspects of their background. Yet post-modernist language would suggest that "identity" is a dated concept with "diminishing" returns. On the whole, post-modernism questions the authenticity and desirability of fused, unitary identities. On the other hand, Giddens (1992, p. 53), writing not long ago, captured the importance of continuity in life by saying that 'it is the reflexively understood by the person in terms of her or his biography. Identity here still presumes continuity across time and space; to be a "person" is not just to be a reflexive actor, but to have a concept of a person as applied both to self and others.'

Birth mothers and their sons and daughters

The views and perspectives on the reunion experience of 78 birth mothers were compared and contrasted with those of their sons and daughters. A key purpose for doing so was to establish how congruent their answers were to similar questions, such as their perception of contact and its outcome. The comparisons identified both high levels of congruence and also important differences. Significant differences were again found between searchers and non-searcher birth mothers and searching and non-searching adopted people, confirming that those who take the initiative to search, be it birth parents or adopted people, are perhaps motivated differently from non-searchers.

Birth mothers and adopted people were in agreement on many aspects of the search and reunion process and outcome, including how helpful contact had been to them and giving credit to the other party for making it turn out like that. High percentages of both birth mothers and their sons and daughters were pleased that they had searched or had been contacted, but searcher mothers were signifi-cantly more pleased than the adopted person who had been sought. As said elsewhere, adopted people preferred to be in control of when to search or make contact. Seven out of 10 birth mothers and adopted people also agreed that their relationship was 'close' or 'very close' but the agreement between them as dyads was mainly congruent in cases where contact had been initiated by the adopted person rather than the other way round. Not unexpectedly, perhaps, the physical health of birth mothers was found to be poorer than that of their sons and daughters, who were on average 21 years younger. However, when it came to emotional health, there was no significant difference between mother and offspring. The birth mother's family were said to have reacted significantly more positively to the idea of contact compared to the adopted person's family. However, around one in 10 from each group also reported some strains developing between themselves and their families. A greater number of birth mothers than adopted people, especially searcher mothers, wanted more contact and more closeness. Those who wanted more contact from each group did not often match, i.e. were not from the same pair. On the whole, reunions seemed more lasting when instigated by the adopted person.

Although high percentages from both groups were glad that they had met, adopted people were more likely to wish that they had not, but few recriminations were voiced. When it came to satisfaction with the overall contact and reunion experience, there was again consider-able agreement between the parties about the high level of satisfaction. Adopted people's expectations, especially those of males, were more likely to be met if they had searched, rather than been sought by their birth mothers. There was also a high level of agreement between both that because of contact they could also relate better to other people. A slightly greater number of adopted people than birth parents reported that their self-esteem had improved after contact (55–44%) with sought mothers appearing to have gained more than searcher ones in self-esteem. However, about an equal proportion of birth mothers and adopted people (a third) had found it hard to cope with the intensity of their feelings aroused by contact, but these were not from the same dyads.

The most common description of the relationship given by both mothers and adopted people was that of friendship, with just over a quarter describing it as filial or parental. Many adopted people distinguished between looking for and welcoming a relationship with a birth parent and seeking a parental-type relationship. The latter was mostly reserved for their adopters. Nor did the majority of birth mothers expect a parent–child relationship, with many of them likening the relationship to that with a friend or an aunt. In other words, when it came to "parent", the blood relationship was important but only relative. Broadly similar findings were reported by Kennard (1991), Sachdev (1992) and March (1995). Unlike a number of adopted people, almost no birth mother described the relationship as distant, or thought of herself as a stranger after continuing contact. What the various findings as a whole suggest is that, in spite of high levels of agreements between the two groups on a range of issues, disagreement was more likely between searcher mothers and sought adopted people, especially a small number of males who, on the whole, did not see things the way their birth mothers did; their birth mothers tended to somewhat exaggerate the positives and minimise the negatives. Two factors appeared to bring this about: the adopted adults' apparent desire to be in control of when to search and the greater loyalty displayed, especially by males, to their adoptive families. In spite of wanting more contact and more closeness, it was a characteristic of both sought and searcher mothers to want to fit in with the adopted person and to appear to be more easily satisfied with the frequency and outcome of contact arrangements, as if they did not deserve better.

Being an adoptive parent

The generation of adopters featuring in this study came into adoption at a time when they were urged to treat the adopted child as their own, as if there was no difference between adoptive and biological parent-hood. The secrecy that was almost guaranteed by legislation helped to reinforce this message, leading perhaps to a "denial" of the difference that was highlighted by studies later on. Writing about US law, which is not very different from British law, Modell (1994) said that 'a made relationship, American law claims, can be exactly like a natural relationship: the child is as-if-begotten, the parent as-if-genealogical' (p. 2). Eventually, by initiating searches and establishing contact with birth family members, adopted people came to challenge the non-recognition of the biological connection. Besides offering optimum parenting, adoptive parents are expected also to acknowledge the difference between adoptive and biological parenting (Kirk, 1964). In a later book, Kirk (1981) reinforced this theme by saying that: 'given that the adoptive situation at the interpersonal level is objectively different from the situation of the family based on consanguinity, the solidarity of the adoptive family's membership is enhanced when their atypical reality is acknowledged in their daily relationship' (xv).

Based on his early study, Triseliotis (1973) suggested that the acknowledgement of the genealogical connection and the sharing of background information could help the child to accommodate in his or her developing personality the concept of two families – a biological and a psychosocial one. Couples who happen to be infertile or childless, as the majority of them are, are also expected to mourn and come to terms with any sadness arising from their position. Infertility implies a big loss and although many of those affected apparently cope well without resorting to outside help, for others it may become a continuing preoccupation that could affect the parenting of the adopted child. Brinich (1990) argues that if the adoptive parents 'are to be able to see their adopted child for whom he is, and if the adopted child is to be able to see his adoptive parents for whom they are, they must mourn the loss of their respective fantasised biological child and fantasised biological parents. The lost (fantasised) relationships must be mourned before the new (real, adoptive) relationships can flourish' (p. 47). Mann (1998) gave the example of how few adoptive parents, unlike adopted people (and perhaps birth mothers), have written their accounts and went on to add that 'the shame and guilt that was so much part of the birth mother's experience in earlier studies is now appearing to be transferred to adoptive parents' (p. 50). The pressures and extra tasks would suggest that adoption can be a stressful process, both for the adopted child and the adoptive parents. However, and as far as those adopted as infants are concerned, outcome studies suggest that they hardly differ from the general population, suggesting that the presumed problems of adoptive parenthood are not too challenging (e.g. Bohman, 1970; Brodzinsky, 1990).

Almost all the adopters in this study found the experience of raising the adopted child rewarding and satisfying and were prepared to recommend it to others. They mostly used superlatives to describe the pleasure that adoption had brought to their lives, believing that it was also good for the child. They reported high levels of closeness and attachment between themselves and their adopted son or daughter during different stages, except for adolescence when a significant proportion of relationships became strained. At the same time, a number of them also reported an element of guilt, wondering if they could have done better. Some difficulties did arise, especially for the small group who had adopted a black or mixed heritage child. A number of them became aware, they said, that they could not fully understand or enter the world and experiences of their child and therefore empathise sufficiently with their pain when at the receiving end of racial abuse and discrimination.

With regard to disclosing and talking about adoption, between 10 and 20 per cent of all adopters delayed the telling or sharing of background information. This small minority still expected the child to take the initiative to ask. A broadly similar percentage was found by Craig (1991) who talked to parents who had been especially prepared some 20 years earlier about how to approach this subject. In this study, those parents who said that their child never spoke about their birth family during adolescence were also more likely to score a poorer emotional health on the GHQ. Grotevant and McRoy (1998) reported from their longitudinal study that open styles of communication about adoption were found to produce significantly higher identity scores among adopted adolescents.

The expectation, from some of the literature, that those who adopted to create rather than to expand their family would report lower levels of emotional health was not borne out. The great majority reported that the adoption experience had 'eclipsed' any continuing feelings of disappointment surrounding their infertility. However, a significant minority (21%) reported that these feelings still lingered. The latter were also more likely to report that they felt less close to the child in infancy, early childhood and adolescence. However, no differences in closeness were reported when their sons and daughters became adults or before or after contact or in current relationships.

Access to information and contact with birth relatives

Considering that the message at the time these parents adopted was that there was no difference between adoptive and biological parent-hood, and that they had been reassured about maintaining secrecy, it was perhaps surprising that the majority in this study reported that they had reacted positively to the legislation that provided for the opening of birth records to adopted people and that they were equally supportive of their son or daughter's search and contact. At the same time, a significant minority reported feeling like spectators or as having been sidelined in much of the discussions and arrangements surrounding contact. It was their view that the focus of adoption had shifted to birth parents and to the adopted person, or as one of them put it:

It appears that the rights of the child and the birth mother rub out all the loving care and devotion to the unwanted infant and the adoptive parents are pushed out into the background.

If a greater number of parents felt like this, they did not say so, appearing to want to act in a way that was supportive of the adopted person. There was a general view, however, that they could have been consulted more or perhaps their contribution in raising the adopted person could have been given more recognition. While around three-quarters of them reported that they had supported their sons and daughters' search, and a significant number had welcomed it, at the same time almost half could not help entertaining concerns and fears about their child or themselves being hurt in the process. Around a quarter of them came to learn about the contact only after the event, which hurt, but was explained, or rationalised, as a protective measure on the part of the adopted person. Those parents who knew about the search and contact beforehand were also more likely to look upon it more favourably. Even though most adopters were certain of the strength of their relationship with their sons and daughters, nevertheless, when it came to actual face-to-face meetings with the birth parent(s), some could not avoid wondering whether they might not in the end be rejected. Their certainty wavered progressively as each step taken by the adopted person led to greater involvement with the birth family. The gradual evolution from enquiry to contact and then to the development of relationships began to shake the certainty of many adoptive parents.

As it turned out, most of the fears either about themselves or of the adopted person being hurt in the process did not materialise. In contrast to the earlier fears and anxieties, the majority of parents came to identify many benefits for their sons and daughters, and some for themselves. For the adopted person, they particularly singled out background information, identity enhancement and the establishment of new relationships. It was surprising to find how many articulated identity issues as a key benefit to the adopted person and were very approving of the outcome. A significant proportion also referred with warmth and approval to the new relationships forged by the adopted person. The main benefits of contact they reported for themselves were a better understanding of her or him and, frequently, a strengthening of their relationship. The reported levels of closeness between them and the adopted person before and after contact and reunion with the birth family hardly changed. Almost nine out of 10 reported very close or close relationships both before and after contact. Any criticisms they had about the outcome of contact were mainly about its impact on the adopted person. No adoptive parent had lost contact altogether with the adopted person, with almost nine out of 10 saying that they had some form of direct or indirect contact at least once a week. In fact, our figures suggested that adoptive parents are more frequently in touch with their children than, perhaps, the general population (see McGlone *et al*, 1996).

Those adoptive parents who had met the birth mother and/or other birth relatives were likely to come to view the search and contact more positively than the rest. In addition, they were pleased to have the birth mother's approval about the way they had brought up her child. Overall, eight out of 10 said they were pleased about their sons and daughters' search and contact, even suggesting having benefited more from contact than the birth mother. The very positive evaluation of their relationship with the adopted person, and equally the good approval rates given to the outcome of contact overall, could raise questions about whether they were denying the fears, worries, anxieties, concerns and doubts they went through at the start, either on behalf of the adopted person or of themselves. As an example, in answer to a different question, around a quarter expressed a fair amount of dissatisfaction and concern, believing that their son or daughter was hurt, or had become unhappy or unsettled mainly as a result of rejection, but this was in relation to the adopted person and not themselves. A handful of them stood out from the rest by having rated the contact experience of their sons and daughters as being negative or being unsure about its value altogether. The great majority, however, were relieved that they were still viewed as "parents" by their sons and daughters and that the relationships that had developed with a birth parent were not on the whole of a parental nature.

Adoptive parents and their adopted sons and daughters

As with birth mothers and their sons and daughters, the perspective of 86 pairs of adoptive parents and adopted people were similarly compared and contrasted. The two groups reached high levels of agreement on a range of variables concerning the experience of growing up and with the search and reunion process, but significant differences also emerged. Almost half the adopted people who grew up in families with biological children said that they had been treated differently from birth children, but only 14 per cent of their parents confirmed this. In spite of this, no significant differences were found in terms of closeness to the adoptive parents, being loved, the overall adoptive experience or sense of belonging. One study that reported on children placed for adoption between the ages of five and nine found that those placed in families where there were already biological children tended to do worse on their measures of stability (Quinton *et al*, 1998).

More females than males in the present study disagreed with their parents and came to feel:

- less close to their adoptive parents;
- less happy about being adopted;
- a lesser sense of belonging;
- less positive about the overall experience of adoption;
- less included by the extended family;
- and scored higher emotional problems on the GHQ.

Sachdev (1992) and Pacheco and Eme (1993) too found that females in their studies were more likely to report an unhappy adoption experience and more identity problems. Interestingly, males in this study came to feel less positive in relation to their birth mothers while females felt less positive in relation to their adoption. The males' descriptive accounts confirmed greater loyalty to their adoptive parents and less to their birth mother, while the opposite appeared true in respect of females. We can only speculate whether females attach less well to substitute parents, and have a greater need, perhaps, to experience the birth parent–child relationship.

There were other areas where significant differences emerged between adopted people and their adoptive parents, such as the timing of the disclosure of the adoption, how openly adoption was discussed, and whether the extended family treated them the same. On the other hand, three-quarters of adopted people confirmed their parents' view that they had been supportive and pleased when contact was initiated. This was much more than the 36 per cent reported by Pacheco and Eme (1993) from their US study. Adopted people usually said that they got more out of contact than their parents, but a significantly higher proportion of the parents reported that they too benefited from it. Equally, parents did not agree with their sons and daughters that they were more worried, upset and angry about the contact. Significantly more adopted people did not agree with their parents' view that the contact experience had proved unsettling for them. Almost all adoptive parents described their current relationship with their sons and daughters as 'close' or 'very close', but only around three-quarters of adopted people agreed. Overall, levels of agreement between parents and children in many areas were high, but adoptive parents tended either to somewhat exaggerate their past and current closeness to the adopted person or, in the case of a minority, tended to magnify the negatives of contact. In the eyes of their sons and daughters, they minimised their own upset and worries arising from contact and stressed setbacks arising from their sons and daughters' relationship with a birth relative. Only exceptionally, however, did an adoptive parent criticise the adopted person directly, such as for not telling them beforehand about the contact, or for having acted disloyally or for not seeing more of them.

The adoption triangle

The impact of contact and reunion on each of the three groups has been a matter for speculation over the last 30 or so years following the opening of the records making contact possible. The general view so far has been that adoptive parents get the least out of contact, having been largely sidestepped (Post-Adoption Social Workers Group of New South Wales, 1988; McMillan and Hamilton, 1992; Mann, 1998). The final part of this analysis was to compare the views of adopted people, their birth mothers and adoptive parents in the 38 families where all three perspectives were available. Depending on who was being asked, the great majority of respondents from each group were pleased that the search and contact had taken place, though this ranged from three-quarters of adoptive parents to nearly all birth mothers. When asked if they wished contact had never happened, hardly anyone agreed: none of the birth mothers wished contact had not happened and only four per cent of adopted people and eight per cent of adoptive parents felt this way. When it came to how positive the overall experience had been, the levels were over 90 per cent for birth mothers and adopted people, but only 72 per cent for adoptive parents, confirming again that adoptive parents had more misgivings. Although their sons and daughters did not always share the negatives perceived by their parents, a minority of parents wanted to stress that their concerns arose from 'watching their child suffer', as some of them put it. On the whole, birth mothers did not appear to want to report negatives, expressing the highest levels of satisfaction compared to the other two groups. In the view of many birth mothers, they had already got a lot out of contact, often against all expectations. Relationships that consequently developed were looked upon as a kind of desired, but unexpected, bonus.

Around half of adopted people and birth parents, but only a quarter of adoptive parents, said that their self-esteem had improved as a result of contact. It is not surprising that significantly fewer adoptive parents reported an increase in self-esteem, as the main issue was between the birth mother and the adopted person. Around half of adoptive parents and adopted people, but two-thirds of birth mothers, also reported feeling more relaxed after contact. Our explanation for this is that birth mothers were more fearful, worried and anxious from the start and the mostly positive results reflected a relief. Members of each group who felt strained by the process were unconnected with each other. Possibly the biggest difference found between the three groups was that around three-quarters of adopted people and birth parents said they felt changed after contact, but only 14 per cent of adoptive parents said the same, suggesting again that the emotional stakes were not, perhaps, as high for them. Although most adoptive parents went through a period of doubt and anxiety about the adopted person's continued loyalty, only a few reported having found it difficult to cope with the intensity of the feelings aroused by contact. This contrasted with a third of adopted people and birth parents. Many of the adopters suggested that, although there were anxieties and worries, and sometimes concerns, they felt they could cope. Considering the good emotional health they scored on the GHQ, perhaps this should not come as a surprise.

All three groups emerged well with regard to their current

emotional health. Adoptive parents scored the fewest severe emotional problems and adopted adults the most, but the difference was not significant. There was no congruence between the triads regarding the presence of severe emotional problems. In other words, it could not be said that if adopted people scored high on emotional problems they reflected the emotional health of either their adoptive parents or birth mothers. Compared also to adoptive parents, adopted people and birth mothers were more likely to ascribe any physical or emotional problems to the adoption. None of the three groups came to view contact as fraught with danger, even though, as seen elsewhere, for a minority of between 10 and 20 per cent of birth parents and adopted people, there was also rejection, disappointment and some disillusionment. Each group concentrated predominantly on the benefits they got out of contact rather than the disappointments. For adopted people, the benefits mainly concerned identity enhancement, the knowledge that they had not been rejected and the establishment of new and productive relationships. For birth mothers, it was the satisfaction that their child had a happy adoption and did not harbour anger towards them, thus allowing them to shed their guilt, as well as a relationship that they had hoped for but which was not central in their expectations. Even though between a quarter and a third of adoptive parents continued to have some misgivings, the main positives for them were the knowledge that, on the whole, their adopted sons and daughters were not hurt as they had feared and that they were still high in their children's estimation and love. They also acknowledged that, in a proportion of cases, the relationship between the adopted person and their newly discovered birth family was working well and they were glad for them.

The law, contact and the future of adoption

A broadly similar proportion of all birth mothers, adopted people and adoptive parents knew about the Adoption Contact Register. However, searcher mothers were more likely to know about the Register than non-searcher ones, even though they did not enter their names in greater proportions. Searcher mothers were also less likely to worry about the provision of the Children Act 1975 for access on the part of the adopted person and more likely to support the idea of birth relatives having a right of access to the adopted person. Overall, the majority of these mothers' responses (60%) suggested feeling mainly a lack of entitlement and fear about the reaction of their son or daughter, preferring to leave the initiative to the adopted person. Searcher mothers were also more likely to support the view that there should be no adoption in society. A small number of them were still carrying a fair amount of anger and bitterness about the "loss" of their child and thus wanted to redress the balance by supporting a right of access by birth relatives.

Of adopted people who knew about the Register, significantly more searching than non-searching ones entered their name, but then a greater number of the latter did not know about the Register. The wish of the majority of adopted people to be in control and have the initiative about who contacted them and when to search, found support from around two-thirds of both birth mothers and adoptive parents. Only a handful of adoptive parents wanted to be asked for their permission first.

In view of questions being raised, mostly outside Britain, about the continuation of adoption as an institution in a modern society, it was interesting to note that hardly any adopted person or adoptive parent subscribed to the idea of abolishing it. Almost all adoptive parents were in favour of continued adoption, as were nine out of every 10 adopted people. It would be understandable that the birth mothers, mostly searchers, would support abolition, but in fact over two-thirds supported adoption (73%). Many respondents from each group, including birth mothers, gave graphic examples of why they thought adoption should be preserved. Not only did they think that the alternatives were unattractive, but they claimed that the need for child care of this kind would always exist.

Final comments

What emerged from this study was that before contact all three members of the triangle, more so birth parents and adopted people, shared feelings and troubling thoughts that had mainly to do with loss, rejection, grief, sadness, guilt, fear and worry. Writing over 10 years ago, Jane Rowe (1991, p. 7) made the comment that 'adoption grows out of grief and is never accomplished without pain'. Nothing found in this study would contradict that statement. Despite the additional tasks that both adoptive parents and adopted people had to accomplish, the outcomes found here about the quality of relationships between the two groups do not appear to differ from those in the general population. Furthermore, their almost total endorsement of adoption also gives additional credence to these findings. However, these findings hold true only for adopted people joining their adoptive families when mostly under the age of 18 months and who searched for or were sought by their birth mothers.

The approach for contact and reunion introduced both excitement and anticipation along with new fears, worries and suspicion, mainly about the other party's motives and expectations. At the same time, each party displayed mostly sensitivity and care to avoid hurting or upsetting the other or their respective families. All three parties were aware that the idea of contact was largely an uncharted area with no script to follow, except perhaps for what they had seen on television, read in newspapers or heard on the radio about contact and reunions. At the end, sufficient evidence was found by the study to suggest that contact contributed significantly to greater peace of mind for most members of the triangle. The new reported feelings, which mostly replaced the earlier ones, now included satisfaction and contentment, no more worry or fear, less or no guilt, feeling more relaxed, enhanced self-esteem, better emotional health, and no more or reduced feelings of loss and rejection.

Contact offered birth mothers the opportunity to satisfy themselves that the adopted person was well and mostly happy and to explain why they had been adopted. For the adopted people it was the satisfaction of finding answers to the many questions that had been troubling them for years and the subsequent linking of the information gained to various parts of their identity. New relationships were formed without it being at the expense of existing or parental ones, but relationships with siblings were particularly valued. Although it would appear that contact and reunion benefited mostly birth mothers and adopted people, adoptive parents insisted that they too got a lot out of it, mostly the satisfaction that many of their anticipated fears about the adopted person or themselves being hurt did not materialise. Even more satisfying for them was the knowledge that their sons and daughters' new relationships were not at their own expense. Considering the assumptions under which they adopted, the majority demonstrated remarkable adaptations, such as coming to recognise the place of the blood relationship in their child's life and their own.

We have no explanations for the finding that males were more likely than females to be loyal to their adoptive families and somewhat more critical of their birth mother. It could, however, explain the fact that fewer appear to search compared to females. Equally, it is a matter for speculation why females in the study came to feel less close to their adoptive parents, less happy about being adopted, conveyed a lesser sense of belonging, were less positive about the overall experience of adoption, felt less included by the extended family and scored higher emotional problems on the GHQ. Whether women have a greater need than men to experience the birth parent–child relationship remains an open question. It could reflect the comment made by about a fifth of birth mothers that something was missing from their relationship with the adopted person, probably because they had not parented him or her.

All the gains reported from contact and reunion should not detract from the intensity of the feelings experienced by many members of the triangle, the complications that at times arose, the anxieties many went through and the continued fluidity and changing nature of relationships giving rise to new anxieties and to a fair amount of stress. A small number from each group were still left with some disappointment or disillusionment. On the whole, the more disappointed the adopted adult or birth mother was, the more likely it was that they would be found among searchers than among non-searchers, but it should not detract from the fact that most searchers were positive or very positive about the contact and its outcome.

Considering the reported benefits of contact and reunion for all parties, the question could be asked whether forms of adoption that are open from the start could have prevented much of the anguish and pain. Since then, changes have been noted in the increasing number of mostly older children who now have contact with members of their birth families after adoption (see Lowe *et al*, 1999; Smith and Logan, 2004). With attention in Britain being focused on the adoption of older children, open adoption for very young children has hardly been debated. Speaking in the early 1990s, Hill (1991) referred to 'the continuing tendency to deal separately with just two periods in an adopted child's life – early childhood and early adulthood'. The reasons for this could be found in Modell's (1994) comment that 'open adoption is disturbing because it does not allow adoptive kinship to be just like biological kinship' (p. 231). Although open adoption is not for everybody, it is perhaps the ultimate in acknowledging the "difference" that the blood connection makes in adoption, with adoption coming eventually to be seen, perhaps, as part of the "gift" relationship.

Finally, adoption touches the lives of millions in Britain either as adopted people, those related by blood to the adopted person and those related by adoption. The present study has explored the connections between experiences across several life stages from the viewpoint of birth parents, adopters and adopted people. Inevitably, such long-term follow-up reflects on circumstances and social conditions now well in the past. Besides demonstrating once again the importance of the blood relationship, the study also showed that psychosocial parenting worked well. The study has also identified the persisting interconnectedness of the three main parties in adoption even after years of total separation and, for the most part, the positive and reparative effects of searching and reunion. The issues will continue to be relevant for children who are reared by those other than their biological families and this includes those who are now adopted when older or from overseas.

References

Andersen R.S. (1988) 'Why adoptees search: motives and more', *Child Welfare* 67:1, pp. 15–19

Bohman M. (1970) *Adopted Children and their Families*, Stockholm: Proprius

Bouchier P., Lambert L. and Triseliotis J. (1991) *Parting with a Child for Adoption*, London: BAAF

Bowlby J. (1980) *Attachment and Loss, Vol. 3: Loss, sadness and despair*, New York: Basic Books

Brinich M.P. (1990) 'Adoption from the inside out: a psychoanalytic perspective', in Brodzinsky D.M. and Schechter M.D. (eds) *The Psychology of Adoption*, Oxford: Oxford University Press

Brodzinsky A. (1990) 'Surrendering an infant for adoption: the birth mother experience', in Brodzinsky D.M. and Schechter M.D. (eds) *The Psychology of Adoption*, Oxford: Oxford University Press

Brodzinsky D.M., Schechter M.D. and Henig M.P. (1992) *Being Adopted*, New York: Doubleday

Brown G.W. and Harris T. (1978) *The Social Origins of Depression*, London: Tavistock

Clapton G. (2003) *Birth Fathers and their Adoption Experience*, London: Jessica Kingsley

Craig M. (1991) 'Adoption: not a big deal', unpublished report, Edinburgh: Scottish Adoption Society

Cushman L.T.R., Kalmuss D. and Namerow P.B. (1997) 'Openness in adoption: experiences and social psychological outcomes among birth mothers', in Gross H.E. and Sussman M.B. (eds) *Families and Adoption*, New York: The Haworth Press

Deater-Deckard K. and Petrill S.A. (2004) 'Parent–child dyadic mutuality and child behaviour problems: an investigation of gene-environment processes', *Journal of Child Psychology and Psychiatry* 45:6, pp. 1171–79

Dominick C. (1988) *Early Contact in Adoption*, Research Series 10, Wellington, NZ: Department of Social Welfare

Fravel D., McRoy R. and Grotevant H. (2000) 'Birth mother perceptions of the psychologically present adopted child: adoption openness and boundary ambiguity', *Family Relations* 49:4, pp. 425–433

THE ADOPTION TRIANGLE REVISITED: SUMMARY AND CONCLUSIONS

ernity and Self-identity, Cambridge: Polity Press

Goffman E. (1969) *The Presentation of Self in Everyday Life*, Harmondsworth: Penguin

Grotevant H.D. (2000) 'Openness in adoption: research with the adoption kinship network', *Adoption Quarterly* 4:1, pp. 45–65

Grotevant H.D. and McRoy R. (1998) *Openness in Adoption: Exploring family connections*, Thousand Oaks, C.A.: Sage

Hill M. (1991) 'Concepts of parenthood and their application to adoption', *Adoption & Fostering* 15:4, pp. 16–23

Howe D. and Feast J. (2000) *Adoption, Search and Reunion*, London: The Children's Society

Howe D., Sawbridge P. and Hinnings D. (1992) *Half a Million Women*, London: Penguin

Kennard J. (1991) *Adoption Information: The repossession of identity*, Wellington, NZ: Victoria University

Kirk H.D. (1964) *Shared Fate: A theory of adoption and mental health*, New York: The Free Press

Kirk H.D. (1981) *Adoptive Kinship*, Toronto: Butterworths

Kubler-Ross E. (1970) *On Death and Dying*, London: Tavistock

Lazarus R.S. and Folkman S. (1984) *Stress, Appraisal and Coping*, New York: Springer

Lewis H.D. (1971) 'The psychiatric aspects of adoption', in Howells J.G. (ed.) *Modern Perspectives of Child Psychiatry*, New York: Brunner/Mazel

Logan J. (1996) 'Birth mothers and their mental health: uncharted territory', *British Journal of Social Work* 26:5, pp. 609–25

Lowe N., Murch M., Borkowski M., Weaver A., Beckford V. and Thomas C. (1999) *Supporting Adoption*, London: BAAF

McGlone M.F., Park A. and Roberts C. (1996) 'Relative values: kinship and friendship', in Howell R., Curtice J., Park A., Brook L. and Thomson K. (eds) *British Social Attitudes: the 13th Report*, Aldershot: Dartmouth

McMillan R. and Hamilton F. (1992) 'Initiating contact with adoptive families and adopted people on behalf of birth parents and relatives', in *Conference Proceedings, Adult Counselling and Adoption*, Ilford: Barnardo's Post-Adoption Centre

309

McRoy R., Zurcher L., Lauderdale M. and Anderson R. (1984) 'The identity of transracial adoptees', *Social Casework* 65:1, pp. 35–39

Mander R. (1995) *The Care of the Mother Grieving a Baby Relinquished for Adoption*, Aldershot: Avebury

Mann S. (1998) 'Adoptive parents: a practice perspective', *Adoption & Fostering* 22:3, pp. 42–52

March K. (1995) 'Perception of adoption as a social stigma: motivation for search and reunion', *Journal of Marriage and the Family* 57, pp. 653–60

Modell J.S. (1994) *Kinship with Strangers: Adoption and interpretations of kinship in American culture*, Berkeley, C.A.: University of California

Neil E. (2000) 'Contact with birth families after adoption', Paper given at the BAAF Research Group Meeting, 20 January

Pacheco F. and Eme R. (1993) 'An outcome study of the reunion between adoptees and biological parents', *Child Welfare* 72:1, pp. 53–64

Parkes C.M. (1975) *Bereavement: Studies in adult grief*, 2nd edition, London: Tavistock

Post-Adoption Social Workers Group of New South Wales (1988) *Experiences of Reunion After Adoption*, Sydney: Post-Adoption Social Workers Group of New South Wales

Quinton D., Rushton A., Dance C. and Mayes D. (1998) *Joining New Families: A study of adoption and fostering in middle childhood*, Chichester: John Wiley & Sons

Robinson E.B. (2004) *Adoption and Loss: The hidden grief*, South Australia: Clova Publications

Roseneil S. and Budgeon S. (2004) 'Cultures of intimacy and care beyond "the family": personal life and social change in the early 21st century', *Journal of Current Sociology* 52:2, pp. 135–59

Rowe J. (1991) 'Perspectives on adoption', in Hibbs E.D. (ed.) *Adoption: International perspectives*, Madison, W.I.: Perspectives Press

Rynearson E.K. (1982) 'Relinquishment and its maternal complications: a preliminary study', *American Journal of Psychiatry* 139:3, pp. 338–40

Sachdev P. (1992) 'Adoption reunion and after: a study of the search process and experience of adoptees', *Child Welfare* 71:1, pp. 53–68

Seligman M.E.P. (1975) *Helplessness*, San Francisco: Freeman

Smith C. and Logan J. (2004) *After Adoption: Direct contact and relationships*, London: Routledge

Sprang G. and McNeil J. (1995) *The Many Faces of Bereavement: The nature and treatment of natural, traumatic and stigmatised grief*, New York: Brunner/ Mazel

Tizard B. and Phoenix A. (1993) *Black, White or Mixed Race*, London: Routledge

Triseliotis J. (1973) *In Search of Origins*, London: Routledge & Kegan Paul

van Keppel M. (1991) 'Birth parents and negotiated adoption arrangements', *Adoption & Fostering* 15:4, pp. 81–90

Washington A. (1982) 'A cultural and historical perspective on pregnancy-related activity among US teenagers', *Journal of Black Psychology* 9:1, pp. 1–28

Weiss R. (1988) 'Loss and recovery', *Journal of Social Issues* 44:3, pp. 37–52

Winkler R. and van Keppel M. (1984) *Relinquishing Mothers in Adoption*, Melbourne: Institute for Family Studies

Witney C. (2004) 'Original fathers: an exploration into the experiences of birth fathers involved in adoption in the mid-20th century', *Adoption & Fostering* 28:3, pp. 52–61

Young L. (1954) *Out of Wedlock*, New York: McGraw Hill

13 Contact between looked after children and their parents: A level playing field?

The final item in this collection questioned what John saw as a trend towards using interactions between looked after children and their birth parents largely as occasions to observe and judge the quality of the relationship rather than to support or improve that relationship. He recognised that sometimes in cases of abuse and neglect it is appropriate to reduce or terminate contact, but quoted experts to indicate that this is exceptional. The article suggests that social workers can misinterpret interactions occurring in artificial and awkward situations and so downplay the significance to a child of contact with a birth parent. As in Chapter 4, he challenged the assumption that children must give up contact in order to attach to a new family. John did not explicitly answer his own question about a level playing field, but the thrust of the article is that often the situation is loaded against the parents and not necessarily in children's interests. The chapter is reprinted from a special edition of Adoption & Fostering *(34:3, pp. 59–66, 2010) that commemorated the 30th anniversary of BAAF.*

Introduction

Over the last 20 years, the quality of contact between children absent in care and their parents has assumed a much higher profile than ever before. Those supervising contact are now expected to keep records on meetings and report on their quality to reviews, courts and, in Scotland, children's panels. When courts are requested to grant a care, placement or an adoption order, a key question almost always asked is the quality of contact. Depending on the evidence, direct contact may be provided for, reduced or stopped altogether.

Yet judgements on the quality of contact lack a coherent and empirically-based theory and guidelines. The recent ascendancy of attachment theory has offered a kind of framework of what to look for, but important as Bowlby's (1969) theory is, there is much more to parenthood and child development than attachments. John Sutherland, former Director of the Tavistock Clinic, co-founder of the Scottish Institute of Human Relations and a close acquaintance of Bowlby, wrote that 'the attachment phenomena are very real, but I do not think these terms are adequate for the ongoing inner processes' (see Scharff, 2007, p. 171).

The introduction of direct contact after adoption in a few selected cases and contact between non-resident parents and children following divorce or separation have raised awareness of the importance of contact and led to a number of studies. However, the details surrounding the subject, which affects thousands of children each year, remain under-researched.

Making judgements on the quality and nature of contact remains a mixture of art and science, possibly balanced more towards art. On the whole, there are no empirically-based guidelines or standardised tests on what to look for and no criteria for evaluating events during meetings. There is also no script for parents on how to conduct themselves, what to do and not do, what to say and not say, and no guidelines for those supervising meetings on how to assess what they observe. The often used Family Relations exercise does not seem to transfer well from the US and has to be adapted. Once this happens, however, it ceases to be standardised. Ticking boxes on forms, as another method, begs the question regarding the accuracy of the perceptions and their interpretation. Yet parents who attend supervised meetings have a right to know on what kind of criteria they are being judged, how these have been arrived at and how reliable they are. When the issue of contact after adoption emerged as an important variable in decision-making around the late 1980s, Triseliotis (1991) set out tentative criteria of what might be looked for. However, recognising these qualities and their strength still remains a problem.

Compared to the thousands of children who are "looked after", contact after adoption is much rarer and usually comes at the tail end of a child's life in care. But what happens with contact beforehand often determines and pre-empts decisions about rehabilitation or permanence outside the birth family, so radically affecting children's lives.

Promoting contact

Child care legislation across the UK places a responsibility on local authorities not only to encourage contact between children in care and their families, but also "to promote" it whenever it is consistent with the child's welfare. It looks upon this as a "right" of the child and not of the parent or other birth relative. Besides encouraging, supporting and making enabling arrangements, the "promotion" of contact would also imply preparing parents and explaining why their visits are important to their children, how they might use contact more productively and how they would be judged. But no preparatory arrangements appear to exist, suggesting that had parents known beforehand how to positively engage, play and stimulate their children, some of their offspring might not have been in care.

The changes in the legislation came about mainly after early studies identified the difficulties experienced by many birth parents when trying to visit their children. For instance, poor organisation, discouraging attitudes and long distances between placements and home communities presented them with significant logistic transport problems and expenses. Millham *et al* (1986) reported that many parents of children in foster and residential care felt unwanted and believed they had nothing more to contribute to the well-being of their children once they were away from home. While most barriers to contact were informal and non-specific, others were ordered by the courts – balancing the wishes of children and families, supervision, timing and venue. More recent studies have noted improved practices, including higher levels of commitment on the part of social workers and foster carers, children increasingly being placed nearer their home communities, easier travel arrangements for parents and the use of venues with better play and other facilities (Cleaver, 1997/8, 2000; Triseliotis *et al*, 2000). However, there are still examples of contact being viewed as if it were arranged for the benefit of parents and continuing obstacles occur. How else to explain why a meeting is cancelled due to a parent who had to negotiate public transport arriving a few minutes late, with the child being left high and dry as the parent leaves after being denied access? Or when contact is arranged at a distant venue, difficult to reach by public transport, to "test" a parent's motivation? When a parent misses a meeting, it is rightly condemned for the distress this causes to the child and is rarely rearranged, but a quite different view is taken when the escort or supervising worker suddenly withdraws.

The claimed benefits of contact to children

Contact is a difficult and highly emotive experience for both children and parents and there are no easy or definitive answers. In spite of increased studies, there is still much to be learnt about whom it is for, its purpose, how to organise it, where it should take place, how to interpret what occurs during meetings, how to make reliable judgements about it and whether it benefits a particular child. Howe and Steele (2004) assert the presence of "strong evidence" pointing to how children benefit from contact, including many who had suffered maltreatment – although they acknowledge that in a 'few exceptional cases' contact would be ill advised due to the effects of previous abuse or risk of recurrence. They cite Weinstein's (1960) pioneering study, which demonstrated how children who were visited were more likely to return home earlier and have a better self-image than those who were not. Equally important was Trasler's (1960) finding that a lack of knowledge of what is happening to their families and themselves 'creates severe anxiety' in foster children, which is then reflected in their behaviour. Other studies relate continuing positive contact for children to fewer fostering breakdowns and better adjustment (Holman, 1973; Berridge and Cleaver, 1987; Thoburn and Rowe, 1988; Wedge and Mantle, 1991). Further benefits identified include: the strengthening of genealogical and physical identity; reassuring the child that the birth parent is well and continues to care; helping to assuage anxiety and possible guilt; demonstrating love and affection; reducing feelings of loss and rejection; promoting a positive sense of self; and helping to avoid fantasising (Weinstein, 1960; Hess and

Proch, 1993; Hetherington and Stanley-Hagan, 1999; Neil and Howe, 2004; Smith and Logan, 2004).

These benefits are not guaranteed, as much depends on the individual child's past experiences, how parents use contact, their relationship with the child, their support for the placement and emotional sanctioning to the child to live there, the relationship between parents and carers and the absence of undermining attitudes and threatening behaviours. Therefore, saying that positive contact benefits looked after children begs the question of what is positive and how benefit is identified and quantified. These qualifications are especially salient for children who have been severely abused or neglected. However, Elizabeth Butler-Sloss, former President of the High Court Family Division, is reported to have said that:

> Violent behaviour alone was not enough to deny a parent contact with a child. It would be for the court to decide, if violence had been proved, how relevant it was. (*The Times*, 10 November 2001)

Nevertheless, concerns remain; the psychotherapist Loxterkamp (2009) has raised the stakes by challenging the notion that post-adoption contact between children and birth relatives who have abused, maltreated or neglected them confers any benefits to the children. Whereas Howe and Steele (2004) carefully stress the need to consider this in 'a few exceptional' cases, Loxterkamp expands the categories of children to include neglect, maltreatment and abuse, without making qualifications about severity and extent, leaving it understood that almost all contact is highly questionable. He appears to dismiss studies, for instance by Smith and Logan (2004), which demonstrate that in the right cases direct contact after adoption on the whole works well. While Loxterkamp is right to question the evidence, his broad categories of neglect, abuse and maltreatment apply to the majority of those entering care and so exclude them from qualifying for contact.

The frequency and duration of contact

There is a presumption in law that contact will be "reasonable", but this is not defined and no study so far seems to have identified the appropriate frequency of contact for each group of looked after children. No doubt when arranging for frequency and duration, account has to be taken of the child's specific circumstances, age, needs, wishes if old enough, and the parent's ability to manage the frequency. In the event of permanency plans being introduced, depending on their stability, contact may be adjusted appropriately. However, any reduction has to be proportionate until the court makes its final decision, especially as the stability of some placements can be very unpredictable.

It is also recognised that after young children are accommodated and placed in foster care, their main closeness will be to their foster carers. As a result, any relationship developed with the birth parent(s) will rely on contact and its quality. Under such circumstances close or strong attachments to birth parents are unusual. Furthermore, the relationship and closeness of such a child to the birth parent can only be relative to that with his or her primary carer. This is especially so when the child has been accommodated from birth. What mostly happens when contact is positive is the development of strong familiarity and a relationship of some strength, together with a degree of emotional connectedness; but even with regular contact, as Katz *et al* (1994, p. 23) point out, this is difficult to achieve if you are not the child's primary carer. Nevertheless, Weinstein (1960, p. 69) stresses that it is wrong to conclude that if a child identifies predominantly with their foster carers, continuing contact with birth parents is not still very important to him or her.

While many practitioners are aware of these qualifications and take account of them when making evaluations on the quality of contact, others still judge the parents as if they were the child's primary carers. Comments such as 'no "strong" attachments exist', 'he does not react to his mother as a person who looks after him', 'when his female carer is present the child goes more often to her than to his mother', are not uncommon. Yet it is understandable that a young child who has been fostered from birth or when a few months old would react in this way, especially if contact is infrequent. In fact, if such a child did not display stronger attachments to his carer than to the visiting parent, questions would have to be asked about the quality of parenting provided. Despite this, the lack of strong emotional links between child and birth parent is likely to be used in court as a strong argument for stopping or drastically reducing contact.

Possibly the most contentious issue regarding contact and its frequency has to do with when it is justified to reduce or even stop it altogether and who makes that decision. Considering the thousands of children affected, research-based guidance is sparse and mainly comes from cases of divorce or separation, and more recently from studies in contact after adoption. For example, should the same criterion be used for stopping contact as for the granting of a care order, namely that continuing contact is likely to cause more harm and distress? In Scotland decisions on the frequency, duration, reduction and stopping of contact are made by lay children's panels, on the recommendation of social workers. Parents may appeal to the court but by the time some cases are heard it can be too late. Furthermore, a finding in favour of the parent can later be reversed by the same panel, making a new appeal necessary, by which stage some parents give up. There is at times too much confrontation between parents and social workers; with some parents resorting to the internet and Facebook (see Fursland, 2010), it is time to move towards more conciliation – provided that contact continues to be in the child's interests.

Professional experiences and studies suggest that it is not at all unusual to blame contact when a child is unsettled before, during or after its occurrence, or is reluctant to attend. Monck et al (2003, p. 187) reported from their study of concurrent placements that the children's carers were particularly sensitive to any signs of distress in the children, and had 'a tendency' to ascribe this to contact with birth parents. Even though there was no doubt that contact sessions were unsettling for a number of children, this may not have been a product of the contact per se but of the surrounding circumstances, such as long journeys, strange environments and disturbed routines.

There can be other explanations for why a child shows reluctance to attend contact meetings or displays unsettled behaviour before, during and afterwards. Who takes a young child to contact and how familiar she or he happens to be to the child could influence the child's reaction and attendance, especially given the high turnover of escort and supervising workers. The same applies to how the carer, on whom the child depends for their physical and emotional needs, prepares, supports and encourages him or her to attend. Exclusive carers may fail to convey the right messages and sufficient encouragement and support (Holman, 1980). Children are usually quick to pick up on a carer or resident parent's emotions; persistent anxiety or mistrust of contact on the part of the primary carer could lead the child to experience similar feelings and a loyalty conflict, and then refuse to attend or display distress. Similarly, a carer may be encouraging the child verbally to attend but emotionally indicate disapproval and disloyalty, so producing unsettled behaviour and pressures from carers on social workers and panels to stop contact (Wilkinson, 1988, p. 236; Ames Reed, 1993; McCauley, 2002).

Separation anxiety from the primary carer, be it a foster carer or a prospective adopter, is not uncommon among young children. A child who does not yet feel secure enough may not trust that the carer will still be there on his or her return from contact. It is common for such children to engage well with the parent during contact and appear content, until the next meeting when the separation anxiety resurfaces. Once the child is satisfied that the primary carer will still be there on return, the anxiety usually fades away. As contact is such an emotive experience for both parent and child, it has to be expected that for a period of time afterwards the child may still be reacting to the engagement, irrespective of whether it was positive or negative. Sinclair (2005) noted that children usually look forward to contact, commonly want more contact than they get, but are nevertheless commonly upset by it – again, given the proviso that there will always be a few children who will be reluctant to take part in meetings from which they gain no benefit or that revive memories of past abuse (see Howe and Steele, 2004).

One explanation offered for the drastic reduction and sometimes stopping of contact is that the child does not talk to their carer and/or social worker about it, often interpreted as a sign of indifference. But, as Cleaver (2000, p. 272) found, 'It was rare for children to make their views on contact known to either carers or social workers.'

Especially in the case of under-five-year-olds, drastically reducing or stopping contact – without evidence that it causes harm or distress or has the potential for doing so, but simply on account of permanency plans and before the case comes to court – inevitably weakens the emotional link between a young child and a parent. So at subsequent hearings, often one to two years later, parents who ask for contact are told that their emotional link or relationship with the child is weak or absent or that the child no longer asks for them.

A further argument for the drastic reduction or cessation of contact is that it will prevent the child from attaching to a new family. Loxterkamp (2009, p. 425) writes:

The later adopted child will inevitably have strong feelings about members of the birth family and longings to be with some or many of them. These longings will interfere with the forming of secure relationships with the adoptive parents and family.

However, studies by Schaffer (1990), Fratter *et al* (1991) and Berridge (1997) all conclude that there is no evidence to support the view that continued contact with birth parents prevents children from becoming attached to new parents, other than in the minority of cases where original parents deliberately set out to wreck a placement. It seems that children are much more capable of sorting out the roles of the various individuals in their lives and sustaining relationships with all of them than they have been given credit for. Children mostly become muddled when the adults in their lives become confused and adversarial. This is not to deny that poor quality contact predicts disruption, and the problems that arise when birth relatives refuse to accept the situation and convey their emotional permission for the child to live with his or her new family and look upon new carers as parents.

Venue

Where children meet their parents for contact varies according to age, preference and level of risk. In a study of foster care, almost half of contact (44%) took place within the parental home, almost a third (30%) within the foster home, a similar proportion at the social work office/centre and 20 per cent elsewhere (Triseliotis *et al*, 2000). (The figures add up to more than 100 per cent as children saw their parents in several places.) Due to changing attitudes and the need to supervise and observe contact, including in situations of potential risk, it is likely that a much higher proportion of contact takes place now within family centres and social work locations. Young children mostly enjoy family centres, which provide appropriate toys and games. However, these are not very suitable for children over about the age of four who tend to prefer activity-type facilities, such as climbing frames, chutes and tunnels which are usually found in adventure centres, or like to go swimming, bowling or ice-skating. Although foster homes still have their place as venues, possibly for babies, they can make visiting parents feel anxious and tense; also, some parents may pose risks to the foster carers. Thus, in spite of much progress parents and children are often thrown back on their ingenuity while simultaneously being criticised for not being more inventive. It is not much fun for the parent and child having contact in an office, or in a storeroom cluttered with office furniture, and expected to make creative and meaningful engagements over several hours. Better play facilities are to be found in some Burger King and McDonald's fast-food outlets.

Supervised contact

Being supervised and observed under contact conditions is an artificially constructed situation, with no script to follow regarding the kind of behaviour to be expected from each participant, including the supervisor. Much of it has to be guessed. Long sessions with one and often more children under such conditions can prove very demand-ing, intense and nerve racking – far more so if watched by one and sometimes two supervisors, even though the parent may have no history of violence or threatening behaviour. When at home, it is unusual for a parent to give so much undivided attention to a single child for so long. More likely they will be engaged in other activities in the kitchen, at the back or front patio, or go out to the park or local shops. What parents can or cannot say during contact can vary between authorities and sometimes between different supervising workers. This only adds to parental anxiety. They may then be criticised for not being spontaneous. Even stricter controls operate when the child is about or has moved to a "permanent" placement. For example, for the parent to mention their new house or say they redecorated a child's room, or stress that the family were missing them, could be interpreted as wanting the child home and therefore inappropriate.

Once a child is accommodated, contact becomes the main, and often the only, medium for observing parental behaviours. In the absence of other evidence, decisions of whether or not to rehabilitate a child home often rely on parental behaviour during contact. The ambiguity of the role of the supervising worker is highlighted when faced with the dilemma of whether to give the parent feedback. In my experience, those who perceive their role as that of a non-participant observer simply observe, record and later report to a review. But it is of no help telling a mother after a period of time that, owing to her lack of parenting skills, her contact will be drastically reduced. Some supervisors do offer support and advice, making suggestions, under-taking modelling or role play and using video playbacks. Adopting the latter role involves striking a balance between support and construc-tive criticism; otherwise it can be experienced as undermining con-fidence. Parents, many of whom already have low self-esteem, are more likely to be receptive to advice and suggestions, and even criticism, if it comes from supervisors with whom they have a positive relationship. With the frequent change of social workers, the lack of time to promote interpersonal relationships and the traditional anti-pathy felt by many parents towards professionals who have been instrumental in the child's removal, a collaborative atmosphere can prove difficult to establish.

While some parental and child behaviours during contact are clearly positive or negative, uncertainty remains. A usual double-bind is the frequently heard comment that if a child does not appear to be upset on parting from a parent after contact, then contact is unimportant to them. The opposite can also be said – namely that if the child is upset at the end, contact may have to be reduced or even stopped. Yet again, there can be a number of possible explanations for these reactions, many of them unrelated to what takes place during meetings. There needs to be awareness of the wider context of past events in a child's life and the current situation, such as what goes on within the foster or residential setting, yet some of those who supervise contact know little or nothing about this dimension.

All of this makes it difficult to establish a fair curriculum as the rules are riddled with contradictions. Parents are criticised for not being sufficiently proactive but also for being too dominant. Too many limits are interpreted as stifling, while laxity is condemned. Children and parents who have not seen much of each other often look upon parental concessions as a sign of affection and on controls as rejection. Parents, who already feel great insecurity about their parenting and guilty for the children being in care, will see enforcing controls as making them feel "bad" and rejecting, especially when they will not see the child for some time to make it up. Not surprisingly, children sense and play into such feelings.

Parents have to feel very secure and convinced that what matters to their child is their presence if they are to resist demands for bigger presents and expensive toys, or for sweets, or to forbid jumping on the furniture or playing with the electric switches. However, had they felt that confident about their parenting and secure in themselves, possibly the children would not have entered care in the first place.

So, can this situation be considered a level playing field?

Conclusion

This review of contact illustrates the difficulties of providing substitute care and the danger of unsubstantiated generalisations. The discussion shows that while we have learned a lot in recent years, there is clearly much more to discover before we can be confident about what we do. BAAF's work is clearly cut out.

Finally, I am aware that this is a special edition to mark BAAF's 30th birthday. I have known the journal under different names for a number of decades before it was relaunched in its present format. It is not an exaggeration to say how fortunate we are in Britain to have a journal of this calibre that has struck a nice balance between the publication of research-based articles and the sharing of practice experience. Long may it continue.

References

Ames Reed J. (2003) *We have Learned a Lot from Them: Foster care for young people with learning difficulties*, Barkingside: Barnardo's/National Children's Bureau

Berridge D. and Cleaver H. (1987) *Foster Home Breakdown*, Oxford: Blackwell

Berridge D. (1997) *Foster Care: A research review*, London: The Stationery Office

Bowlby J. (1969) *Attachment and Loss, Vol. I*, London: Hogarth Press

Butler-Sloss E. (2001) reported in *The Times*, 10 November

Cleaver H. (1997/8) 'Contact: the social worker's experience', *Adoption & Fostering* 21:4, pp. 34–40

Cleaver H. (2000) *Fostering Family Contact*, London: The Stationery Office

Fratter J., Rowe J., Sapsford D. and Thoburn J. (1991) *Permanent Family Placement: A decade of experience*, London: BAAF

Fursland E. (2010) *Social Networking and Contact: How social workers can help adoptive families*, London: BAAF

Hess P.M. and Proch K.O. (1993) *Contact: Managing visits to children looked after away from home*, London: BAAF

Hetherington E.M. and Stanley-Hagan M. (1999) 'The adjustment of children with divorced parents: a risk and resiliency perspective', *Journal of Child Psychology and Psychiatry* 40:1, pp. 129–40

Holman R. (1980) 'Exclusive and inclusive concepts of fostering', in Triseliotis J. (ed), *New Developments in Adoption and Foster Care*, London: Routledge & Kegan Paul

Holman R (1973) *Trading in Children*, London: Routledge & Kegan Paul

Howe D. and Steele M. (2004) 'Contact in cases in which children have been traumatically abused or neglected by their birth parents', in Neil D. and Howe D. (eds), *Contact in Adoption and Permanent Foster Care*, London: BAAF

Katz L., Maluccio L. and Cordes K. (1994) *Concurrent Planning*, Seattle, WA: Lutheran Social Services

Loxterkamp L. (2009) 'Contact and truth: the unfolding predicament in adoption and fostering', *Clinical Child Psychology and Psychiatry* 14:3, pp. 423–35

McCauley C. (2002) *Children in Long Term Fostering*, Aldershot: Avebury

Millham S., Bullock R., Hosie K. and Haak M. (1986) *Lost in Care*, London: Gower

Monck E., Reynolds J. and Wigfall V. (2003) *The Role of Concurrent Planning*, London: BAAF

Neil E. and Howe D. (eds) (2004) *Contact in Adoption and Permanent Foster Care*, London: BAAF

Schaffer H.R. (1990) *Making Decisions about Children*, Oxford: Basil Blackwell

Scharff S.J. (ed.) (2007) *The Psychodynamic Image: John D. Sutherland on self in society*, London: Routledge

Sinclair I. (2005) *Fostering Now: Messages from research*, London: Jessica Kingsley

Sinclair I., Baker C., Wilson K. and Gibbs I. (2005) *Foster Children: Where they go and how they get on*, London: Jessica Kingsley

Smith C. and Logan J. (2004) *After Adoption: Direct contact and relationships*, London: Routledge & Kegan Paul

Thoburn J. and Rowe J. (1988) 'Research: a snapshot of permanent family placement', *Adoption & Fostering* 12:3, pp. 29–34

Trasler G. (1960) *In Place of Parents*, London: Routledge & Kegan Paul

Triseliotis J. (1991) 'Maintaining the links in adoption', *British Journal of Social Work* 21:4, pp. 401–14

Triseliotis J., Borland M. and Hill M. (2000) *Delivering Foster Care*, London: BAAF

Wedge P. and Mantle G. (1991) *Sibling Groups and Social Work*, Aldershot: Gower

Weinstein E.A. (1960) *The Self-image of the Child*, New York: Russell Sage Foundation

Wilkinson C. (1988) 'Prospect, process and outcome in foster care', unpublished M.Phil. thesis, University of Edinburgh